Palgrave Macmillan's Critical Studies in Gender, Sexuality, and Culture

Highlighting the work taking place at the crossroads of sociology, sexuality studies, gender studies, cultural studies, and performance studies, this series offers a platform for scholars pushing the boundaries of gender and sexuality studies substantively, theoretically, and stylistically. The authors draw on insights from diverse scholarship and research in popular culture, ethnography, history, cinema, religion, performance, new media studies, and technoscience studies to render visible the complex manner in which gender and sexuality intersect and can, at times, create tensions and fissures between one another. Encouraging breadth in terms of both scope and theme, the series editors seek works that explore the multifaceted domain of gender and sexuality in a manner that challenges the taken-for-granted. On one hand, the series foregrounds the pleasure, pain, politics, and aesthetics at the nexus of sexual practice and gendered expression. On the other, it explores new sites for the expression of gender and sexuality, the new geographies of intimacy being constituted at both the local and global scales.

Series Editors:

PATRICIA T. CLOUGH is Professor of Sociology and Women's Studies at Queens College and The Graduate Center, CUNY. Clough is on the editorial boards of *Women's Studies Quarterly*, *Body and Society*, *Subjectivity*, *Cultural Studies/Critical Method*, *Qualitative Inquiry*, and *Women and Performance.* Clough is the coeditor of *Beyond Biopolitics: Essays in the Governance of Life and Death* (with Craig Willse, 2011); author of *The Affective Turn: Theorizing the Social* (with Jean Halley, 2007); *Autoaffection: Unconscious Thought in the Age of Teletechnology* (2000); *The End(s)of Ethnography: From Realism to Social Criticism* (1998); *Feminist Thought: Desire, Power and Academic Discourse* (1994); *The End(s) of Ethnography: From Realism to Social Criticism* (1992).

R. DANIELLE EGAN is Professor and Chair of the Gender and Sexuality Studies Program at St. Lawrence University. Egan is the author of *Dancing for Dollars and Paying for Love: The Relationships between Exotic Dancers and Their Regulars* (2006) and coauthor of *Theorizing the Sexual Child in Modernity* (with Gail Hawkes, 2010), both with Palgrave Macmillan. She is also the coeditor of *Flesh for Fantasy: Producing and Consuming Exotic Dance* (with Katherine Frank and Merri Lisa Johnson, 2006). She is on the editorial board of *Sexuality and Culture.*

Titles:

Magnus Hirschfeld and the Quest for Sexual Freedom: A History of the First International Sexual Freedom Movement
Elena Mancini

Queer Voices: Vocality, the Uncanny, and Popular Music
Freya Jarman-Ivens

On the Literary Nonfiction of Nancy Mairs: A Critical Anthology
Edited by Merri Lisa Johnson and Susannah B. Mintz

Antarctica as Cultural Critique: The Gendered Politics of Scientific Exploration and Climate Change
Elena Glasberg

The Parallel Lives of Women and Cows: Meat Markets
Jean O'Malley Halley

Positioning Gender and Race in (Post)colonial Plantation Space: Connecting Ireland and the Caribbean
Eve Walsh Stoddard

A Critical Inquiry into Queer Utopias
Edited by Angela Jones

Young People and Pornography: Negotiating Pornification
Monique Mulholland

Juliet Mitchell and the Lateral Axis: Twenty-First-Century Psychoanalysis and Feminism
Edited by Robbie Duschinsky and Susan Walker

Women on the Role of Public Higher Education: Personal Reflections from CUNY's Graduate Center
Edited by Deborah S. Gambs and Rose M. Kim

Sex, Ethics, and Young People
Moira Carmody

Postfeminist Digital Cultures: Femininity, Social Media, and Self-Representation
Amy Shields Dobson

Postfeminist Digital Cultures

Femininity, Social Media, and Self-Representation

Amy Shields Dobson

palgrave
macmillan

POSTFEMINIST DIGITAL CULTURES

First published in 2015 by
PALGRAVE MACMILLAN®
in the United States—a division of St. Martin's Press LLC,
175 Fifth Avenue, New York, NY 10010.

Where this book is distributed in the UK, Europe and the rest of the world, this is by Palgrave Macmillan, a division of Macmillan Publishers Limited, registered in England, company number 785998, of Houndmills, Basingstoke, Hampshire RG21 6XS.

Palgrave Macmillan is the global academic imprint of the above companies and has companies and representatives throughout the world.

Palgrave® and Macmillan® are registered trademarks in the United States, the United Kingdom, Europe and other countries.

ISBN: 978–1–137–40839–6

Library of Congress Cataloging-in-Publication Data

Dobson, Amy Shields, 1981–
Postfeminist digital cultures : femininity, social media, and self-representation / by Amy Shields Dobson.
pages cm.—(Critical studies in gender, sexuality, and culture)
Includes bibliographical references and index.
ISBN 978–1–137–40839–6 (hardback : alk. paper)
1. Internet and women. 2. Social media. 3. Femininity. 4. Women—Identity. 5. Feminism and mass media. 6. Mass media and women. I. Title.

HQ1178.D63 2015
302.23082—dc23 2015008657

A catalogue record of the book is available from the British Library.

Design by Newgen Knowledge Works (P) Ltd., Chennai, India.

First edition: September 2015

10 9 8 7 6 5 4 3 2 1

For GM

Contents

Acknowledgments

This book and the research projects it draws on have involved much work from others that I am greatly indebted to. In particular, Anita Harris has been an invaluable colleague and mentor, initially supervising my doctoral research, and continuing to provide feedback on drafts of several of the chapters in this book. I am most grateful for her razor-sharp intellect, her detailed and keenly perceptive feedback, and her generous all-round support. I am also most grateful to Denise Cuthbert for her ongoing mentorship and support. I am in awe of Denise's insight and wisdom about so many pressing issues of our time, and her generosity, dedication, and critical eye as a scholar and research supervisor. Mark Davis and Grant Bollmer both kindly agreed to read chapters of this book and provided me with most insightful, crucial feedback. I am grateful for their time and passion for theory.

This manuscript is much indebted to Leo Keith, who has supported me with all things in life, work, and play ("support" may be an understatement). Leo helped proofread this manuscript, as well as download and categorize comments from YouTube, sort out computer-related problems and formatting issues along the way, and provided reassuring hugs at frequent intervals. His insights, time, and all-round love and care are invaluable. My parents, Candice Shields and Robert Dobson, also continue to provide me with the love and support that has enabled me to grow as a person and scholar, and I am indebted to them.

I'd like to thank all my colleagues and students in the Sociology Department and the Centre for Women's and Gender Studies in the Monash School of Social Sciences. In particular, conversations with JaneMaree Maher and Akane Kanai at the Centre for Women's and Gender Studies have been invaluable to my thinking over the past three years while I worked on this manuscript. I'd also like to thank

Rachel Fensham, for getting me started and inspired on the path of feminist research, and Peter Snow, for all his help along the way. The Monash School of Social Sciences, the Sociology Department, and the Arts Faculty provided funds for the research on sexting and cybersafety discussed in chapter 4, as well as the research on YouTube videos discussed in chapter 6. My doctoral research was funded by an Australian Postgraduate Award scholarship, and I am most grateful for all of this support.

Two conferences in the UK, and the colleagues I was fortunate enough to meet there, have been very valuable sources of inspiration and motivation to keep working in this field. First, the Pornified conference in London in 2011, organized by Meg Barker, Rosalind Gill, Emma Renold, and Jessica Ringrose, provided much stimulus. My continued conversations with Jessica Ringrose about the issues discussed in this book have been most valuable to my thinking. I greatly admire her approach to research and to life, and am thankful for her collegial support and friendship. Second, the Girls and Digital Culture conference, in London in 2012, organized by Ofra Koffman and Rosalind Gill, was a fantastic event where I was inspired by so many presentations and conversations with feminist researchers from around the world. I am particularly grateful to Rosalind Gill for her scholarship and for her generous support.

Many thanks go to the team of researchers involved in the project discussed in chapter 4, "Youth, Mobile Technologies, and Gender Politics," Danielle Tyson, Mary Lou Rasmussen, and Adrian Farrugia. Their enthusiasm and hard work on this research is much appreciated, and these colleagues have provided valuable insights about youth, media, and sexuality along the way.

The team at Palgrave has been most helpful and professional and I am grateful for their assistance throughout the process. Many thanks to Lani Oshima, Nicola Jones, Mara Berkoff, and Elaine Fan. Thanks also to the series editors R. Danielle Egan and Patricia Clough.

Very special thanks goes to all the young people and the two schools who participated in the research projects discussed in this book.

An earlier version of chapter 3 appeared as: Dobson, A. S. (2011). Hetero-sexy representation by young women on MySpace: The politics of performing an "objectified" self. *Outskirts: Feminisms Along the Edge*, 25(November). I am gratredful to the journal, *Outskirts: Feminisms Along the Edge*, for permission to use this material here. Sections of chapter 2 have been reworked from an early version of the article: Dobson, A. S. (2014). Performative shamelessness on young women's social network sites: Shielding the self and resisting gender melancholia. *Feminism & Psychology*, 24(1), 97–114.

Paragraphs from chapter 6 have been published previously in the chapter: Dobson, A. S. (2015). Girls' "pain memes" on YouTube: The production of pain and femininity in a digital network. In Sarah Baker, Brady Robards, and Bob Buttigieg (eds.), *Youth Cultures and Subcultures: Australian Perspectives*. Farnham: Ashgate.

Chapter 1

Introduction

This book explores some social media practices and digital self-representations commonly engaged in by girls and young women. One of the central concerns of the book is to take girls and young women seriously as media and cultural producers. Cultural commentators quite often treat girls' and young women's media practices and self-representations not only with panic but also with disdain and contempt. The female "selfie," now that it has been named as such, has become the subject of seemingly endless editorials and "think pieces" questioning the narcissism of this generation, and female youth in particular (Senft and Baym, 2015), and questioning the self-esteem, mental health, and moral values of girls and young women today—as well as their value to society. In one such piece, noted technology writer John C. Dvorak writes in *PC Magazine* that "the only thing worse than selfie snapshots are the hordes of teens, again, usually female, who set up a webcam and begin to 'produce' commentary to post on YouTube. They are usually alone and grumbling about one thing or another in a way that's coy, cutesy, and often hipsterish." According to Dvorak (2013), "There are few guys, including adults, who partake in this sort of amateurish rant." When commentary about girls' and young women's digital media practices and self-representations does not fuel moral panics about their safety and well-being, it often mocks their interests and abilities in cultural production, as Dvorak's piece exemplifies. Hence, the only thing seen as "worse" than teenage girls' selfie photos are publicly posted videos made by girls and young women in which they *speak* to a camera. Their media practices and self-productions are framed as cringe-worthy, as well as risky or dangerous, and these deficiencies are often implicitly constructed as a weakness of their sex. Dvorak's derisive comments help to illustrate a central impetus behind this book: girls and young women are seen as active users and media producers in the social media landscape, but they are often judged as being active in the "wrong" ways—thought to be engaged in projects of self-representation driven by vanity, or incessant social communication driven by insecurities and trivialities.

A growing body of scholarship addresses girls and young women as active users and producers in the social media landscape, speaking back to these kinds of hegemonic discourses, by tracing their practices of media and cultural production. The present book contributes to this work. But my main goal is to build on it and extend understandings of what it is to perform young femininity in contemporary digital cultures by focusing specifically and critically on gendered media practices and representations that are controversial and often framed as "wrong" for various reasons—hotspots of recent attention and sometimes panic. Young women produce media and culture of many different kinds and in many different spheres and genres. This book attends to the sphere and "genre" (Thumin, 2012) of social media self-representation. It does not attend to the extensive ways in which young women are producing media and culture in explicitly political or creative spheres; several other anthologies and authors have documented and analyzed this arena fruitfully (Piepmeier, 2009; Mazzarella, 2010; Bae and Ivashkevich, 2011; Kearney, 2011; Keller, 2012, 2015; Powell, 2015). This book is concerned with some media practices and representations that have largely been framed as "problematic" areas of heat; sexual self-representations on social network sites (SNSs); sexting; constructions of highly confident, "out there" feminine selves via SNS profiles' "Am I Pretty or Ugly" videos; and video-blogs (vlogs) describing girls' pain and suffering. These are media practices and representations that are not usually obviously "resistant" or politically "subversive" but, I suggest, can be seen as cultural modes of "survival" and "getting by" (Berlant, 2008, p. 27) and are politically significant in terms of what they reveal about negotiating the conditions of postfeminism and femininity in contemporary techno-social mediascapes.

Coming to the study of digital media cultures from a background in feminist theater and performance studies, I became interested in girls' and young women's self-representations on SNSs. When I first joined MySpace back in 2006 (before Facebook had become dominant in Australia) and became interested in self-representation on social media, I encountered a lot of sparkling, flashing fashion brand logos, Playboy bunny wallpapers, and cartoons of sexualized lips and mouths on young women's publicly visible profiles. Common profile decorations included images of shiny red lips with cherries sitting precariously on protruding tongues with the words "so hot" flashing beneath, logos inviting viewers to "pop my cherry," or warning them, "don't stick your tongue out unless you plan to use it." Images of Paris Hilton were popular at the time: Paris Hilton sucking a red phallic-shaped lollipop, or naked but for black stilettos and tied up, Paris Hilton pretending to clean a pool, or crouching on the floor like a tiger. I also encountered a lot of photos of young women in brightly colored satin cocktail dresses laughing, smiling, and shouting, and young women with their limbs spread out across front lawns in the nighttime, and across each other, surrounded by half-filled bottles and casks of wine. The greeting texts on these profiles were often friendly and flirtatious invitations to view, friend, and message the profile owners, but this went along with disclaimers of "I don't give a f*** what you think," or "If you don't like what you see, leave." Blocks of text with distinctly "pErsoNaliZd" use of spelling and capitalization were made harder to read by common practices of switching colors and fonts every few words. Such text described the profile owners in tones of self-belief and confident self-promotion.

I was interested in, or perhaps more truthfully, *concerned* about the political implications of such self-representational practices by young women. When I first started browsing the public SNS profiles of young women, I viewed these profiles and their owners with a mixture of self-consciousness (at being in what felt very much like "their" space[1]) and self-righteousness (about my "feminist research" purpose and intent), fascination and concern, admiration and disapproval, curiosity and confusion. I was tempted to conclude that I did not approve. But how could I confidently disapprove of something that I did not, and still do not, really understand? I will never understand what it is to be ten years younger than I am and to have grown up in the age of Paris and the infamous bunny rather than Cyndi Lauper, Madonna, and Janet Jackson.

I was also interested in the question of what, if anything, might make such online self-produced representations of contemporary femininity different, politically speaking, from mass-produced images of women? Do young women's self-representations that are often seemingly gender-typical, "sexualized," or in other ways controversial and politically contested, indicate the power of popular culture in shaping youth and gender identities? Following a Foucauldian feminist line of thought (Bartky, 1988; Gill, 2007), might such mediated *self*-representations point to the narrow regulation and disciplining of female bodies and feminine gender identities? What kind of other important significations might such self-representations hold about living young femininity today that feminists like myself perhaps miss through these kinds of quick and apparently intuitive appraisals? I wanted to explore the question of whether seemingly sexist and stereotypical representations of women could or should be read by feminist cultural scholars differently because of their *framing* within new, "participatory," "interactive" (Banet-Weiser, 2012), and "demotic" (Turner, 2010) digital media cultures, "self-produced" by girls and young women. In short, might the premise self-production (discussed further later) of even sexist media tropes perhaps disrupt long-standing gendered binaries of object and subjecthood and gaze relations, following feminist representational theories? This book attends to such questions about the politics of self-representation for girls and young women in the age of social media. It is driven by an effort to understand the ways in which media representations and practices of girls and young women simultaneously utilize and complicate the kinds of strong and sexy, hot and assertive, autonomous and confident constructions of a "postfeminist" young femininity that have become ubiquitous in globalized mediascapes through advertising, music videos, film, TV, and celebrity culture in recent years (Aapola, Gonick, and Harris, 2005; Harris, 2005; Levy, 2005; Gill, 2007, 2011; Tasker and Negra, 2007; McRobbie, 2009; Negra, 2009; Zaslow, 2009; Douglas, 2010; Ringrose, 2013; Evans and Riley, 2014; Harris and Dobson, 2015).

As Sarah Banet-Weiser outlines, the notion that girls and young women now produce, rather than just consume, media has been embraced (although not unconditionally) by many feminist scholars as a kind of "empowerment" (2012, p. 62). That girls and young women are now media producers themselves has meant we need to seriously reconsider research approaches and agendas that position girls as cultural dupes, or victims of negative media influence and effects like "sexualization" in straightforward ways. But scholars (such as Banet-Weiser among others) remain *ambivalent* about the kind of "empowerment" it is possible for girls and young women to achieve through media production practices and digitally enabled self-representations. In a media landscape that is increasingly "convergent," where the lines between media producers and consumers have been seriously complicated (Jenkins, 2006; Bruns, 2008), and where "participation" and content creation is actively encouraged as a profit strategy by social media companies and marketers, scholars of media and culture have argued we need to stay alert to, and seek refreshed understandings of, power, coercion, cultural influence, and exploitation (Turner, 2010; Andrejevic, 2011; Driscoll and Gregg, 2011; Banet-Weiser,

2012; Hinton and Hjorth, 2013; Marwick, 2013; van Dijck, 2013b). In short, individuals are asked to submit to new forms of control in order to participate in new media freedoms. I am primarily interested in the implications of girls' and young women's media practices and representations, especially those framed as sexualized, risky, or even pathological, for debates about flows of power and influence. This book addresses the areas of media practice and representation mentioned via an approach that does not see such media production a priori as evidence of girls' sexualization or poor mental or psychical health, and does not a priori seek to "protect" girls and young women through surveying their digital practices. Rather, my examination of hotspots of girls' and young women's digital cultures is conducted with the intent to illuminate the complexities, tensions, and shifting flows of power in media and in gendered subjectivity production in postfeminist digital cultures.

Contested and controversial aspects of cultural production are vitally important for what they tell us about "getting by" in the conditions of postfeminism (these are explicated in chapter 2). In all of these chapters I ask how media practices and representations framed as sexualized, risky, cringe-worthy, or pathological enable girls' and young women's daily survival in postfeminist digital cultures. How do girls and young women navigate the conditions of postfeminism and construct feminine selves that help them attain the relational and peer support, social legitimation, and pleasure needed to get by? In this particular framing of my key concerns and questions I am influenced by Lauren Berlant's suggestion that many people's interests are "less in changing the world than in not being defeated by it, and meanwhile finding satisfaction in minor pleasures and major fantasies" (2008, p. 27). The social media practices and representations discussed in this book can be seen as "juxtapolitical," following Berlant. In stating that a central concern here is to take girls and young women seriously as cultural producers, it is in this sense of giving attention to the juxtapolitical in postfeminist digital cultures that I mean. Berlant suggests the term juxtapolitical to describe a cultural sphere located next to, but not in politics, and responding to it. In this book I investigate representations and practices that are not overtly political in the way that, for example, online Slut Walk organizations or feminist forums are (see Keller, 2012; Cook and Hasmath, 2014; Powell, 2015), but may be politically significant in what they reveal about the quest to get by, to survive, and to *not be defeated* in/by postfeminist neoliberal Western societies. Like Berlant, I am interested in "the defensive, inventive, and adaptive activity of getting by, along with the great refusals to go through power to attain legitimacy" (Berlant, 2008, p. 27).

I explore SNS self-representations, sexting, and YouTube videos drawing on data collected and analyzed using tools from feminist performance theory and cultural studies. I am less concerned with putting forth an argument about the meaning of girls' and young women's media practices and representations in postfeminist digital cultures overall, or for a particular scholarly discipline, than I am with answering questions about each of the specific media practices and representations discussed. What is it about particular media practices and representations engaged in by girls and young women that has become a source of fear and/or public concern? Why are certain, sometimes common, gendered media practices often constructed in public discourse as narcissistic, vain, or stupid?[2] What values are being contested? I also question political and critical assessments of young women's cultural practices, including my own, that feel intuitive, easy, fast, or heated, and to try to untangle causes of potentially justified political and psychosocial concern from hype and panicked reactions.

The chapters and discussions focus on the key areas of "heat" mentioned previously: heterosexy SNS profile representations (a term I explain in more detail in chapter 2), youth sexting, representations of confident and "excessive" youthful feminine selves on SNSs, the question asked by young girls on YouTube "Am I Pretty or Ugly," and girls' YouTube vlogs describing gendered pain and suffering. These media practices and representations are critical because they are not just catalysts of moral panic but also areas of political contestation and debate for feminists and those concerned with the politics of representation and gender politics more broadly. I include myself here. The kind of feminist stance with which I am aligned is concerned with women's social equality and empowerment, as well as with challenging the gender binary and heterosexual matrix (Butler, 1990); and, put simply, sees the representation and sexual objectification of women in media as deeply connected to women's social status. When I first began my research into young women's MySpace profiles, I wanted to see what shifts and reworks were required in feminist representational theory and analysis in relation to this new domain of female-driven cultural representation. But I was also driven by the urge to weigh-up and critically *evaluate* the self-representation I found on young women's profiles against these kind of feminist concerns about challenging the gender binary and disrupting conventions of sexual objectification; not entirely conscious, perhaps, of my own investment in girls and young women as "the future subjects of feminism" and the future of feminism itself (Bae and Ivashkevich, 2011). In my analysis here I try to hold on to the former question, and, if not let go of the latter approach entirely, at least remain conscious of it. I argue that an open, curious, and "slow" approach to the analysis of girls' cultures and youth digital cultures more broadly is what is needed in future research also.

Slowing Down the Approach to Girls, Young Women, and Digital Cultures

By way of beginning with a key conclusion, I want to offer a simple suggestion about the kind of analytical disposition, or approach, needed in research exploring girls and young women's digital cultures. As adults concerned with the well-being of girls and young women, we need to *slow down* when it comes to assessing youth digital cultures on political, social, and psychological levels, and in constructing potential interventions. We need to be extra slow and careful in our evaluations when media practices of representing, and thus producing/constituting, a female self in some way appear to be new, potentially dangerous, and of "*urgent* concern." That is, we need to be *slow* when we are affectively *heat up*. A central issue in girlhood studies is the question of how to study and critically analyze girls' and young women's cultural practices, and the meanings that girls and young women give to them. We must be cognizant, scholars have argued, not to simply impose adult meanings onto youth cultural lives and values. At the same time, we must remain aware of the temptation to uncritically report the accounts girls and young women provide of their lives and cultural practices without attention to the discursive and material conditions that enable and produce personal "choice and agency" as a primary, largely depoliticized, mode of self-understanding and narration (Duits and van Zoonen, 2006, 2007; Pitcher, 2006; Best, 2007; Gill, 2007; Driscoll, 2008; Baker, 2010; Lamb and Peterson, 2012; Ringrose, 2013; Lamb, Graling, and Wheeler, 2013; Harris and Dobson, 2015). In suggesting the need to look closely, critically, but also slowly and curiously, at young women's more controversial digital media practices, I do not mean to suggest that there is nothing concerning about the practices I have mentioned for feminists and for others with a stake in the well-being of girls and young women. Rather, I mean that in the complicated terrain of postfeminist girlhood (outlined in chapter 2) and digital cultures where choice and agency operate as dominant frameworks for understanding lives, identities, and media practices, untangling interplays of power takes time and steady effort, and, as Banet-Weiser (2012) suggests, often results in *ambivalence* rather than certainty.

Lisa Henderson calls for feminist and queer scholars to "slow down" that is, to be slow to judge, and "slow to discover meanings or to package sexual experiences and sexual cultures" (2008, p. 223). This is particularly important, Henderson suggests, when new cultural practices seem at odds with our own values, preferences, and politics. She terms this a call for "slow love." Describing the qualities of the slow food movement that Henderson wishes to imagine for "slow love," she notes that it is "place-based; it occurs in networks of producers, distributors, and consumers who know each other and who negotiate, in some contexts, in terms intended to protect an environmental and social future. Who slow down." (2008, p. 223). In response to feminist critiques of what I have described elsewhere as "participatory raunch" involving young women, such as *Girls Gone Wild* (Dobson, 2014c), Henderson writes, "I don't know whether to expect a lot of girls gone wild in the slow love movement, but if they show up, I'll learn something."

It is this kind of open, ambivalent, disposition I seek to bring to the investigations of girls' and young women's apparently provocative media practices and representations, and that I want to suggest as the kind of disposition needed in future analyses of such media. We need to actively invoke curiosity about such practices. Scholars and other stakeholders need to approach girls' and young women's cultures with a view to *learning something* about their lives within particular social, cultural, geographical, and political contexts, rather than with the intent to *evaluate* their media practices against preexisting theoretical criteria or ideals, including those associated with various strands of feminism. This is not to suggest that as feminists and scholars we should let go of our values, ideals, and projects associated with our particular disciplines, and theoretical and epistemological standpoints. It is to suggest that for myself, as for other scholars of girlhood, it remains crucial to remember to ask how our investigations of cultural practices and groups with whom we do not fully identify challenge and inform our views (Best, 2007); how our investigations of youth cultures and lives teach us things about our own beliefs, values, and theories, and add to them, rather than just measuring (or failing to measure) up. There are a lot of girls going wild in various ways on social media, not all of them expressly sexual, as we see in the following chapters. By examining their media practices and representations, and debates and discourses about them, slowly and carefully, by curbing impulses toward quick judgment, we can learn something, I suggest, about gendered subjectivity and about living youthful femininity in postfeminist Western cultures. We can also learn something about the limitations of current feminist theory and analysis, and where our own views are challenged and potentially require shifts and revisions in relation to new youth cultures and practices.

Self-Representation and the Premise of Self-Production in Social Media

Scholars have suggested that social media and SNS profiles can be viewed in terms of "identity performance" (boyd and Ellison, 2007; Buckingham, 2008; Liu, 2007; Westlake, 2008; Cover, 2012a). The ideas of sociologist Erving Goffman about the "performance of self in everyday life" have been taken up in scholarship on social media to explain processes of identity construction and management. SNS profiles have been theorized as conscious, reflective performances of the self for particular audiences. Visual and textual expressions including images, graphics, and texts are constructed to give off impressions about the self and foster particular narratives about one's life and identity for a particular audience, most often for peers (boyd, 2008). This process is theorized as similar to how one usually presents the self appropriately for one's audience and context in daily life offline, through dress, speech, embodiment, and so on. However, Nancy Thumin suggests that it is important to distinguish between the presentation or performance of self as something we all do all the time, in a way that is "neither bounded nor indeed a necessarily conscious process," and "self-representation" produced by individuals as a "bounded text, however fleeting and ephemeral that text might be." In other words, Thumin uses the term "self-representation" to distinguish between more general notions of the presentation and performance of self, and the conscious, mediated representations of selves that can be found on social media, as well as other kinds of media. The key difference for Thumin is that "When a self-representation is produced it becomes a text that has the potential for subsequence engagement" (2012, p. 6). I add that another key difference is the level of conscious intent and reflectivity typically assumed by audience members/viewers. Via media, one is required to use text and images to symbolize the self, and I suggest that this is generally assumed by viewers to require a higher degree of consciousness and reflectivity about the self than conventionally required in face-to-face self-presentation.

Further, Thumin suggests that self-representation can be thought of as a "genre." A genre is a contract or "tacit understanding" between audiences and cultural producers, and the genre of self-representation is centered on conveying notions of authenticity (Thumin, 2012, p. 163). Thumin suggests that, as a genre, self-representation usually includes certain generic conventions or elements of focus, including focus on ordinary people or communities, experience, personal histories, journeys and interior worlds, emotion, as well as conventions such as speaking to a camera in close-up, scrapbook-style aesthetics, family photographs, and personal artefacts (pp. 166–167). The genre of self-representation is thus not specific to social media, nor is all social media use self-representation, but it is increasingly and particularly prevalent in social media. I follow Thumin's use of the term "self-representation" here to delineate a cultural genre and to distinguish conceptually between general notions of performativity and self-presentation, and the mediated self-representational texts, communications, and expressions with which I am concerned in this book.

Thumin suggests that in self-representation there is an implicit or explicit claim that "people are '*doing it for themselves*'" (2012, p. 8) rather than being represented by another implicitly more powerful group or individual. This claim, I suggest, effects how self-representation *via social media* is viewed, understood, and engaged with in a way that requires some further explication. Self-representations via social media most often proceed from a premise of agentic, conscious, and "authentic" self-authorship. The tacit understanding at work in social media self-representations between viewers and viewed means that members of a networked public generally take a SNS personal profile as an indicator of someone's self-chosen and "authentic" identity, produced for personal use. The term "networked public" is discussed further, but in brief, it is used to describe the way in which social media audiences can be thought of as members of a public, bound together by their use of a common platform such as Facebook. Grant Bollmer has suggested that increasingly, legitimated, socially accepted participation in networked publics is dependent on the extent to which users are willing and capable of representing their "true selves" to the exclusion of more playful and fluid notions of identity (Bollmer, 2012; see also van Zoonen, 2013).

Thinking more specifically about self-representation on social media platforms, there is perhaps a higher-level claim to "authenticity" assumed on personal social media profiles because the contract, or tacit understanding, between producers and audiences is usually also that the self-representation is produced primarily for personal use, for social and intrinsically motived, rather than commercial, purposes and intents. I describe this understanding as the "premise of self-production" that I suggest frames the way personal social media profiles are contextualized and understood by viewers, particularly on the SNSs discussed in this book. When deceptions around identity and *purpose or intent* in creating a personal profile occur on social media platforms they disrupt the conventions and expectations of the community, as was the case with, for example, pseudo-vlogger Lonelygirl15[3] and A Gay Girl in Damascus,[4] as well as many other cases. This is both because the kind of self-representation occurring in social media is usually assumed to be tied to a singular, stable identity, and *also* because the self-representation is tacitly assumed to be produced primarily for the purposes of intrinsically motivated self-expression and sociality rather than commercial or explicitly political purposes. In referring to the "premise of self-production" I suggest is at work in much social media use, I mean to foreground it as precisely that—a *premise* of, or assumed claim to, "authenticity," rather than a "truth" of how things are. Regardless of the degree to which social media practices of self-representation are actually "self-produced," agentic, chosen, conscious, tied to "real" bodies/selves, and primarily used for socially and personally motivated, noncommercial purposes, they are important to examine because of this implicit claim to truth and authenticity on multiple levels.

The premises operating in different media representations inform the ways in which much feminist media and cultural scholarship has interpreted and critiqued representations of women in media. This premise of self-production contrasts the kind of premise underscoring representations, particularly representations of women, in mass-broadcast and commercial forms of media. There is evidence from feminist research that mass-media and commercially produced representations often depict women in sexist and demeaning ways, from film, to fictional TV shows, and now reality TV and video games (Gill, 2007; Thornham, 2007; Pozner, 2010; Ross, 2010; Sarkeesian, 2013). It is often suggested that perhaps this would be less the case if more women were themselves involved in media production processes, as I explain in chapter 2. It is in this context that self-representation, as made easily accessible by social media, has been theorized as potentially "empowering" for girls and women, and thus also a political tool (Brandes and Levin, 2013; Dean and Laidler, 2013; Tiidenberg, 2014). My thinking about the politics of social media self-representations proceeds from this understanding of self-representation as a genre concerned primarily with claiming and depicting "authenticity," and the "premise of self-production" as primarily for social purposes which frames audiences' interpretation of personal social media self-representations. In many ways, however, neat binaries between commercial or "mainstream" media and social media do not hold up in the contemporary context, and much self-representation via social media complicates notions of greater freedom, authenticity, and empowerment in social media self-representation, as I argue in the chapters to follow.

As Nick Couldry states, all kinds of media representations make "truth claims, explicit or implicit." Because of these truth claims, "the gaps and repetitions in media representations, if systematic enough, can distort people's sense of what there is to see in the social and political domains" (2012, pp. 21–22). In this sense, and following poststructuralist theorists, we need to understand media as not reflective of a preexisting "reality" but as producing and constituting our sense of the real through repeated discourses and representations, and in concert and "intra-action" (Barad, 2003) with the material world of resources, objects, and bodies. As Couldry states, "Representations are a material site for the exercise of, and struggle over, power. Put most simply, our sense of 'what there is' is always the result of social and political struggle, always a site where power has been at work." (2012, p. 30). I would suggest that these ideas about power and the importance of media representations are particularly important to understand in relation to *social media self-representations.* Social media self-representations make explicit and implicit claims to truth and authenticity on multiple levels, and this makes them vitally important to critically analyze as representational texts.

Girls and young women are centrally caught up in power struggles as they interact with, via, and in postfeminist techno-social mediascapes to produce self-representations in the course of everyday life. Further, the feminist poststructuralist epistemology with which I am aligned understands gendered bodies and identities not as inherent properties of bodily matter, but as constituted and produced in concert with performative and discursive acts of self-articulation that give rise to the *illusion* of stable and bounded material bodies with stable "inner cores" (Butler, 1990; Barad, 2003; Cover, 2012a). As such, social media self-representations provide rich data for an analysis of *gender* as it is constituted and produced performatively and discursively, through symbolic, repetitive, and normative expression.

* * *

Chapter Outlines

In chapter 2, I provide an overview of the key contextual factors I wish to highlight in situating the media practices and self-representations discussed in this book within a "postfeminist" cultural context. I begin by outlining some of the key problems and concerns around the representation of women identified by feminist scholars of media and culture working in the 1970s and 1980s in order to better situate current cultural and techno-social shifts in the representation of girls and women. I then discuss four cultural conditions that I argue are key to the postfeminist context and idealized femininity within it. These are: 1) continued and prominent objectification of female bodies in Western visual culture, now framed as "chosen/agentic"; 2) the prominence of "new femininities" in culture and representations that construct and address girls and young women as strong, confident, capable, and fun-loving subjects in contrast to earlier models of weak femininity; 3) highly publicized debates about the sexualization of girls in Western cultures, which have positioned girls and young women as in need of protection, surveillance, and regulation; and 4) the psychopathologization of femininity and the institutionalization of "gender melancholia" (McRobbie, 2009). In the final sections of this chapter, I outline some of the new possibilities and pressures for girls and young women opened up by social media in order to situate my own investigations into particular digital media practices and representations in the chapters to follow.

Chapter 3 explores a hotspot of sexualization debates by examining what is arguably the most contentious aspect of young women's SNS content: heterosexy and sexual profile decorations and self-imaging. I analyze different types or categories of heterosexy visual material encountered on young women's SNS profiles: digital animations, soft-porn-type images, celebrity images, self-images, and "hot and hostile" images. I explore possible meanings of each of these types of heterosexy iconography. The feminist potentialities of such representation in a premise of self-production are debated, with reference to Schneider's theorization of explicit body performance art produced by women. I conclude by elucidating my ambivalence about the particular postfeminist "brand" (Banet-Weiser, 2012) of visual heterosexiness, and the work and resources potentially required for girls and young women to signify "sexual subjectification" (Gill, 2003) in cool and legible ways.

Chapter 4 examines the issue of sexting practices and gender. Here I look at the prevalence of youth sexting, how it has been approached in prevention messages aimed at young people, as well as how young people themselves perceive the gender dynamics of sexual digital communication in recent research on this issue, including my own. This issue highlights a key contradiction in the postfeminist cultural context between the positioning of girls and young women as empowered and powerful postfeminist sexual subjects, and the positioning of them as "at risk" and vulnerable to the harms of cultural sexualization. Research into youth sexting makes it clear that longstanding sexual double standards and beliefs about male and female sexuality are still the basis for harassment and abuse. I argue that symbolic and discursive acts that disempower women and implicitly authorize male violence are perpetrated too when we assume women and girls' victimhood status and act to "protect them" from their own sexuality and from men's assumed reactions on this basis. Both in the panic that has ensued about sexting and its damaging consequences for girls, and in girls' experiences of gendered bullying and violence, we can see that we are still a long way from being able to safely assume women's sexual empowerment. We are also, it seems, still a long way from making the space necessary for an actualization of women's and girls' sexual empowerment through our discursive approaches to this issue. This chapter shows why it is so important that we find a way to assume and discursively position girls as *sexual agents* in our approaches to youth sexting, while addressing current gendered power imbalances in relation to the circulation of sexual and bodily images.

In chapter 5, I discuss the common features of the decorative textual "mottos" and self-descriptions posted on the SNS profiles I analyzed. As well as being strikingly forthright, self-assured, and unapologetic in their articulations of self, the profile creators often highlight the "random," changeable, imperfect and unfinished nature of their identities. I examine these texts in relation to broader discourses of individualization, self-actualization, transparency, and self-esteem for girls. The texts work overall to foster a sense of confidence and self-acceptance—two highly valued traits of postfeminist femininity. Such self-representational texts, I suggest, perhaps work to enable young women to negotiate conflicting demands of digital self-representation to construct a self that is fluid and open to revision, and yet also "authentically" youthful and feminine, and stable in its gendered attributes. I suggest that the textual mottos and self-descriptions by young women discussed in this chapter indicate both the value and sociocultural currency of confident, self-assured, youthful, feminine self-representations, as well as the harshness and hostility experienced by many young women in postfeminist digital cultures as sites of "incited judgment" (Nurka, 2014).

In chapter 6, I explore what might be seen as the polar opposite of such girl-powered performative digital selves. If the texts and mottos young women post on the SNS profiles I analyzed represent and construct "can do" girls, the girl media producers explored in chapter 6 represent "at risk" girls (Harris, 2004). In this chapter I discuss two examples of girl figures I suggest are both positioned as fitting within a broader rubric of "digital girls in crisis," but between whom there are important differences as well as commonalities I unpack. First, I discuss girls seeking appearance-related feedback in networked publics through an exploration of the "Am I Pretty or Ugly" videos. I then consider the case of 15-year-old Amanda Todd, whose YouTube video posted just weeks before her suicide in Canada in 2012 went viral, and similar videos made by teenage girls on YouTube narrating experiences of emotional pain often tied to bullying, depression, and various practices of self-harm including self-injury and eating disorders. I argue that discursive and affective responses to girls seeking appearance feedback publicly suggest a concern about the *value* and *values* of these girls, who seem to be judged as either having an *excess* of self-focus, or a *lack* of self-esteem, and thus, little value. Girls who narrate and mediate pain publicly are positioned slightly differently, as already fully pathological subjects, and thus a key concern about their digital self-productions appears to be that their pathologies and emotions will spread virally and contagiously (Kramer, Guillory, and Hancock, 2014) and infect or "trigger" other girls in networked publics. Public response to both girl figures, I argue, suggest a broader gendered devaluation, and increasing pathologization, of media practices of seeking feedback, connectivity, and relationality.

I conclude *Postfeminist Digital Cultures* with a critical assessment of the kind of postfeminist, girl-powered femininity that still prevails in media and cultural representations of, and addresses to, girls and young women. I suggest particular ambivalences and concerns around the ideals of visibility and self-exposure that are so central to postfeminist femininity, and weigh up the cultural promises made to girls and young women about digital visibility and self-exposure against some potential costs. I summarize the complex and contradictory pressures on girls and young women in postfeminist digital cultures to tell and show the self and body as heterosexy, but not sexualized, and confident, independent, "authentic," and "transparent," but not narcissistic; to be markedly visible and exposed in very specific and conditional ways.

The Research Projects Discussed

In two of the chapters here I report on a study of MySpace profiles conducted in 2007 and 2008, which looked at contemporary postfeminist feminine gender performativity through SNS self-representation. My study was of visual and textual data from 45 MySpace profiles selected out of a viewing of over 300 profiles conducted between September 2007 and February 2008. Criteria in these searches limited the search results to public profiles marked as owned by Australian women aged between 18 and 21. Profiles were selected after a preliminary browse, looking at the general page aesthetics and checking to see that sufficient expressive features were contained. Profiles were included for further analysis in the study, first, because of the way these young women performed their identities within current conventional models of femininity in Western popular culture. One of the aims of this research was to examine the meanings of young women's own engagements with, and appropriations of, mainstream and currently popular models of mediated feminine performativity. As such, profiles were included in this study based on visual and aesthetic indicators of engagement with "femininity"; for example through use of pink and purple colors, feminized graphics and wallpapers such as hearts, stars, glittered logos, or images of currently popular feminine celebrities. Profiles with overtly subcultural or alternative themes, or profiles which did not obviously engage with feminized aesthetics or visual culture, were not included in the study. Second, profiles were included for analysis based on the amount of rich, expressive public data they contained. In other words, I selected profiles with sufficient expressive material to indicate a publicly oriented and "expressive" approach to SNS use. For example, when members utilized features and affordances on MySpace such as personalized profile decorations, descriptive or creative text, lists of personal likes and dislikes, and the public posting of pictures, music, videos, and other media, this I suggest constitutes a more "expressive" rather than "instrumental" approach to SNS use. Some public profiles contained many pages of comments between friends, but little text directed toward a public audience, and minimal decorations, photos, or other visual expressions, and were excluded on this basis. I conducted a textual and semiotic analysis to investigate the performative construction of femininity on SNSs through signs and symbols, photos, self-descriptive text, publicly circulated blog posts, and lists of "likes" and "dislikes." In this research I was not looking at interpersonal communication documented on the profiles or interviewing profile owners about their self-representations.

All of the profile owners were contacted via their MySpace profiles. They were informed about the details of this project, including the details of de-identification processes. They were asked to voice any concerns about the research, and to give their *implicit* consent to the inclusion of their profiles for de-identified analysis in the study. I informed the owners that if I did not receive any objections from them, their profile would be included for analysis. No objections were received, and six profile owners replied to voice their best wishes for the project. The names of all the profile owners and the friends they mention have been changed and any identifying information has been altered or removed from material discussed to protect the identities of the profile owners and their friends. I do not show visual material from the profiles analyzed in this book. The pseudonyms I use have been constructed to give readers a sense of the kind of names chosen by the creators. They are in keeping with the spirit of the names used by these young women, but they do not reveal the individuals' MySpace aliases. This research received ethics approval from the Monash University Human Research Ethics Committee.

This research is of interest in this book not because this site is still the latest trend with young women, but because it provides us with examples of how young women mediate common aspects of contemporary postfeminist femininity. The profiles I analyzed in 2007 are now mostly abandoned, deleted, or they have been made private, accessible only to those who have been accepted as "friends" by the owner. Facebook is now the most widely used SNS in Australia, and worldwide. At the time of writing Facebook was second only to Google in Australian and global web traffic (Alexa.com, 2014). With Facebook comes a different kind of use and functionality to that of MySpace, one more centered on social communication and the sharing of media rather than visual self-representation to a public audience. As Brady Robards suggests, MySpace use appears to be more aligned with the "performative model of the personal homepage," while Facebook appears to be a more social space where "biographical details are less important than regular interactions." (2010, p. 392). These MySpace profiles thus have much to tell us about the self-representational requirements of postfeminist femininity and how these are negotiated by girls and young women themselves.

In chapter 4, as well as discussing international research on sexting, I discuss data collected by myself along with Danielle Tyson, Mary Lou Rasmussen, and Adrian Farrugia in 2013 for the project "Youth, mobile technologies, and gender politics: Young people's beliefs about gender and ethical use of communication technologies." We showed

Tagged—a short film about cybersafety and digital reputation—to students in Years ten and eleven (aged 15 to 17) at two rural schools in Victoria, Australia. This film is produced by the Australian government and used widely in schools. A week after screening the film, we conducted focus groups with the students. With the help of teachers, these groups were friendship-based and mostly gender segregated, resulting in two mixed-gender groups, one group of all boys, and one of all girls, with a total of 24 participants across the two schools. One school was relatively small in size, with less than 80 students in Years Ten and Eleven combined. The other was a large school with 184 students in Year Eleven only. The group discussions focused on general impressions of the film, what they remembered most from it, and what is communicated in the film about gender roles. Our discussions also asked for participants' views about the issues raised in the film of sexting and cyberbullying, and their views on the gender roles depicted around these incidents. The film *Tagged* provides what we thought might be a "believable" narrative account of various incidents relating to digital reputation management that allows young people to reflect on the actions and the characters presented, and develop their own thoughts and critical evaluations of the scenarios depicted. Sexting practices, and student's opinions about various practices relating to the mediation and circulation of sexual images in networked publics, emerged as one of the key themes of these discussions. In the legal landscape in 2013, legal minors (those under 18 years of age) in Victoria could be charged with offences relating to child pornography for various sexting practices. We were very conscious that talking to young people about gender roles and experiences around technology might bring up stories of activities or experiences that potentially position young people as criminals. We took care to clarify with the young people involved that our discussion was focused on their understandings and opinions about gender roles in relation to technology use, and not on people's personal experiences or stories involving sexting. At the same time, we made sure there were protocols in place that would allow teens to discuss issues troubling them privately, with their school counsellors, if these did arise. The student participants were assigned pseudonyms in the focus groups. This research received ethics approval from the Monash University Human Research Ethics Committee and from the Department of Education and Early Childhood Development.

In chapter 6, my discussion and arguments stem from research on YouTube that began as background research for the project, "Youth, mobile technologies, and gender politics." I viewed and analyzed online cybersafety campaigns from Australia, Canada, and the UK as part of this project. I became interested in the way in which several of these campaigns drew from, attempted to imitate, or directly responded to gendered stories of digital abuse and harassment told by young people, primarily teenage girls themselves (see Dobson, 2015; Dobson and Ringrose, 2015), and I began searching for young people's own digital stories of online bullying and harassment via YouTube. Naming conventions emerge around the telling of such stories on YouTube. For example, a search for "my bullying story" brings up around 384,000 videos. I searched for videos based on this, and other common titles such as "my self-harm story," "my secrets," "if you really knew me" and "hi my name is [. . .]." I browsed through hundreds of these videos, most of which appear to be made by young teenage girls, and analyzed in detail a small sample of 20 videos depicting girls holding up flash/cue cards for the camera in order to narrate their stories of pain to music, stories most often related to gendered bullying and self-harm of various kinds. Elsewhere I have analyzed in more detail the conventions of these "pain meme" videos and their significance for those charged with caring for youth (Dobson, 2015).

Some Key Definitions

Some key terminology used in this book requires explanation before proceeding. First of all, I refer to "girls" and "young women" as the subjects of research discussed in this book. The research I conducted on SNSs examined profiles identified as owned by women aged between 18 and 21 at the time of viewing. The young people with whom we spoke about cybersafety education, gender, and sexting were aged between 15 and 17. The videos I viewed on YouTube in the course of research into bullying and self-harm vlogs depicted female subjects who appeared to be aged in their early to mid-teenage years, but age was not often specified on the vlogs. I refer in this book to both "girls and young women" when specific boundaries between adulthood and childhood are not of key import. I use "young women" when I am referring specifically to women older than 18 and thus no longer legally considered minors in Australia, where this research was conducted. I use "girls" when specifically referring to subjects aged under 18.

I describe the digital media discussed in this book as both "representations" and "practices." I find it helpful to think of "media as practice" following Nick Couldry (2012). Couldry argues that the central focus of media research needs to shift in the digital era toward questions of practice: "what types of things do people do in relation to media" and "what types of things do people say (think, believe) in relation to media?" (Couldry, 2012, p. 40). He suggests that such questions cannot be clearly answered "simply by starting out from the 'text' of, say, a televised game and the various ways people read that text" (2012, p. 43). Rather, "By moving media research's center of gravity away from texts (and their production or direct reception) and towards the broader set of practices related to media, we get a better grip on the distinctive types of social processes enacted through media-related practices." (p. 44). I am still concerned with unpacking significations in media representations themselves that appear to be made by girls and young women to represent the self. I keep representations central to my discussions here despite the acknowledgment that representations can be seen to fit within a broader category of "media practices." Representations still matter vitally, as Couldry suggests. Couldry advocates for a media sociology approach that is "interested in actions that are directly oriented to media, actions that involve media without necessarily having media as their aim or object; and actions whose possibility is conditioned by the prior existence, presence or functioning of media" (2012, p. 35). This describes well my angle of approach to the study of digital media cultures in this book, concerned as I am with issues of gender and the shaping of social ideas about young femininity that occurs around and in relation to digital media practices and representations produced by girls and young women. Examining social media representations that are apparently self-produced by young women and girls provides a way to try to understand the "truth claims" made about young femininity in Western, postfeminist social contexts, via and with media. In chapters 3 and 5 my aims are to unpack, explore, and explain constructs of gender in young women's self-representations on SNSs, while in chapters 4 and 6 I am more centrally concerned with understanding social and cultural *life with media* (Couldry, 2012, p. 34).

It is not necessary for this book to provide an extensive discussion of various media and technological terms and functions, but a few media practices discussed require brief definition. I utilize boyd and Ellison's definition of SNSs as "web-based services that allow individuals to: (1) construct a public or semipublic profile within a bounded system, (2) articulate a list of other users with whom they share a connection, and (3) view and traverse their list of connections and those made by others within the system." (boyd and Ellison, 2007, p. 211). I also follow them in referring to such sites as social *network* sites rather than social *networking* sites to draw attention to the fact that for the majority of users, and especially young people, such sites often function as ways of displaying and connecting one's existing social networks rather than as tools used primarily for the purpose of networking (boyd and Ellison, 2007). As Hinton and Hjorth outline, "social media" is a term that has developed with the rapid growth of SNSs, and the increasing ubiquity of mobile media devices, and it helps to encompass the "growing and often unwieldy sphere of contemporary online media practice" (2013, p. 1). Social media, as they note, "bleed across platforms (desktop computers, mobile phones, tablets, and on modern network-capable televisions), across social and media contexts," and across public and private, personal and professional spheres (2013, p. 1).

It is worth outlining here briefly the key affordances of digital mediation. Understanding the affordances of digital mediation is key to comprehending the significance of media practices that *occur in* and *produce* digitally networked spaces, or "networked publics"—a term I use throughout this book. As danah boyd explains, via digital mediation, our interactions, representations, digital artefacts, and traces are *persistent* across time and place, *visible* to potentially large and mostly invisible audiences, easily *spreadable* across contexts (and thus often transported out of the intended social context), and much more easily *searchable* and locatable thanks to the help of large and powerful search engines (boyd, 2014, p. 11). Ideas of what information is, can be, and should be shared "publicly" and what is "private" and "personal" have become complicated, and are still shifting in relation to the popularity and widespread use of social media (Lange, 2007; Hartley, Burgess, and Bruns, 2013; Senft and Baym, 2015; Salter, forthcoming). So too, ideas of the boundaries between public and private spaces and contexts are also complicated in this techno-social context (Gregg, 2011). Most SNSs allow users to make their posts and profiles publicly available on the Internet or semiprivate and broadcast only to select networks of friends and contacts. The profiles and videos posted via the SNSs I discuss in this book were publicly available on the Internet at the time I accessed them. But as scholars have pointed out, the affordances of digitally networked media complicate such simple distinctions, primarily by increasing the ease with which media can be shared. The term "networked public" best describes both the space and the techno-social context in which media practices take place. As boyd writes, "Networked publics are publics both in the spatial sense and in the sense of an imagined community" (2014, p. 9). Social media allow people to gather, connect, and be present with each other, similarly to public physical spaces; and, similarly to how an audience of popular TV shows might imagine itself as "an audience" connected through their viewing of the show, users of social media might imagine themselves as part of broader communities (boyd, 2014, pp. 9–10). The term "networked public" as I use it following boyd, is not centrally a way of distinguishing between "public" and "private" space or information, but describes "(1) the space constructed through networked technologies and (2) the imagined community that emerges as a result of the intersection of people, technology, and practice" (boyd, 2014, p. 8).

For further elaboration on various technological terms and affordances to do with social media and digital culture I point readers to Sam Hinton and Larissa Hjorth's book *Understanding Social Media* (2013), which provides an excellent introduction. Other excellent existing books have also covered the key concepts, research questions, and issues at play in social media scholarship across a range of disciplines, including youth studies, media studies, and anthropology, and I point readers to these sources for further information (Weber and Dixon, 2007; Buckingham, 2008; Papacharissi, 2011; Horst and Miller, 2012; Hartley, Burgess and Bruns, 2013; Hunsinger and Senft, 2013; boyd, 2014; Robards and Bennet, 2014).

Chapter 2

Postfeminism, Girls and Young Women, and Digital Media

Introduction

This chapter provides an overview of the key contextual factors I wish to highlight in situating the media practices and self-representations discussed in this book within "postfeminist" digital culture. It is helpful to remember some of the key concerns of feminist media scholars working in the 1970s in situating the current cultural and techno-social context as postfeminist. I thus begin this chapter by outlining some of the key problems and concerns around the representation of women identified by feminist scholars in various spheres of visual culture—television, art, theatre, and film—in the 1970s and 1980s. I then describe some of the changes feminist scholars of media and culture have noted in the cultural landscape of the late-1980s onward, positioned centrally as postfeminist in terms of cultural, political, and social shifts that were provoked in key ways by the second wave feminist movement. Here I am concerned primarily with cultural shifts. A central shift in representations of women in visual culture noted by Rosalind Gill (2003) is from sexual *objectification* to sexual *subjectification*, as I explain. New modes of youthful femininity have been identified in media representations of women, and media and culture aimed at girls and young women. Along with more "active" and "desiring" constructions of sexuality, cultural scholars have noted that in postfeminist mediascapes girls and young women are depicted and addressed as fun-loving, consumption focused, and more "empowered," active, and bold, physically, socially, and psychologically. Such constructions of femininity can be seen as a response to feminist critique of earlier, weaker versions of femininity portrayed widely in media and cultural representations (Hopkins, 2002; Harris,

2004; Aapola, Gonick, and Harris, 2005; Gonick, Renold, Ringrose, and Weems, 2009; Zaslow, 2009; Hains, 2012).

At the same time as more active, assertive, and sexually desiring representations of girls and young women have become quite prevalent, a panic around the "sexualization" of culture has erupted (Attwood, 2006, 2009), focused on Western mediascapes, and particularly concerned with the well-being of Anglophone and middle-class girls and young women (Egan, 2013). This has put girls and young women in the awkward position of being called toward active and assertive sexual performativity and displays of strong self-confidence on the one hand, and policed for signals of sexualized self-representation, as well as signals of "low self-esteem" that are thought to result from immersion in a sexualized media culture, on the other. It is important to understand these broad shifts in modes of feminine representation and address to girls and young women in order to understand the meaning and significance of girls' and young women's self-representations and media practices today. In the final sections of this chapter, I explain how girls and young women are engaging with digital media, and social media in particular. I outline some of the new possibilities and pressures for girls and young women opened up by social media in order to situate my own investigations into particular digital media practices and representations in the chapters to follow.

Women and Representation: Second-Wave Feminist Concerns

> More and more, women have been cast on the periphery as whores, sisters, wives, or they are there to be screwed, quarreled over or slapped around. [...] There are no contemporary stories with strong-willed mature heroines. (Edgar and McPhee, 1974, p. 17)

A body of feminist-inspired research into gender roles in the media, and gender socialization through representation, gained momentum in the Anglophone West in the early 1970s, consisting mainly of content and textual analysis of film and television. This work aimed to demonstrate from a feminist perspective how forms of visual and textual representation contributed to the socialization of women and men into normative gender roles (Greer, 1970; Kustow, 1972; Butcher et al., 1974; Edgar and McPhee, 1974; Busby, 1975; Janus, 1977; Williamson, 1978; Goffman, 1979; Tuchman, 1979). At the same time, in the study of Western "high" cultural forms such as visual arts and theatre, feminism was inspiring research into images of women and the social construction of feminine subjectivity in Western culture, as well as into the history of female artists, or lack thereof (Nochlin, 1971/1989; Hess and Baker, 1973; Callaghan, 1989; Ferris, 1990). Feminist scholars highlighted the broader question of how it is that women are socialized to be both consumers of their own image and objects of consumption, rather than *producers*, even of their own image and representation (Berger, 1972/2008; Hess and Nochlin, 1973). Thus, early research into "images of women" in media and culture, and gender or "sex-role socialization" through representation spans across a wide range of media and cultural forms including television, newspapers, magazines, radio, advertising, films, novels, and paintings.[1] In brief, in feminist scholarship of the 1970s and 1980s, images of women, and female gender roles in both the mass media and in "high culture," are found to be very limited, weak, and passive. Representational and cultural products are seen as major vehicles for the communication of gender norms that privilege men as a group, and the male-biased political ideologies which serve to uphold and sustain gender normative roles and subjectivities. In relation to eroticism in nineteenth-century art, Linda Nochlin summates, "The male image is one of power, possession and domination, the female one of submission, passivity and availability" (Nochlin, 1973, p. 14). The Women's Studies Group at the Centre for Contemporary Cultural Studies at the University of Birmingham summarizes women's mass media representation as follows:

> We find that woman's re-presentation in the media is orientated round the images of "mother," "housewife," "wife," and "sexual object." These are the "norms" within which women are pushed to conform, which individual women have to negotiate. They all represent woman as negativity, woman as oppressed: she only exists through her relationships to men, she can only be consumed by men. (Butcher et al., 1974, p. 17)

Patricia Edgar and Hilary McPhee (1974) strongly critique the kinds of stereotypical roles afforded to women in television in Australia, and Hollywood movies, arguing that such representation serves to socialize women into prescribed and very limited avenues for appropriate femininity. They call for more "realistic" images of women in the mass media, for more female roles, and for "better"—meaning stronger, more active—female roles in all types of representational and artistic forms, arguing that women are *misrepresented* in the media. However, they uncritically contrast representation in the mass media with a notion of representing "real women" (1974, p. 2), implying that media simply *reflects* identities and subjectivities rather than *constituting* them. This is typical of much work in this early stage of feminist media and cultural inquiry. Images of women in representation are often theorized by feminist scholars working in the 1970s as the product of a media and cultural production arena controlled overwhelmingly by men. In such critiques of the mass media, there seems an underlying hope, or assumption, that when more female producers of media are able to successfully infiltrate the media and cultural landscape, representation of women will progressively diversify, and more possibilities will open up as to how women are represented. For example, Linda Busby writes in 1975:

> Since the mass media have been dominated primarily by one group—white, American males—it is not surprising to find a similarity of imagery in all the media. The media sex-role studies that have been completed in the 1960s and early 1970s can be used as historical documents to measure future social changes. (Busby, 1975, p. 127)

This statement demonstrates the expectation that in the aftermath of the women's liberation movement, social change in terms of female representation will occur, largely as the result of a presumed breakdown of the male monopoly over cultural representation. We have seen women's entry into many areas of commercial media production over the last 30 years. Although, as feminist scholars have documented, much work remains to be done and many media industries are still overwhelmingly male-dominated (Gill, 2007). While I do not have space for a detailed account here, Lousie North (2009), for example, documents ongoing male-domination in newsrooms, among and despite radical industry changes, and Alice Marwick (2013) outlines the US digital media industry, and male-domination within it.

Girls and women's prominent participation in cultural production through digital and social media has been theorized in some recent feminist work as contributing to the weakening or porosity of media and cultural production industries dominated by men and modes of female representation within them (Molyneaux, O'Donnell, Gibson, and Singer, 2008; Szostak, 2013; Boler, Harris, and Jacobson, forthcoming; Keller, 2015). However, the following chapters of this book complicate any simplistic conceptualizations that tie progressive or subversive gender representation to the "democratization" of media production and women's increased participation in the spheres of digital cultural production and self-representation. Questions were raised in the 1970s by Marx-influenced feminists, such as Noreene Janus (1977), regarding: first, what actually constitutes "realistic" or "better" portrayals and images of women; and second, whether women's entry into media production should itself be seen as a determinant of progressive changes in the representation of women, or whether there are other more significant determinants of cultural change and repetition. These questions remain important today, especially in relation to social media. Janus argues that women's socialized roles in society—as subordinated housewives, mothers, consumers, and lower-paid workers—are instrumental to the functioning of the capitalist economy, and the sustaining of a ruling class (Janus, 1977, p. 24). She suggests that the causes of change in female representation are often material and profit-based. Janus writes: "While the home products industries, for example, may still find the traditional housewife to be their best market and strive to keep women in that role, other industries whose products are not so tied to home use, may now find it expedient to avoid such role stereotyping in their communications or even to promote other roles for women" (Janus, 1977, p. 26). As she suggests, it is important to remain aware that representational changes that appear to offer something new and more diverse, or more socially progressive, do not necessarily or inevitably serve gender and social justice purposes. Women's entry into media production in and of itself, and the proliferation of digital self-representation, may not be the cause of lasting or deep shifts in ideologies of gender, as representations and self-representations are tied to markets and systems of profit-making, and gendered identities intersect with racialized identities and socioeconomic-based positions of status (Jhally, 2006; Gill, 2007; Banet-Weiser, 2012). Further, women hold various psychosocial investments in gender-typical feminine self-representations (Hollway, 1984) that intersect with raced and classed identities, and that do not swiftly or easily disappear because of the widespread availability of the tools of media production, and techno-social calls toward self-representation (Thumin, 2012).

Feminists in the 1970s and 1980s also pertinently questioned from a psychological perspective whether it was possible for female "subject positions" to originate within narrative cultural forms and structures developed within a patriarchal system of knowledge (Mulvey, 1975/1989; Cixous, 1980; de Lauretis, 1984; Case, 1988; Diamond, 1997). Sue-Ellen Case documents the processes and theories by which feminists in the late 1970s and early 1980s began to deconstruct the historical, material, and *psychological* semiotics of representation within dominant patriarchal sign systems, rather than simply campaign for "more," "better," and different types of female representation (Case, 1988, pp. 112–117). The pertinent realization of this time, explored by scholars such as Mulvey (1975/1989), Kaplan (1983), and de Lauretis (1984) is that "the sign 'woman'" is constructed not just by but *for* a male heterosexualized gaze (Case, 1988, p. 118). The protagonists of major narratives—the *subjects* of representation—are constructed as "universal" subjects, while being imbued with specifically masculine "psychosexual anxieties." Feminist scholars of film and theatre suggest that there is little room for the representation of female desires, meaning both sexual desires and "drive" or motivation more broadly, and thus, no real female *subjects* of representation within this system. This work both draws from and critiques the Freudian psychosexual theories so influential in film and theatre. For example, Laura Mulvey (1975/1989) influentially argues that in film, the gaze of the camera itself is encoded as "male" (and heterosexual) and thus in film viewers, whether male or female and regardless of sexuality, are asked to identify with the male protagonist and *his* desires. Similarly, John Berger (1972/2008) explains the way that the *subjects* of classical European oil paintings are never themselves painted, but are constructed as heterosexual males through the nude, performative poses of the female bodies. These nudes seldom represent a *desiring* body, and nearly always signify a body merely "on display," as if there only to satisfy a viewer's desire, according to Berger (1972/2008, pp. 48–49). Case explains how theatrical texts and performances construct the protagonist of the dramatic action as male through an analysis of the various signifying aspects of theatrical performance that takes the gender-specificity of Freudian theories into account. She writes,

> Within this order of male desire and castration, the only role for women is as the objects of that desire. The result is that women become fixed in the position of object of the gaze, rather than as the subject directing it; women appear in order to be looked upon rather than to do the looking...Thus, women on stage never represent the subject position—their desire is not symbolized in patriarchal culture...The audience becomes the male subject, exiled in the system of theatrical representation and driven by unfulfilled desire. (Case, 1988, p. 120)

For many feminist scholars of media and culture, the representation of women's desires is essential for the construction of female *subject* positions in representation, and the constitution of a more empowered and active feminine subjectivity. It is beyond my scope here to detail the critiques that have been made of these theories, particularly of Mulvey's claims around the gaze[2] (see Mulvey, 1989). I have outlined only in brief some key concerns around the representation of women in feminist work that can be broadly classified as part of the second wave of feminism. This is because it is important to ground our understanding of recent shifts and debates about women's representation in the postfeminist cultural and historical context in this history of feminist thinking about gender roles, sexual objectification, desire, and the gaze.

The cultural context I want to highlight and operationalize as "postfeminist" in this book is one which I suggest is characterized by four conditions that appear to be prominent. I use the term "conditions" to invoke the notion of a particular climate that must be navigated. These are: 1) continued and prominent objectification of female bodies in Western visual culture, now framed as "chosen/agentic"; 2) the prominence of "new femininities" in culture and representations that construct and address girls and young women as strong, confident, capable, and fun-loving subjects in contrast to earlier models of weak femininity; 3) highly publicized debates about the sexualization of girls and young women in Western cultures, which have positioned girls and young women as in need of protection, surveillance, and regulation; and 4) the psychopathologization of femininity and the institutionalization of "gender melancholia" McRobbie (2009) describes. These are four significant cultural, social, political, and historical conditions that I suggest girls and young women must currently traverse, and negotiate a pathway around or through, in the process of constructing legible feminine subjectivities. In the sections to follow I outline each of these conditions, starting with the framing of women's sexual objectification as chosen and agentic, which is key to how postfeminist cultural "sensibilities" (Gill, 2007) have been theorized.[3] I am primarily concerned in this book with the cultural, and thus mainly refer in what follows to the postfeminist "cultural" context, with the provision that the cultural is tied inextricably to the social, political, and historical. (When I wish to draw attention more specifically to one of these other broad contextual factors I do so.)

Postfeminist "Agentic Objectification" or "Sexual Subjectification"

In the contemporary Western and Anglophone cultural context, the representation of "female desire" does not hold the same meaning as it did in the 1970s and 1980s. In many forms of commercial culture, a certain kind of assertive, sometimes aggressive, image of female desire is now as common a trope as feminine passivity and demureness once was. Rosalind Gill suggests that in media culture since the late 1980s there has been a shift in the way women and women's bodies are represented, a move away from the passivity and submission once associated with female bodies on display for a masculinized gaze, toward the presentation of "desiring sexual subjects who choose to present themselves in a seemingly objectified manner because it suits their liberated interests to do so" (Gill, 2007, p. 258). Gill and several other scholars and cultural commentators have noted that female sexual *objecthood* in visual culture today is most often constructed in and through discourses of, and textual and meta-textual references to, choice, self-pleasure, desire, and authenticity. Women's bodies are still on display, and may still be constructed as on display for male heterosexual viewers, but semiotic signals and explicit references to the "choice" and "agency" of the body on display are a central part of postfeminist cultural constructions of female sexiness and desirability (Goldman, 1992; Gill, 2003, Levy, 2005; Atwood, 2006; Pitcher, 2006; Thornham, 2007; McRobbie, 2009; Gill and Scharff, 2011; Evans and Riley, 2014). This shift can be seen as a direct response to the concerns raised by feminists in the 1970s and 1980s about women's sexual objectification in media and culture. In the postfeminist era women are now often represented as "subjects" with powerful and active sexual drives and desires, and also as sexual "objects" who make choices about their own sex object status. But they are still on display, and it is in part the representation of women's supposed desire and active choice-making that positions female bodies as *desirable* within the postfeminist cultural context, as Gill (2003) argues. This element of choice and the presentation of female bodies as "agentically objectified" or rather, as Gill suggests, women's "sexual *subject*ification" is a key shift in the representation of women and in broad cultural discourses that address girls and women. As Gill suggests, "Subjectification, it might be argued, is just how we 'do' objectification today. But women are still located in their bodies, indeed *as* bodies, albeit voraciously heterosexually desiring ones, as in conventional pornography" (2007, p. 111).

Journalist Ariel Levy (2005) has made a similar argument regarding cultural leisure trends and practices which she groups together as "raunch culture." She suggests that women in the Anglophone West are now invited to willingly participate in a range of cultural practices that position female bodies as objects on display. She documents, for example, women's attendance at strip clubs under a guise of "knowing" fun and "irony," as well as the repositioning of pole-dancing as a legitimate leisure and fitness activity for women (see also Whitehead and Kurz, 2009). For Angela McRobbie, such cultural practices might be said to "invoke" feminism only to dismiss the need for it. McRobbie suggests that popular cultural representations of women and cultural trends marketed to them in the postfeminist context "actively invoke hostility to assumed feminist positions from the past in order to endorse a new regime of sexual meanings based on female consent, equality, participation, and pleasure, free of politics" (2004, p. 9). McRobbie (2009) describes how the "aftermath" of feminism sees young women positioned in government and educational discourses as subjects who are best placed to succeed in the neoliberal political climate that emphasizes personal responsibility rather than social and state support.[4] Provided they do "succeed" within the strictures of middle-class norms, by achieving high educationally and delaying motherhood until establishing a career for themselves, they are invited to participate in the masculinized hedonistic sexual and leisure culture of commercial clubs and youth party scenes, McRobbie suggests. At the same time, in visual culture women's bodies are emphatically feminized, objectified, and disciplined through hyper-feminine fashion culture, and via often vicious makeover television shows that position feminine fashion and the pursuit of bodily perfection as empowering "care of the self" (McRobbie, 2009; see also, Ringrose and Walkerdine, 2008; Gill and Scharff, 2011). Critical accounts of postfeminist popular culture such as these are helpful in unpacking new framings of female *desire*, choice, empowerment, and agency that complicate earlier feminist theories about "objects" and "subjects" in representation. Powerful images of "active" rather than passive, desired and *desiring* female bodies are now common across mediascapes and in certain cultural scenes. We can no longer rely upon the representation of "desiring" females to provide the kind of cultural openings or progressive change many second-wave feminists perhaps envisioned. These are shifts that complicate the object/subject binary itself, as women are presented as, and invited toward agentic objectification or rather sexual subjectification that still involves, in short, a lot of disciplined gendered body work and display. Further, a relatively narrow range of young, slim, white, able bodies are still fetishized in postfeminist popular culture.

Confident "New" Postfeminist Femininities

I now discuss the prominence of representations and cultural discourses that address girls and young women as strong, confident, and capable in the postfeminist cultural context, in contrast to understandings of femininity as weak and submissive. I agree with Gill's assertion that in the postfeminist era, femininity has become more focused on the body and on "hotness" as a key characteristic of femininity (Gill, 2007, p. 255). But, as I suggest here, other physical and psychological traits are also significant and work to distance and distinguish ideal contemporary feminine subjectivities from older, weaker models, as well as from notions of *victimhood* and *dependence* so reviled in contemporary neoliberal political discourses of self-governance (see Harris and Dobson, 2015). Scholars of girlhood and culture have theorized the kind of youthful "new femininities" that have come to prevail as centered around energy, vitality, capacity, and entrepreneurial spirit, along with public visibility and self-exposure (Hopkins, 2002; Aapola, Gonick, and Harris, 2005; Harris, 2004; McRobbie, 2007; Banet-Weiser, 2012; Ringrose, 2013; Dobson, 2014c). This kind of idealized femininity is theorized as well aligned with broad neoliberal political discourses of individual responsibility and meritocracy, and thus in work on new femininities, postfeminism, individualization, and neoliberalism are often emphasized as a "matrix" (Gill and Scharff, 2011; Evans and Riley, 2014). Shifts toward young feminine strength, confidence, and capacity are positioned as accompanying "girl power"; a cultural movement that, as Harris (2004) describes, has explicitly feminist political origins as a phrase used by Riot Grrrl bands in the early 1990s to raise awareness of sexual and gendered violence and subvert cultural norms of feminine fashion and bodily discipline. Girl power was swiftly appropriated for more commercial purposes, and gained momentum in the 1990s through pop girl groups such as the Spice Girls, Destiny's Child, and several others (Harris, 2004; Aapola, Gonick and Harris, 2005; Currie, Kelly, and Pomerantz, 2009; Zaslow, 2009; Hains, 2012). As Emilie Zaslow writes, "At its core, girl power is a commodification of opposition to traditional femininity. It takes feminist ideas and feminist language, and makes them popular, accessible, and sometimes, less potent" (Zaslow, 2009, p. 159). Girl-powered shifts have occurred in media representations of girls and young women, as well as in public discourse about them, and addresses to them in marketing, education, health, and politics.

For example, the prevalence of media representations of young women as physically strong, tough, assertive, and confident in popular television shows and films in the 1990s has been well documented (Inness, 1999, 2004; Hopkins, 2002). Scholarly work has examined the popularization and meaning for feminism of characters such as

Lara Croft from *Lara Croft: Tomb Raider* (Hopkins, 2002), Buffy from *Buffy the Vampire Slayer* (Daugherty, 2001; Playdon, 2001; Ross, 2004; Sherman, 2004; Jowett, 2005; Williamson, 2005), and the women of the remade *Charlie's Angels* films, among several others. Scholars have also noted the ways in which popular television shows centered around female characters in the 1990s depict women as confident, successful, and high-achieving in terms of their careers, and assertive/demanding in relation to the pursuit of heterosexual relationships: *Sex and the City*, *Ally McBeal*, and the *Bridget Jones's Diary* films are notable in this regard, and have received significant attention from feminist scholars concerned with evaluating what such representations of femininity have to offer women (Arthurs, 2004; Akass and McCabe, 2004; McRobbie, 2004, 2009; Taylor, 2012). At the same time as female strength and capability have been powerfully visualized, and women feature as subjects of representation driving the action, scholars note the repetitive and exclusive whiteness, heterosexuality, and gender-typical attractiveness of most of these characters, the commodification and sexualization of racial difference and sexual diversity (Gill, 2007), and intense focus on consumption (McRobbie, 2009) within popular contemporary postfeminist narratives.

Some scholarship has also noted media depictions and commentary decrying young women as "newly" loud, vulgar, and "more masculine" in their social behavior in the postfeminist cultural context. Such constructions and constitutions of young femininity occur most notably via reality television shows such as *Big Brother*, *Ladette to Lady*, and *Jersey Shore* and in news media coverage of binge-drinking "ladettes" (Day, Gough, and McFadden, 2004; Skeggs, 2005; Jackson, 2006; Jackson and Tinkler, 2007; Dobson, 2014c; Skeggs and Wood, 2012). Young women have also been commonly portrayed in reality television over the last decade as excessively bitchy, mean, and competitive toward other women (Pozner, 2010). Similarly, in popular psychology texts (from the United States in particular), and in news media stories that follow their lead, concern has been generated over girls' apparent "meanness" and "relational aggression." The film *Mean Girls*, based as it was on Rosalind Wiseman's (2002) book *Queen Bees & Wannabes: Helping Your Daughter Survive Cliques, Gossip, Boyfriends, and Other Realities of Adolescence*, exemplifies such concerns, and also makes clear that "mean girls" are a raced and classed figuration, as scholar have noted (Chesney-Lind and Irwin, 2008; Ringrose, 2008, 2013): middle-class white girls are produced as a little too "girl-powered" and in need of some psychological support, while racialized and poor girls remain more straightforwardly framed as "deviant," and criminalized. "Ladettes" and "mean girls" are media figures that perhaps constitute the *excessive* limits—the borders—of contemporary ideal femininity (Skeggs, 2005). Elsewhere I have suggested that while such figures are not framed as representations of "ideal" new femininities, the reality shows in which they feature are exceedingly popular, and do present contemporary young womanhood to girls and women as, in short, much more fun than it was in the past, reinforcing ideas of ***unambiguous*** social change vis-à-vis femininity and girlhood (Dobson, 2014c).

Postfeminist, girl-powered versions of femininity can be said to incorporate aspects of both femininity and masculinity physically, psychologically, and socially. As Zaslow writes, "In this new model [of femininity], some elements of traditional femininity (beauty, care, and sexiness) are retained while others (passivity, weakness, and dependence) are met with a feminist reimagining so that girls are repositioned as active, choice-making agents." (Zaslow, 2009, p. 158). Tough female characters in TV and film are often aligned with exaggeratedly feminine and "sexy" bodily properties, while aligned with physical and attitudinal strength and toughness, and playful, fun, "laddish" attitudes toward sex, leisure, and hedonistic consumption (Tincknell, Chambers, Van Loon, and Hudson, 2003; Jackson, S., 2006; McRobbie, 2007; Day, 2010; Dobson, 2014c). Particularly in the twenty-first century, idealized femininity is popularly constructed around the bodily property of sexiness (Gill, 2007, p. 255), but it is also centrally about performing strength, independence, achievement, and confidence, as well as being "spontaneous and fun rather than sensible and sober" (Brown and Gregg, 2012, p. 364).

Independence and *confidence* in particular emerge as qualities strongly tied to ideal young femininity in broader social and political discourses that produce girls and young women as the success stories and high-achievers of late modernity. As McRobbie (2007) suggests, girls and young women are positioned in governmental and educational discourses as the beneficiaries of feminist activism allowing them new opportunities in schools and workplaces. They are also positioned as the beneficiaries of moves toward "flexible" (unstable), service-based neoliberal economies (Walkerdine, Lucey, and Melody, 2001). Anita Harris (2004) examines the ways in which neoliberal political discourses and ideologies of individual responsibility dovetail with the kind of idealized postfeminist femininity I am describing in the requirements of achievement, self-betterment, and success for young women. Young women, she suggests, are now under pressure to live up to these prominent cultural narratives of girls as girl-powered, self-governing success stories, subjects of capacity and confidence who are able to navigate their way through new economic and social conditions with ease, despite intensified social inequalities. Harris has argued that public self-disclosure for young women is seen as key in the process of their self-actualization and achievement. They are encouraged through media, educational, and political discourses, to "voice themselves" toward this end; that is, to express themselves loudly and confidently, and to demonstrate not only educational and economic capacity but also *psychological* qualities of self-acceptance, self-esteem, and high confidence. Sarah Banet-Weiser (2012) suggests that girls and young women are also increasingly called to make themselves publicly visible via digital media production and "brand" their self-representations in line with the kind of qualities and traits described previously. For her, such qualities constitute the postfeminist brand of femininity. In this landscape, these scholars suggest, failure to succeed in education or in labor markets, as well as failure to express and make visible a *confident* postfeminist feminine self is increasingly pathologized for girls and young women.

Girlhood and Sexualization

At the same time as this investment of girls and young women with sexual agency, strength, capacity, and confidence through media representations and public discourses, we can observe in recent news media, online commentary, and political and educational debates, panicked protectionist and moralist discourses about cultural sexualization and its supposed effects on girls and young women. Over the last decade, reports on sexualization have been commissioned and written by government bodies, policy think tank groups, and other special interest and lobbying groups in Australia, the United Kingdom, and the United States (Rush and La Nauze, 2006; American Psychological Association, 2007, 2010; Australian Parliament Senate Standing Committee, 2008; Bailey, 2011; Papadopoulos, 2010). While there has also been increasing debate about "porn chic," "pornification," and "raunch culture" over the last decade (McNair, 2002; Levy, 2005; Paul, 2005; Paasonen, Nikunen, and Saarenmaa, 2007; Attwood, 2009), these influential reports on sexualization and its possible impacts upon children (mainly girls) seem to have anchored the term "sexualization" at the center of these debates about sex and gender in media and visual culture. Childhood sexualization, and the sexualization of girls in particular, has been discursively constituted as one of the key issues with and in media and culture over the last decade.

In Australia, Emma Rush and Andrea La Nauze published two reports for The Australia Institute in 2006 condemning what they saw as the sexualization and "corporate pedophilia" at work in contemporary media culture and marketing to children. Their concerns are about the ways in which the media and marketing to which they refer, aimed at children, "captures the slowly developing sexuality of children and molds it into stereotypical forms of adult sexuality" (Rush and La Nauze, 2006, p. 1). They are concerned that girls in particular "face a sexualizing pressure unlike that faced by any of today's adults in their childhood" (2006, p. viii). Along with several other commentators (for instance, Maguire, 2008; Lumby and Albury, 2010), I struggle to see what is primarily or overtly *sexual* about many of the examples they discuss of clothing advertisements featuring children. What is clear is that the cultural representations they analyze model gender and heteronormative roles to children through the poses of the models and the gender-typical aesthetics employed. Femininity appears to be encoded through pinkness, interest in beauty products and appearance, and sinuous poses connoting passivity and availability, while masculinity appears to be encoded through dark colors and upright, more stable poses suggesting strength, and protectiveness of the girls pictured with boy figures (as well as interest in sports and academically oriented activities). Children *are* sexualized in such media in the sense that their bodies are strongly encoded with norms of masculinity and femininity, which are forcefully tied to cultural scripts of heterosexuality (Butler, 1990, 1993).

Meg Barker and Robbie Duschinsky (2012) have pointed to a similar issue in their critique of the Bailey Review conducted in Britain, *Letting Children Be Children* (Bailey, 2011). In research undertaken for this report, parents and other concerned groups raised issues with the prevalence of sexual material in visual culture *as well as* the intensely gendered nature of marketing aimed at children. But the report appears to dismiss the later and foreground the former as a new phenomenon, somewhat disconnected to gender representation. Reg Bailey, head of the Christian family charity The Mother's Union, apparently objects to such material not so much on the grounds of the perpetuation of outdated heterosexual norms and the continuing objectification of women, but for the sake of protecting children from references to sex in general.

The American Psychological Association (APA) issued a report in 2007 on the sexualization of girls which I suggest makes somewhat clearer that the problem being debated is not so much a new one of girls' being sexualized, but the ongoing issue highlighted by feminists for decades of the primacy of sexually objectified representations of women and the limited range of sexist roles and stereotypes on offer to women in Western media cultures that are increasingly globalized. The authors describe media content and coverage from the late 1980s through to the early 2000s as sexist and objectifying, clearly highlighting incidences of the distinct sexual objectification of women that occurs regularly across various media. Their reports (2007, 2010) provide a summary of content analyses on music videos, magazine covers, in television and movie content, as well as in advertisements, computer games, and Internet content, showing that the last few decades have seen an invigoration of sexism in a range of media, an increasing focus in representations of women on sex and the body, and continued fetishization of slim-but-curvaceous, white, youthful, able feminine bodies. What the APA reports make clear is that, despite the postfeminist framings around "choice" and "empowerment" noted, there are severely limited roles and aesthetics for women on offer in popular and commercial media culture. What is less clear is that the media and the cultural objects described necessarily function to sexualize girls and young women any more so than they have been in the past through the very limiting gendered socialization processes strongly tied to a particular notion of heteronormativity. In this regard the key issues at stake in much of the contemporary media and cultural examples mentioned in these reports on childhood sexualization stray beyond the boundaries of childhood and affect the lives of individuals, especially those whose identities do not fit into the narrow terms of gender embodiment and sexuality commonly set out (Barker and Duschinsky, 2012), more broadly than the prominent moralist and child protectionist discourses of sexualization imply.

Protectionist and moralist discourses have invoked fear about the damaging effects of sexualization on girls in particular, and have tended to associate any forms of so-called self-sexualization with pathology and "low self-esteem" for girls and, more implicitly, young women also. For example, the *Australia Senate Inquiry into the Sexualization of Children in the Contemporary Media Environment* saw parent groups writing in to express their concern to the government that girls' magazines feature "sexually promiscuous" stories which may "awaken" the sexuality of girls "before they are mentally able to be responsible for their actions or have a morally formed conscience only to be deeply hurt leading to an increase in teenage pregnancy, sexual diseases and mental breakdown" (Australian Parliament Senate Standing Committee, 2008, p. 52). In media commentary accompanying news of an Australian study which finds that girls dance "exotically" at primary school discos in attempts to copy their pop idols, the psychologist quoted warns parents of "the possibility of long-term damage of their children's self-esteem if they buy into a sexualized image of themselves" (Stokes, 2012). These discourses around girlhood, sex, and self-esteem also frame dominant understandings of older teens' and young women's self-presentation and sexuality. This is evident in recent debates about young women's selfies (photos of their own faces taken with a camera held at arms' length) posted on social network sites (SNSs), as I discuss in the following chapter. In much news media commentary pouting at one's camera phone or posing in flesh-revealing clothing is normatively understood as misguided, attention-seeking behavior, and an indication of young women's ill-advised participation in the "sexual rat race" (e.g., Nelson, 2013). An assumption underlies discourses about girls and sexualization that we can clearly distinguish a child who has been artificially "sexualized" through their contact with media and marketing culture from a "normal" child. Through such discourses a moral framework has become attached to certain styles of dress, self-presentation, and also to *desire*, for girls and young women (Egan and Hawkes, 2008a; Valenti, 2011; Egan, 2013). Egan and Hawkes's critique of the *Corporate Paedophilia* report (2008a) makes clear the very exclusionary and faulty framework of sexualization as a measure by which to judge girls' development, whereby any signs of sexuality supposedly suggest that girls have been damaged by media culture. The prominence that has been given in media to the issue of girl children and sexualization means that in the process of negotiating a legible feminine subjectivity girls and young women must now actively position themselves in relation to protectionist and moralist discourses; discourses that, at the same time, position them within preestablished and dichotomous frameworks of legibility.

A growing body of ethnographic work with girls and young women, as well as theoretical and historical work, complicates these protectionist/moralist discourses around girls and young women and sexualization. Girlhood and childhood scholars have made important contributions to this debate by complicating the notion that sexualization affects girls in clear and direct ways. Research by Jackson, Vares, and Gill (2013), in which the authors asked eleven-to-thirteen year-old girls to make video diaries and talk about the cultural objects in their bedrooms, suggests that sexual media is not necessarily as monolithic in the lives of girls as some commentators suggest. They suggest that girls appear to regulate themselves and each other carefully in terms of their sexual identities, often distancing themselves from other girls or celebrities who are seen as "too sexy" or "slutty." Duits and van Zoonen suggest that the sexualization discourse ignores decades of audience reception scholarship unpacking the ways in which individuals negotiate media and culture differently based on a range of factors, such as social and familial context, class, race, ethnicity, and personal history (2011, p. 504). Their research with teenage girls suggests the ways in which girls from different family backgrounds appear to negotiate sexualized notions of femininity differently. Renold and Ringrose (2011) suggest that as girls negotiate conflicting discourses of sexual knowingness and innocence, their performances of femininity are always "in-movement," but are always shaped heavily by the classed and raced social contexts in which they occur. Egan and Hawkes (2008b, 2009, 2012), in their scholarship on historical constructions of childhood, have pointed to the classed assumptions contained within sexualization discourses about "childhood innocence." As they point out, the sexualization panic tends to ignore the sexuality of children and divide girl children into the classed binaries of "innocent" and "corrupted/sexualized" child. Kehily (2012) has illustrated through historical case studies of girls' life stories the way in which the "innocent" versus "sexualized" binary disregards the material conditions of girls lives. And Egan (2013) further suggests that sexualization panics are related to broader social anxieties about changing markers of socioeconomic status, and the diminishing power of the middle class in late modernity. I side with Egan and Hawkes in contending that this panic is frequently sexist in its implications about the sexuality of girls, and also perhaps somewhat overblown. However, this contention is tempered by the acknowledgement of continued and intense sexual objectification of women's bodies in postfeminist popular culture, which is now framed as "self-chosen" and a source of fun, pleasure, and empowerment for women.

Heterosexy As a Descriptor

Too often, I suggest, the term "sexualization" is used to *imply*—without directly stating—the way that girls and women are socialized in line with femininity and heteronormativity. The visual lexicon and symbols that constitute the dominant *kind* of sexualization to which the authors of the reports discussed implicitly refer connote and signify conformity with appropriate *gender* performances. It is not just that contemporary popular feminine aesthetics are often sexualized, but that common and popular feminine fashions and sensibilities are aligned with specific stereotypes of heterosexual sex appeal and desirability, often to the exclusion of any other kinds of sexual appeal. For example, the body of a Barbie Doll is not so much sexualized as it is heterosexy. The phenomenon of marketing padded bras to eight year old girls (Cook and Kaiser, 2004) does not simply or automatically sexualize young girls, but I would suggest that such clothing serves to construct girls' bodies in a specific, heterosexy manner. Following Egan and Hawkes (2008a, b), I think that sexualization as a term suggests too general an investment of girls' and women's bodies with sexuality, as if this were unnatural. I use the term "heterosexy" in this book as a general descriptor to indicate the kind of symbols, fashions, poses, and behaviors invested with current gendered ideals of sex-appeal. Heterosexiness is constantly changing rather than static, and it is culturally specific. We might in brief suggest that it is currently constituted in the Anglophone West for girls and women as an aesthetic derivative of both traditional femininity (pink, delicate, decorative, cutesy, and so on) and mainstream heterosexual pornography (overly large artificial looking breasts, high heels, excessive makeup, flesh-revealing clothing and clothing which draws attention to sexual and erogenous zones). The narrow current construct means that slim, young, white, hairless (except on the head), able bodies continue to be fetishized.

Femininity As Pathology

We can see then that, as Renold and Ringrose (2011) and Jackson, Vares, and Gill (2013) suggest, girls and young women must negotiate complex "pushes and pulls" within this sociocultural terrain. In brief, a narrow version of heterosexiness still appears to hold an immense amount of social currency, but at the same time "sexiness" for girls is equated with victimhood, low self-esteem, and/or deviancy in public debates and regulatory discourses of sexualization. In this context feminist scholars have acknowledged the contradictions girls and young women face to present themselves as "sexy," but not "slutty" or "sexualized." At the same time, young women are called to present their identities in line with the girl-powered neoliberal ideals discussed of girls as confident, strong, capable, fun, and up for a good time. They are called toward public self-representation, visibility, and self-exposure, and encouraged to express and represent their life narratives in terms of personal and professional choice, success, and achievement.

Within these postfeminist conditions of contradicting invitations and pressures on girls and young women we can also note a broad and related cultural understanding of normative femininity as pathological. Feminists have long pointed to the ways in which trying to meet the demands of femininity makes one ill (Brownmiller, 1984; Bordo, 1993; Fredrickson and Roberts, 1997). Further, Susan Bordo (1997) argues that diseases that predominantly effect women are matched to the traits of femininity itself at the time of prominence, constituting femininity itself as pathological in the psychological and medical discourses so influential in modern societies. She maps links between hysteria and nineteenth-century Victorian constructs of femininity, agoraphobia and the idealized femininity of the 1950 and 1960s, and anorexia and femininity in the 1980s. In the late twentieth century, as she notes, women are expected not only to be physically very slender and fragile, but to also take on the qualities of men as "tough" and "hard" as they enter the spheres of work and public life, amounting to a "double bind" (Bordo, 1997, p. 97). Barbara Brickman sheds light on the construction of self-cutting practices as a "feminized" syndrome, demonstrating that the gesture of cutting has been described in medical journals in highly feminized language, and theorized by psychologists as a "passive" act of aggression and a "mute protest" against the female subject's own body (Brickman, 2004, p. 95).

What I think worth highlighting as at least somewhat distinct in recent years is the level of *normalization* surrounding ills that are widely acknowledged as related to feminine embodiment. This is something Angela McRobbie has pointed to: the way that symptoms of "gender distress" have "come to be established as predictable, treatable, things to be managed medically rather than subjected to sustained social scrutiny" (McRobbie, 2009, p. 112). Beyond highlighting the social construction of self-cutting, eating disorders, and certain drug addictions as feminine, she usefully articulates the *un-remarkability* of such conditions as they affect young women, and the cultural resignation that "gender distresses" are a part of gendered embodiment. "Popular culture," McRobbie suggests, "is asking young women to get used to gender melancholia, and to recognize themselves and each other within its terms" (2009, p. 115). In explaining this point McRobbie uses fashion photography as an example. We might add to this the spate of recent successful films featuring rather melancholic, if also strong, young heroines such as the *Twilight* series, *The Hunger Games*, and Lars von Trier's aptly named *Melancholia*, in which the lead young female character, despite being newly married, from a wealthy family, and "tracking well" in her career, is portrayed as so alienated and depressed that she is the only one who is able to face somewhat rationally and bravely the impending end of the world. McRobbie suggests that melancholia is constructed in public discourses and popular culture as arising from the pressures involved in "being a girl" today (p. 117), which are acknowledged as immense, but which are also constructed as personal and psychological grievances to be managed individually.

The relationship of melancholia with the political and economic conditions of neoliberalism, and with the other postfeminist cultural conditions I have outlined, is obscured. Prominent public discourse suggests that young women's melancholia and/or rage has no social or structural basis since women's entry into the spheres of education and work in the West, and young women are asked to consider themselves the winners in neoliberal societies. Thus for young women the possible structural sources of their grievances have become "opaque," McRobbie suggests (p. 116). She refers to a broad range of "gender disorders" that are on the rise such as eating disorders, self-harm, and drinking and drug addiction, and suggests that these can be framed in terms of "illegible rage." That is, rage that may be of social/political origin but can only be currently understood as individual/psychopathological. "Shameless self-exposure" through digital media may be part of this broad phenomenon of normalizing melancholia for young women, she suggests. In the age of social media, as McRobbie notes, it is hard to differentiate between "female agency in the many opportunities for self-advertisement of pain, anxiety and self-loathing, and those mechanisms which are pre-emptively deployed across the commercial media which produce the framing for the institutionalization of melancholia" (p. 116). McRobbie's articulations around "gender melancholia" contribute valuable insights into what I suggest is a key condition of postfeminist girlhood and young womanhood: the pathologization of femininity, or rather, the *normalization* of feminized grievances as psychopathologies. But I think there is more going on in young women's "shameless self-exposure" online than just the intensification of this condition. I unpack and explore girls' and young women's shameless self-exposure in networked publics in more detail in the following chapters, through textual analysis and empirical research dealing with some of the more controversial, sexual self-representations and media practices, highly self-confident self-representations, and expressions of pain and suffering.

* * *

Girls, Young Women, and Digital Media

In the concluding part of this chapter I provide an overview of recent scholarship that seeks to understand girls' and young women's engagements with digital media and cultures, and how gender is operationalized in digital media practices and self-representations. There are contrasting ideas about the meaning and value of girls' and young women's engagements with digital media in the postfeminist cultural context. Some empirical work in this area positions the Internet as a "safe space" for girls and young women to experiment with self-expression, including styles of gender performativity that deviate from traditional feminine modes of expression. Some scholarship has documented the opportunities for control over one's representation and suggests a kind of empowerment available to girls and young women in this sense. Other scholarly work has noted the dominance of gender-typical styles of self-representation that occur online, and the continuation of gendered gazes and economies of visibility, particularly in the changing *social* media landscape since the rise of SNSs in the mid-2000s. I provide an overview of this work to situate my own investigations into girls' and young women's media practices and self-representations in postfeminist digital cultures.

SNSs are widely used among teenagers and young adults with regular access to the Internet, and it appears that teenage girls and young women are the largest demographic of active users. Recent statistics from the Australian Communications and Media Authority on young people's Internet use suggest that by the time young people with Internet access are 17-years-old, 99 percent of them have used SNSs at some stage, and 71 percent report daily use (Australian Communications and Media Authority, 2013, p. 8). No significant gender differences are found for overall use rates of SNSs reported, but significantly more girls than boys report *frequent* SNS use: 34 percent of teenage girls compared with 25 percent of teenage boys report checking SNS profiles more than once a day (Australian Communications and Media Authority, 2013, p. 38). A study of undergraduate-age students from a midsized American university found that 91.6 percent of female students use SNSs, while 74.5 percent of male students do (Tufekci and Spence, 2007). Thelwall's (2008a) study of MySpace demographics, using a random sample of over 20,000 profiles, finds a small majority of female-owned profiles, with a median age of 21 years. Data from the Pew Internet and American Life Project also suggests that older teenage girls and young adult women are the largest demographic of SNS users (Lenhart and Madden, 2007;

Lenhart, 2009; Lenhart, Purcell, Smith, and Zickhuyr, 2010). Pew report that in the United States 76 percent of women with Internet access and 72 percent of men use SNSs, with young adults the biggest group of users: 89 percent of those aged 18–29 use SNSs (Duggan and Smith, 2013). Some research indicates that girls and women use the Internet primarily for social interaction (Drotner, 2001; Tufte, 2003; Molyneaux, O'Donnell, Gibson, and Singer, 2008), and that girls and young women are predominant participants in online activities such as blogging, chatting, and sharing photos. Orlowski (2003) reports on a Polish study which finds that 62 percent of Polish blogs are authored by women, and three quarters of these are by teenage or younger girls. Lenhart and colleagues report that 35 percent of all American female teenagers with Internet access practice blogging, compared with 20 percent of online teenage boys (Lenhart, Madden, Smith, and Macgill, 2007, p. 9). Young women are suggested as the demographic who engage most in photo and video-sharing online, according to Pew's statistics from the United States (Duggan, 2013).

Qualitative research on girls and young women's Internet use has investigated a range of online environments and activities such as home-page creation, web design, blogging, vlogging, and webcam culture (Stern, 1999, 2002; Takayoshi, Huot, and Huot, 1999; Reid-Walsh and Mitchell, 2004; Bortree, 2005; Kearney, 2006; Dobson, 2008; Keller, 2012; Boler, Harris, and Jacobson, forthcoming), as well as use of SNSs (Elm, 2009; Tsoulis-Reay, 2009; Leage and Chalmers, 2010; Ringrose, 2010; Stokes, 2010; Dobson, 2011, 2014b; García-Gómez, 2011; Ringrose and Barajas, 2011; Brown and Gregg, 2012; Hall, West, and McIntyre, 2012; Brandes and Levin, 2013; Dean and Laidler, 2013). Studies have also been conducted into how girls interact with peers and express identity in online environments such as chat rooms, instant messaging (IM), forums, and games (Davies, 2004; Grisso and Weiss, 2005; Clark, 2005; Thiel, 2005; Kelly, Pomerantz, and Currie, 2006). Much of the research on young women's online activities conducted before the widespread take-up and popularization of SNSs seems to suggest the Internet as a place where girls and young women can express themselves freely, often in ways, it is suggested, that it would be more difficult for them to do in offline environments where "real" gendered bodies and feminine norms can be the cause of self-censorship. Scholars such as Susannah Stern (1999, 2002) and Pamela Takayoshi (Takayoshi, Huot, and Huot, 1999) position the Internet as a safe place for girls to express needs and desires, and to construct and perform their identities creatively and innovatively. Through online interactions and participation in chat rooms, IM, girl-oriented forums, and games, girls explore and push the boundaries of their performed feminine identities in several ways. Deidre Kelly and colleagues (Kelly, Pomerantz, and Currie, 2006) document instances of girls taking on assertive roles in communication with the opposite sex in chat rooms and on IM boards. Shayla Thiel finds of girls' IM conversations that they are "using foul language, saying what they wish, and experimenting with sexual tones in conversation" (2005, p. 197). Similarly, Grisso and Weiss (2005) observe girls talking openly about sexual practices and desires in the forum gURL.com. Digital environments have thus been theorized as places where teenage girls in particular can experiment with identity, gender, and sexuality, testing the limits of normative gender behavior with less social risk than offline. The Internet is thus suggested as a vehicle for girls' empowerment in much scholarship on girls' and young women's digital engagements, although not unreservedly.

Such scholarship also notes critically the online reproduction of "offline" modes of gender performance, patterns of communication, and gender politics that position girls' and women's bodies and sexuality as central to their identities. For example, Grisso and Weiss (2005) find that while frank and open discussion of sex and of girls' sexual practices are commonplace on the girl-oriented forum site they examine, so too are discussions about body image, weight, and how to please one's male partner sexually. Further, when girls express too much sexual freedom, pleasure, or agency, the authors suggest, they are "reined in" or chastised by other girls on the site (2005, pp. 40–41). This leads the authors to suggest that even in female-oriented spaces such as gURL.com, preconceived notions of gender and sexuality linger, in which girls remain sexually submissive and body-image focused (pp. 45–46). As Kelly and colleagues conclude:

> Pushing the boundaries of girlhood—of what constitutes acceptable femininity—does not necessarily mean that unequal gender relations are being transformed. For emphasized femininity and hegemonic masculinity to be challenged at the collective level, girls need access to feminist and other oppositional discourses that name their experiences and feelings and link these to the ongoing quest for gender justice. (2006, p. 22)

A broad shift can be noted in research agendas and findings about girls and young women's Internet use since the widespread take-up of SNSs. The kind of social media platforms that have come into wide use post-Web 2.0[5] have changed the way in which many people use the Internet to communicate and socialize. Digital technologies have become more widely adopted in many parts of the world, domestically integrated, and convergent with other kinds of communication and media since the mid-2000s. As Sonia Livingstone notes in 2008, "the simple distinction between offline and online no longer captures the complex practices associated with online technologies as they become thoroughly embedded in the routines of everyday life" (2008, pp. 395–396) for many people.[6]

With prevalent use of SNSs to communicate among teenagers, young adults, and increasingly older adults too (Madden, 2013; Duggan and Smith, 2013), contemporary techno-social landscapes can be seen as potentially characterized less by experimentation and anonymity and more by "connectivity," and both social and architectural imperatives toward coherent narratives of the self (van Dijck, 2013a, p. 204). Conventions have developed around SNS use that tie bodies, or images of bodies, and offline identities and social networks to online SNS profiles, sometimes forcefully. For example, in 2014, many transgender and gender-queer Facebook users shut down their profiles in response to Facebook's "real name only" policy that required them to tie their trans and/or gender-queer identities to their legal names (Rodley, 2014). Grant Bollmer (2012) argues that Internet users are increasingly called to be good "networked citizens" by performing only an "authentic" identity online—one that is clearly tied to a stable and unified offline identity. Liesbet van Zoonen (2013) suggests that as identity has widely come to be understood as fragmented and necessarily multiplicitous, a range of technologies and social forces work to counter this by fixing and pining down coherent and singular identities. Jose van Dijck (2013a) suggests that the interface and architecture Facebook, currently the most popular SNS in the world, supports such processes and narratives of identity coherency, singularity, and stability.

These theorizations of digital culture, and recent research on girls' and women's use of SNSs, to some degree deflate the optimism and excitement generated by scholars in the early years of widespread Internet adoption. Scholars such as Donna Haraway (1991) and Sherry Turkle (1995) theorized the possibilities for identity transformation, and the transgressing of the boundaries of material bodies limited by gender, race, ethnicity, ability, geography, and socioeconomic status in cyber worlds often used anonymously, and popularly conceived of as *separate* and *nonphysical* worlds/realities. In this post-Web 2.0 mediascape that can be characterized as more *social* and also perhaps more *surveillance-oriented* and regulatory in regard to identity (Marwick, 2012; Kanai, 2015a), shifts in research concerns and findings about girls and young women can be noted away from notions of gender experimentation and conceptualizations of digital "safe spaces," toward mappings of complex lives *with and through* the Internet and social media, involving certain opportunities and gendered pressures. For example, Jennifer Rubin and Sara McClelland note the way Facebook produces "uneven consequences for people already labouring under the weight of Otherness in their everyday lives" (2015, p. 522). They map the emotional labour queer young women must perform to participate in SNS, including worrying over self-outing or unintended exposure of sexual identity. As they note, many queer youth remain in "the virtual closet" online, for fear of cyberbullying (p. 513) (see also Duguay, 2014; Albury and Byron, 2014). Jessica Ringrose's work on girls' SNS profiles demonstrates the pressure to present an appropriately sexually knowledgeable but not "slutty" self on the SNS Bebo, along with girls' creative strategies for negotiating these demands of postfeminist femininity. This is a balancing act that can be difficult to get right both on and offline for girls, and Ringrose argues that "the increasing normalization of pornography and sexual commodification of girls' bodies online has a direct relationship to girls' 'real-life' experiences and relationships at school" (2010, p. 180). Antonio García-Gómez's (2011) work explores girls' relational aggression on SNSs and notes the normative gendered and sexualized nature of aggressive communication among girls online, and the ways in which girls regulate each other's sexual identities at the same time as subverting gender norms through language use. Sigal Barak Brandes and David Levin (2013) have suggested that SNSs provide a space for expressions of friendship, and allow the Israeli girls with whom they spoke a means of tangibly managing their social circles and identities. They suggest that a degree of empowerment accompanies the kind of playful and social uses of SNSs in which their participants engaged, as well as a sense of control over their identity construction. They also find that girls are concerned about prevalent online racism, and some also feel "addicted" to using SNSs. The authors note the "constant maintenance and work" required to participate, as well as girls' expressed "fear of missing out," which they suggest sometimes results in "a high degree of stress in the girls' lives" (Brandes and Levin, 2013, p. 12).

Recent scholarship has provided rich and detailed accounts of the complexities, opportunities, freedoms, pitfalls, and pressures of girls' and young women's participation in postfeminist digital cultures. However, tendencies are still present in some work on SNSs and gendered media production to position girls' and young women's participation as radically free from social context, rather than *shaped by and in relation* to broader postfeminist media culture and neoliberal discourses of individualization. In their research on girls' and young women's use of SNSs in Hong Kong, Marissa Dean and Karen Laidler (2013) suggest in relation to competing discourses of postfeminist girlhood as "either in a state of emergency or offering unprecedented promise" that SNSs offer girls "wholly new spaces to create, experiment, and express unique forms of identity" that fly "under the radar" of such prevalent understandings of contemporary girlhood. In outlining the discourses and conditions that constitute and shape postfeminist girlhood and young womanhood as I have in this chapter, I suggest that the self-representations girls and young women create and circulate in networked publics are produced *directly in relation* to such dominant understandings of girlhood. Dean and Laidler suggest that SNSs allow girls and young women to "create identities of choice." Their participants describe enacting a high degree of control over their online identities, feeling like they can "be themselves" on SNSs and be "more real" than offline. However, left unexplored are the ways in which such processes of controlling digital identities and producing self-representations that can be claimed as "authentic" and "real" can also be seen as the very processes by and through which power operates (Harris, 2005; Kanai, 2015a). I argue elsewhere (Dobson, 2014a, b) that in postfeminist cultures marked by contradiction—where girls and young women are called toward sexual subjectification, and confident, fun, and hedonistic performativity on the one hand, and addressed via discourses inviting moral and sexual self-regulation and shame on the other—"performative shamelessness" and claims of agency and authenticity become necessary for girls and young women to adopt. Living with and through social media and the demands of femininity in postfeminist cultures perhaps requires a performance of "shamelessness" by girls and young women in order to constitute pleasurable SNS experiences, and also to protect the self when a high degree of self-exposure is normalized and called for as a condition of participation. Claims of control, agency, and choice are also perhaps necessary in order not to position the self as a victim, as Joanne Baker suggests in a different context (Baker, 2010). When scholars uncritically position the voices of their participants describing self-construction and self-representational practices online through the terms of choice, control, and personal empowerment as uncomplicated accounts, we risk reproducing the postfeminist and neoliberal social structures and technologies of subjectification we seek to understand (Evans and Riley, 2014).

Some scholarly research has traced gendered harassment and violence online, a topic that Emma Jane (2012) suggests has received too little attention. A small but growing number of studies document the ways in which girls and women's participation can be severely hampered in online spaces by harassment that is specifically sexualized and gendered (Powell, 2010; Jane, 2012; Salter and Crofts, 2013; McGarry, 2014; Powell and Henry, 2014). A recent Pew report into online harassment suggests that young women aged 18 to 24 are the demographic group that experience the most severe kinds of harassment online: a quarter of female Internet users in this age range report being stalked online, and a quarter also report being harassed in other ways online (Duggan, 2014). Some feminist cultural studies work argues that the gendered gaze conventions and economies of visibility and specular judgment and evaluation noted in second-wave feminist theorizations of visual culture are intensified in postfeminist digital cultures. Several scholars have suggested, for example, that women are disciplined via comments and feedback on the self and body that they themselves invite in network publics. As I discuss further in chapter 6, the highly publicized "Am I Pretty or Ugly" videos posted by girls on YouTube have been theorized as exemplary of the way in which gendered gaze relations can be intensified via interaction in networked publics (Banet-Weiser, 2014; Nurka, 2014; Rossie, 2015). Camille Nurka argues that "judging publics" are called forth in postfeminist digital cultures through a proliferation of ratings sights and dating sites such as "Hot or Not," in which women's bodies are positioned as central objects of a "specular democracy." Nurka sees girls' own "Am I Pretty or Ugly" videos as a continuation of such gendered logics of visual and appearance-based judgment. She suggests that the democratic potential of Internet technologies "are inevitably bound to gendered forms of representation" (2014, p. 2) and, like scholars concerned with gendered harassment and violence online, questions women's ability to be full participating members of networked publics in such conditions.

Sarah Banet-Weiser (2011, 2012) suggests that gendered economies of visibility structure girls' and young women's video production on YouTube. "Interaction" and "visibility" are called forth by the logics of "self-branding" and individualized entrepreneurship that, she argues, structure postfeminist digital cultures and popular social media platforms. Further, interaction, visibility, and the value of the "self-brand," are increased via heterosexy and gender-normative bodily properties and performativity. This perspective echoes my earlier about cam girl cultures (Dobson, 2008), in which young women maintain websites centered on a webcam, usually set up in their bedroom, and ask for material gifts and money in exchange for their everyday visibility. In YouTube video production today, as in earlier cam girl cultures, the narrow visual aesthetics, bodily properties, and girl-powered fun, confident, and "up for it" personae that have achieved celebrity, attention, and visibility in commercial postfeminist media are those that also achieve high visibility and circulation on social media, as Banet-Weiser suggests (see also Bailey, Steeves, Burkell, and Regan, 2013). This is not to say that there are not simultaneously many kinds of creative and innovate media production by girls and young women occurring, as the work of Kearney and other scholars documents (Kearney, 2006, 2011; see also Bae and Ivashevic, 2011; Keller, 2012). Banet-Weiser suggests, however, that "For every radical statement, there are many more that are shaped by a confluence of commercial and sexual codes," such as the dancing videos so numerous on YouTube that feature girls singing and dancing to popular music that profits from selling "hegemonic female sexuality" (Banet-Weiser, 2012, p. 65). Banet-Weiser's arguments imply that it is questionable as to whether spheres of representational visibility can be widened in postfeminist digital cultures structured by logics of branding and marketization and the grammars of marked racial and bodily exclusion they contain (2012, p. 89). These ideas bring us back to some of the key concerns of second-wave feminists I outlined at the start of this chapter. The question of how and to what extent girls and women are able to challenge gendered representational conventions of visibility and the gaze via self-representation and other kinds of digital media production within patriarchal and capitalist systems is especially important to keep in mind in the context of widespread availability of media production technologies, and prominent calls toward visibility and self-exposure for girls and young women.

Conclusion

In this chapter I have outlined some relevant concerns of feminist media and cultural scholars working in the second wave, as well as four conditions that I suggest are key to understanding the postfeminist cultural context, and the complexity for girls and young women navigating their way around and into feminine subjectivities in this context. I have also outlined both new possibilities and new pressures for girls and young women engaging with digital media and communicating in networked publics. The early hopes of some feminists about the Internet's potential for enabling radical challenges to gendered identities and power dynamics through widespread identity play are still playing out in many online communities and spaces, particularly virtual worlds. However we might tentatively surmise that in many everyday digital youth cultures centered on social media and SNSs, online identities are often strongly tied to offline bodies and social lives. Gendered representational structures of gazing at and evaluating women's bodies noted by second-wave feminists still prevail in many of these digital spaces and cultures. It is vital to explore what girls' and young women's own public self-representation and media practices can tell us about the requirements of contemporary postfeminist femininity, as well as its boundaries and "constitutive limits" (Skeggs, 2005). Likewise, it is important to investigate how girls and young women themselves negotiate the postfeminist conditions I have outlined via their digital media practices and self-representations. How does one present one's self to an audience of both peers and a potentially wider public in the context of the complex pushes and pulls, pressures, and contradictions that have been theorized and empirically documented by feminist scholars of media, culture, femininity, and girlhood? The following chapters illuminate the ways in which young women's media practices and self-representations simultaneously utilize and complicate the kinds of heterosexy, and strong, assertive, fun, confident, and capable constructions of femininity prevalent in contemporary Western mediascapes in the postfeminist era. We also see how imperatives toward *self-regulation* (particularly around sexual identity) and *control* on the one hand, and toward *visibility* and intense *self and body exposure* on the other, play out in girls' and young women's own media practices and self-representations, and discourses that circulate prominently about them.

Part I

Sexual Self-Representations

Chapter 3

Heterosexy Images on Social Network Sites

Digital Dreamgirls

On the social network site (SNS) profiles viewed in my study, animated heterosexy dreamgirls abound, punctuating text on young women's self-representational profiles like love-hearts drawn on letters, or stickers decorating notebooks.[1] One might see a little flashing pair of lips here, a little sparkling "pretty lady" figure there, a cartoon shopper-girl carrying a handbag and sunglasses, or a sinuous cartoon female figure posed undoing her bikini top. I use the term "dreamgirl icons" to refer specifically to decorative cartoons, animations, and digitally rendered or digitally altered feminine body imagery, after Rebecca Schneider's (1997) conceptualization of the "commodity dreamgirl" seen so often in advertising and other forms of visual culture. Commodity dreamgirls live in the dreamworld of media images. The dreamgirl is one and many simultaneously, in that she represents a notion of *the* one, essential, ideal "woman" (Schneider, 1997, p. 125) at the same time as her possibilities for transformation and replication are endless. The commodity being branded with dreamgirl icons and images on SNSs is the self. As Alison Hearn (2008, p.198) suggests, branding involves creating a "detachable, saleable image or narrative, which effectively circulates cultural meanings."[2] As I discuss in this chapter, different kinds of dreamgirl images brand the self in different ways. The animated and digitally rendered dreamgirl icons that decorate the MySpace profiles I viewed represent generic decorative depictions of a heterosexy feminine form. This type of profile decoration depicts feminine bodies that are perfect, idealized, and unidentifiable as individuals in their digital perfection and lack of specificity. These kinds of decorative graphic icons were often referred to as "bling" or "glitter" for one's MySpace profile, and could be procured from websites specializing in selling layouts and decorative icons to embed in SNS profiles. In this way, images of women's bodies were commodified and traded on SNS, just as they have long been in the sphere of commercial media. They were used as profile decoration, and also sometimes as humorous "greeting-cards." For example, friends might paste such images onto each other's profile walls with a "Happy Hump Day" message,[3] or similar. Such icons evoke the aesthetics and conventions of mainstream heterosexual pornography.

For example, Bite Me and Glamourbitch (accessed 30/10/07) both feature digital dreamgirl icons prominently on their profiles that signaled a kind of feminine sexuality that has become conventional in visual culture. The digital figures on both their profiles have slim-but-curvaceous body types, and are depicted in sinuous body poses, wearing scant apparel, with their legs in the air, and their genital regions exposed. Signifiers of sexual arousal are often communicated by digital dreamgirls. For example, Bite Me's decorative icon is depicted clutching her hair with one hand, and her other hand between her legs. Glamourbitch's is posed with her finger in her mouth. The facial expressions depicted may be described as somewhat indifferent or blank. A vacant gaze is typical of the quintessential commodity dreamgirl used in much advertising, as described by Schneider and other scholars of gender and visual culture (Schneider, 1997, pp. 92–93; see also Goffman, 1979; Goldman, 1992). Decorative, disinterested vixens such as these were common on the girls' and young women's MySpace profiles I viewed.

MJ Love's profile is decorated almost exclusively with small, close-up, digitized feminine mouths, with lips made-up in a variety of different ways and signifying a variety of expressions. These digitized, detached mouths may be said to exemplify visual fetishization. This singular part of the body has been separated from all else, and elevated above all else, making it the center for desire and fantasy. Through visual repetition, these kinds of mouths become commodified and objectified. On MJ Love's profile, the mouths are presented as would be products in a display case or shop window. They come in a range of colors and shapes. The variety of different styles, colors, and poses eludes any notion of which is the "real" or "original," and rather, all are foregrounded as artifice, play, and "simulacra" (Baudrillard, 1983) of heterosexy female bodies. These qualities of a playful, up-for-it sexiness and casual attitudes to commodification are suggested as key "sensibilities" common in postfeminist visual culture in commercial forms of marketing and popular culture (Gill,

2007) and self-branding undertaken by young women online (Banet-Weiser, 2012). The lips produce both an excess of possible malleable feminine masks suggestive of play and irony, as well as a kind of standardized, generic "raunchy" femininity.

Other researchers have also found that on girls' and young women's SNS profiles heterosexy digital dreamgirls commonly greet viewers (Ringrose, 2010; Stokes, 2010; Ringrose and Eriksson Barajas, 2011). Other images I encountered depict female models posed in G-strings and high-heels. An image featuring a pair of sparkling red lips with a cherry sitting precariously on a protruding tongue, and the words "so hot" flashing beneath was popular at the time of my study. The text accompanying digital dreamgirl images invites viewers, for example, to "pop my cherry," or warns them, "don't stick your tongue out unless you plan to use it." There also appear to be seemingly endless visual and graphic variations on the theme "Playboy Bunny," an icon Jessica Ringrose also commonly encountered in her research with teenage girls on their use of the SNS Bebo in the United Kingdom (Ringrose, 2013, p. 129). Playboy bunny icons appear on MySpace in the traditional black and white form associated with the Playboy brand, as well as in hot pink, pastel pinks and purples, glitter-encrusted, sparkling, and "winking" at viewers. One image I encountered several times while analyzing young women's SNS profiles depicts a semi-naked female model in a G-string and stockings, straddling the Playboy bunny logo. In addition to these kinds of heterosexy visual representations, Ringrose (2010) and Carla Stokes (2010) both found sexually themed quizzes to be prominent on teenage girls' SNS profiles. On the public SNS profiles of young teenage Black girls in the United States, Stokes found results displayed for quizzes such as "What sexual position are you" and "What type of nipple are you"(2010, p. 52). In the United Kingdom, Ringrose found on young teenage girls' SNS profiles quiz results for "What type of kisser are you," "What type of lingerie are you," and "Are you sexy, flirty, or a slut" (2013, p. 118). Some of these quizzes also appeared on the profiles in my study of Australian young women's MySpace self-representations.

On the profiles in my study several different types of dreamgirls can be identified: "classic" fetishized digital dreamgirls posed for a viewer's pleasure (this is how I describe the kind of decorations discussed so far); depictions of heterosexual couples performing sexual acts; highly posed images of youthful feminine celebrities such as Paris Hilton; "camera seduction" selfies by some of the profile owners themselves (commonly referred to as "duckface" pictures); and finally, "hot and hostile" dreamgirls. Some images visually reference the conventions and characteristics of mainstream pornography or centerfold-style imagery; some are overtly decorative spectacles of the feminine heterosexy body, idealized and fantastically unreal, as said. Some images seem self-referential and aware, and some direct a kind of hostility toward viewers, play with the conventions of viewer–viewed relationships, and reference or signal acknowledgment of an obtrusive masculinized and sexualizing gaze, perhaps not dissimilar to the work of feminist artists such as Barbara Kruger. This heterosexy self-representation evinces the kind of postfeminist "sensibilities" (Gill, 2007) and modes of feminine performativity described in the previous chapter; modes in which the idealized and desirable has shifted toward a tougher, shrewder, and more sexually assertive performativity (Gill, 2003, 2007; Aapola, Gonick, and Harris, 2005; Levy, 2005; Attwood, 2006; McRobbie, 2009; Zaslow, 2009; Banet-Weiser, 2012; Dobson, 2014c; Ringrose, 2013; Winch, 2013; Kanai, 2015b).

In this chapter I describe the heterosexy profile decoration and imagery I viewed and analyzed using feminist performance theory. My discussion addresses the question of how the premise of self-production I suggest operates in this kind of social media (discussed in chapter 1) may open up new meanings of this material. I discuss the political and social significance and possible functions such self-representation may serve when it is framed as "self-production." Female artists, particularly performance artists, have long employed the sexually explicit female form as a way to subvert and complicate notions of "passive" female objectification, as Rebecca Schneider documents. As I explain, Schneider's work suggests that a purposeful construction by a female artist of her specific, individual body in "the object's" role can be understood as disruptive to object–subject binaries by making visible the object's own "eye", and "showing the show" of her own objectification and commodification. Or perhaps, as Schneider puts it, marking the historical terms of her commodification across her own body (Schneider, 1997, p. 86). Following on from this theory, I explore how the premise of self-production commonly at work in personal SNS profiles may serve to alert viewers to the "eyes" of the individual subjects behind such imagery, who are also understood as having agentically chosen/constructed this self-representation for viewers, although not in an "artistic" context. As such, I explore how the premise of self-production may function productively as a signifier of specific, material bodies in the context of heterosexy self-representative imagery on SNSs.

I go on to address the question of whether this kind of boundary blurring around sexual object and subjecthood is still politically productive in the postfeminist cultural context. In the contemporary mediascape described by scholars such as Gill (2003), where women's bodies have been re-sexualized specifically in ways that denote knowingness, desire, activity, and autonomy, it would be problematic, I suggest, to conclude that heterosexy self-representations via social media, in all their various forms, function straightforwardly as "productively disruptive" to conventional ideologies of gender and gaze relations. Young women are invited to participate in mediated sexual subjectification on the one hand, and sexual self-regulation on the other (Ringrose, 2010; Renold and Ringrose, 2011). Examining heterosexy digital self-representations in the different forms they commonly take provides some insight into the complexities of self-representational processes in the postfeminist cultural and technosocial context.

Heterosexy "Love": Soft Pornographic Imagery

Depictions of heterosexual couples engaged in sexual acts constitute another common kind of heterosexy representation used by young women on the profiles I analyzed. Most often the bodies depicted in such acts are Anglophone in appearance, and echo hegemonic gendered ideals of slimness and curvaceousness for women and muscularity for men. These images of sexual acts are illusory and mimetic. That is, rather than being constructed specifically as poses, for example by positioning a model looking directly into a camera, these images are meant to look as if the couples are actually engaged in, and enjoying, the sexual acts depicted. Thus, this kind of profile decoration may be described as closer to soft pornography than to advertisements in the kind of aesthetics, bodily poses, and camera shots conventionally employed. For example, Goldylox and Bec (accessed 29/11/07) feature images of couples on their profiles that may be said to call forth a kind of "voyeuristic" gaze from viewers, drawing from Laura Mulvey's (1975/1989) work on cinema: it is as if neither the camera nor the viewers are there, so that viewers become voyeurs, seeing moments of apparently private, real sexual pleasure between the man and woman depicted. There is nothing particularly remarkable about such sexual imagery itself. These images may be read as sexualized and typically gendered ones that produce sexual desire for a masculinized and heterosexualized gazing subject. This is still how much postfeminist popular and visual culture has been theorized, with the added complication that in some ways the power of the masculinized gaze has come into question. It has been suggested by several scholars that in a postfeminist cultural context the power of the male gaze has been complicated, as many women are themselves encouraged to, and agentically take up, "raunchy" sexual subjectivities and practices, and sexual representations of women in popular culture now also foreground signals of female agency and choice (Pitcher, 2006; Gill, 2008, 2009; Evans, Riley, and Shankar, 2010; Banet-Weiser, 2011; Hatton and Trautner, 2011; Hall, West, and McIntyre, 2012). But ultimately, many scholars suggest, this amounts to a situation where women are incited through discourses of "choice" and "empowerment" to surveil themselves (McRobbie, 2007, p. 724), sexualize themselves, and keep their consumption choices, desires, and bodies in line with those dominant in the commercial and patriarchal sphere (Gill, 2007, p. 91), amounting to no substantive challenge, then, to the kind of masculinized gaze relations theorized in the second wave of feminism.

But varied meanings are possible to read in imagery such as that discussed so far (of both digital dreamgirls and heterosexy love) depending on whether a viewer interprets the female bodies in this material as standing in for the profile owners themselves, or as imagery *consumed* and *liked* by the profile owners. In the former interpretation, the profile owners are perhaps positioned as gazed upon sexual objects, with the complicating factor that they have put themselves in this position, and thus may be presumed to take some pleasure and/or power from it (Dobson, 2008; Attwood, 2011). In the later interpretation, more tributaries of meaning are opened up. The display of such images, when read as connoting taste or interest on the part of profile owners, may indicate complicity and self-alignment with a historically male, heterosexual gazing subject position (Mulvey, 1989). As such, the display of desirous digital dreamgirls or images of heterosexual couples engaged in sexual acts may suggest a kind of reciprocity with a (heterosexual male) viewer's supposed/imagined desire on the part of the profile owners. Sue Thornham suggests that such reciprocity is conventional in visual images of women gesturing toward any kind of sexuality (Thornham, 2007, p. 37). If women are going to be depicted as sexual beings, she suggests, they must be depicted, and depict themselves, as sexual beings whose desires are in line with those already articulated in a patriarchal framework that is extended in and by postfeminist popular culture.

Such readings invariably suggest a degree of false consciousness on the part of the profile owners who use such imagery in a premise of self-production. It has been argued by Ariel Levy that young women are now consumers and participants within "raunch culture," in that they too engage in consumption and viewing choices that sexually objectify other women (Levy, 2005), and sometimes themselves too, for example through participation in pole-dancing classes or burlesque dancing, or pornography consumption. The specific ways in which *women* participate in raunch culture has received less attention, although the work of Evans and Riley (2014) and Whitehead and Kurz (2009) are notable exceptions. I suggest that to interpret this kind of sexual image display on SNSs within a framework of straightforward sexual objectification, or even a kind of postfeminist "sexual subjectification," is to shut down possibilities of sexual self-expression here through a new medium, and to foreclose on further thinking about the function this kind of imagery serves for young women. Viewed through a premise of self-production, digital dreamgirl icons and soft-pornographic images open up other questions that should be considered. Asking such questions allows us a way of moving beyond simplistic, perhaps somewhat instinctive, appraisals of the "hypodermic" effect of heterosexy media imagery, allowing the possibility of less "uniform and dangerous" (Egan and Hawkes, 2008a, p. 297) meanings to emerge. Such images in a context of self-representation may be a way for young women to show an interest in sex, and experiment with their sexual identities (Stokes, 2010). It is important to keep in mind the possibility that display of such imagery may signal desire and interest in sex on the part of the profile owners themselves, despite the very limited and narrow kinds of bodies and sexual desires represented here.

For instance, if such images are understood primarily as "profile decoration," perhaps this indicates a display of personal taste or pleasure in female-body iconography. Whether such images may be seen to express desire for women, for men, or are read more broadly as indicators of sexual feelings/interest itself, it is important to centrally include desire in discourses about young women's sexual SNS decorations and self-representations. This is especially important in the context of prominent debates about cultural sexualization, in which girls and young women are heavily policed for signs that they have become "sexualized" (Egan, 2013; Albury, Crawford, Byron, and Mathews, 2013). In this context, Louisa Allen (2013) argues that the "imaging of desire" by girls and young women, for men or women, can be understood as "queer." In a visual landscape of limited, often homogenized, sexual aesthetics and gender representations it becomes perhaps even more important to make space for the possibility of young women's articulation of sexual desire (McClelland and Fine, 2008), and important to remember that such articulations will likely take the shape of heterosexy and "pornified" visual forms (Ringrose, 2010). In order to better comprehend young women's participation in postfeminist digital culture, feminist scholars must find ways to balance an acknowledgment of young women as cultural producers and desiring subjects in their own right, with acknowledgment of the cultural and historical conditions that shape and limit their sexual self-representations.

Undeniably Paris: Defending Feminine Self-Production with Celebrity?

As well as the kind of "unidentified" dreamgirls such as those discussed so far, Paris Hilton featured prominently on many of the profiles. On one profile in particular, that of Penny Darling, Paris Hilton constituted the main visual theme (accessed 06/11/07). In the series of images displayed on this profile, Paris appears in several different costumes and settings, again foregrounding masquerade, artifice, and playful performativity. We see Paris posed sucking a long red lollypop, overt in its phallic implication; Paris as pool cleaner; Paris as an angelic naked figure surrounded by white, with her chin lowered bashfully and her long blonde hair covering her bare breasts; and Paris dressed in a negligee and stripper-heels, posed in the doorway to what appears to be a sex work venue, to describe but a few of these images. In popular photo shoots circulating on young women's profiles of Paris, the artifice of femininity is made apparent. In the images of her there is often a clear framing of mask, costume, and femininity as a construction. There is no original, "authentic" Paris, only Paris posing for the camera in a variety of different sets and costumes. In one striking image seen on Penny Darling's profile, Paris wears black stiletto boots, and appears naked and tied up in black cord that, on closer inspection, reveals itself to be electrical lead with a microphone on the end of it. Rather than implying distress or submission, in this image Paris looks as if she has a degree of control over the situation, and over her representation. The microphone is, after all, pointing at her mouth and the brick wall and curtains behind her suggest that she is on a stage. Her expression is one of calmness, even pleasure, as she gazes flirtatiously at the camera. The markers of construction in these images of Paris may serve as reminders to viewers that, ultimately, Paris is in control. The signifiers of control here are similar to those identified by Railton and Watson (2007) in music videos to suggest a female artist's authorial voice and agency. Somewhat paradoxically, through this foregrounding of play and artifice, I suggest, Paris has come to signify a kind of "authenticity."

Unlike many of the other heterosexy dreamgirl images found on young women's SNS profiles, Paris is identifiable as an (in)famous individual. She may represent feminine artifice, masquerade, pornification, and hyperfemininity itself, yet unlike images of digitally rendered and anonymous dreamgirls, like the lips and mouths, or the bodies of couples engaged in heterosexual acts, her performance of malleability and idealization is somewhat tempered by the reference to her material, specific body. It is hard *not* to recognize her as "Paris," with the connotations that such identification brings. Paris is a celebrity who attained fame because of her position as a rich, white, young heiress who made a sex tape. Her classed and raced position is significant in how she has been able to generate a celebrity brand. Her position as an heiress enabled her celebrity status through the power of financial resources and cultural capital, and it also made the sex tape circulation online an event that could be harnessed to support her self-branding as somewhat of a "rebel." The digital circulation of a sex tape would not function in the same way, for example, if the celebrity in question was a porn star or a soap opera star rather than an heiress. Naomi Wolf has suggested that Paris is an "empty signifier" that "you can project absolutely anything onto" (Wolf, cited in Esch and Mayer, p. 107). But my point is precisely that she is not an empty signifier in the way that unidentified decorative female bodies in gif files circulating on social media are. She is not an anonymous or generic but, rather, infamous female body. In the postfeminist context Paris has come to signify quite specific qualities as a young female celebrity.

As Esch and Mayer suggest, after the release of her home sex tape, "Hilton has parlayed her literal exposure into a self-made, highly mutable brand exposure" (Esch and Mayer, 2007, p. 107). I suggest that her brand is indeed mutable, but not completely so. Paris has come to symbolize an ideal of not caring about one's social reputation, of "being yourself" and disavowing social approval in favor of "authenticity." What I suggest perhaps makes Paris so popular is that her "brand of authenticity," her "self-brand" (Banet-Weiser, 2012), mirrors precisely the narrow aesthetics, taste, and bodily qualities of heterosexy femininity. The Paris self-brand is hyperfeminine, slim, white, and blonde; consumer focused, with a taste for luxury and expensive high-fashion brand names that is *naturalized*; and it has a sensibility of fun playfulness around identity itself. In a postfeminist context these aspects of femininity with which Paris is aesthetically and ideologically aligned are fetishized at the same time as they are subject to criticism from adults (Fritzsche, 2004; Duits and van Romondt Vis, 2009; Zaslow, 2009; Lamb, Graling, and Wheeler, 2013; Jackson and Goddard, 2015), including parents, teachers, journalists, and feminists. Her self-branding supports a popular postfeminist narrative about hyperfeminine embodiment, fashion, and makeup, as "playful," as something women "choose" to participate in for fun and pleasure in contemporary culture, at the same time as it is something claimed as "authentic" and essentialised. Several profile owners appear to idolize Paris without saying precisely what it is they like about her. Penny Darling tells viewers that she wants to be identified as "Paris," and describes herself as having similar perceived likes and dislikes to Paris, and also owning a Chihuahua, like Paris. Another profile owner writes in her self-description: "my hero is paris hilton love her to death... shes f*^%ing awesome!!" (Laaanni, accessed, 05/03/08). I suggest that Paris's imaged and imagined identity may be appealing to young women as a symbolic representation of someone who appears to be agentically engaging with the aesthetics of femininity and heterosexy consumer culture in a way that is signaled as both *playful* and *authentic*. Her self-branding is "mutable" (albeit within the narrow restrictions of ideal femininity) in the way artifice and feminine masquerade are often foregrounded in her images. Yet Paris also projects a cool indifference, facilitated by her wealth and power, to what others think of her, in this way signaling a sense of "authenticity."

It is important, I suggest, to try to understand the different possible functions of different *kinds* of heterosexy imagery girls and young women engage with in their digital self-representations, rather than dismissing girls' and young women's identifications with female celebrities such as Paris (and now Miley Cyrus, Kim Kardashian, and several others) as signaling an unquestioned or unambiguous acceptance of commercial, "sexualized," culture. These aspects of culture have been heavily critiqued, and are increasingly surveilled by adults concerned about the influence of sexualized celebrities (see Jackson and Goddard, 2015). Images of Paris Hilton displayed in a premise of self-production may function to allow girls and young women to identify with policed aspects of femininity and popular girl culture in a way that signals some acknowledgment of, and implicit defense against, adult critique and regulation.

"Hot and Hostile" Hyperfemininity: Talking Back?

Some sexual images of women found on the profiles in my study signal a kind of hostility toward viewers. But whether this "hostile" imagery highlights, plays with, or questions traditional gendered gaze relations, or whether it simply provokes idealization, fetishization, and distance between viewed objects and viewing subjects is debatable. For example, an image displayed prominently on Glamourbitch's profile (accessed 30/10/07) provides an example of what could be read as a self-referencing, viewer-aware presence in much of the heterosexy iconography. It also exemplifies a key performative mode of postfeminist, popular femininity—a mode that might be described as "hot and hostile." In this image, a digitally rendered, too-perfect, slim, white, and curvy headless dreamgirl poses lifting her hot pink tartan skirt to expose her bare bottom to the camera. This image is displayed in a decorative pink frame, as would be a portrait, but the dreamgirl's head is cut off, out of the frame, so that her torso is positioned as the focus. The words "Dream on Baby!" are written across the top of the image, across the bent arms and back of the dreamgirl, in hot pink italicized font. A teasing, flirtatious mockery of viewers is suggested here: viewers are shown what is supposedly desirable, fantasized, and "dreamt" of, only to be alerted to the impossibility of possession. Desire is provoked and invited, but satiability is denied. The lack of a face or head makes the image generalized as the 'ideal Woman' with no reference to a specific identifiable body, but with signals of whiteness (as invisible; see Dyer, 1997). The digital skin is flawless/perfect, normatively white and tanned, and can never be grasped by viewers, but is rendered to create an illusion of tactility (Schneider, 1997, p. 89). Satiability is further denied to viewers because of the hostility the object herself appears to be signaling toward viewers through the combination of a decidedly "show-off" pose with the words "Dream on Baby!" as if spoken by the dreamgirl herself.

In another image, displayed on Bitch Cunt/Janine's profile (accessed 04/09/07), two women turn their heads in the direction of the camera, possibly as if they have been interrupted by its presence, or taken by surprise. They are posed with one on top of the other, as if engaged in a sexual act. One is Darling Nikki, a promotional model from LA with a small following on MySpace, and she has one arm gently embracing Christine Dolce, another MySpace celebrity model who, at the time of my study, had a growing social media following. Darling Nikki's other arm shields her exposed breasts, supposedly *from the camera*. Christine Dolce looks slightly predatory, protecting the body of her "pseudo lover" beneath her. Both women have straw-like, bleached blonde hair, and are made-up with blackened eyes and whitened, luminescent lips. They wear black studded cuffs around their wrists, suggestive of S and M. This tough, bondage-themed image of heterosexy women posed homoerotically, and also directing a potentially seductive glance toward viewers that borders on aggression, is not an uncommon one in advertising and pornography produced in the postfeminist cultural context.

Another common "hot and hostile" image circulating on social media, seen on She's Infamous's profile (accessed 06/08/08), depicts a slender, young, white female with long blonde hair, wearing tight, low-cut jeans that appear unzipped at the front. The top half of her body is bare. She is posed with her back to the camera, but with her head and shoulders turned around to look into it. She is shielding her bare breasts from viewers and bearing her teeth in an aggressive facial expression, and also making an "up yours" gesture with her finger toward the camera. Just enough flesh and conventional femininity is displayed through her body to flirtatiously spark a heterosexualized viewer's supposed desire. The curve of the back and torso, the bottom peeking out of the top of the jeans, the side of one breast, partially covered by an arm and turned away from the camera, and the hanging fabric of the open jeans are symbols of feminine heterosexiness. At the same time, the pose is constructed to communicate hostility explicitly toward a masculinized and sexualized gaze. All of these images play into social and historical gendered and raced gaze conventions whereby the bodies of white women are idealized and fetishized, but rarely signified as completely and unconditionally sexually "available" to viewers (Railton and Watson, 2005) in popular cultural tropes.

These images evince the way in which representations that depict more strength, self-awareness, and even aggression or hostility to viewers have been somewhat co-opted in postfeminist visual culture over the past 20 years. Gill writes of this shift, "The figure of the autonomous, active, desiring subject has become [. . .] the dominant figure for representing young women, part of the construction of the neoliberal feminine subject. But sexual subjectification, I would argue, has turned out to be objectification in new and even more pernicious guise" (Gill, 2003, p. 105). These postfeminist female objects of desire are perhaps "stronger," posed to suggest a willing, playful, or "aggressively defended" sexual self-exposure (Gill, 2007, p. 89), rather than a passive mode of being "on display" for a male gaze. But an object's gaze which appears to signal a degree of hostility to viewers does not hold the same disruptive power it may once have. Further, this fantasy of choice and playful, active sexuality nonetheless disavows satiation and "graspability," deferring instead to a circulation of desire and idealization by keeping material, finite bodies forever "just out of reach." Abstracted, headless, and hostile representations such as those I am describing invite viewers to gaze in racially prescribed ways, without ever possessing, to look but never to touch, to "Dream On." That is, to dream the dreams suggested, only to be continually disappointed, unfulfilled, and never satiated by a "reality" that is constructed as opposed to such fantasies and never adequate.

It is important to also consider the ways in which, in a premise of self-production, such images might also communicate an unambiguous *lack* of "comforting reciprocity" to the imagined normative desires of viewers, unlike the images of women in advertising, discussed by Thornham (Thornham, 2007, p. 37) who also gaze assertively, sometimes threateningly, at the camera. It is perhaps unsurprising in the postfeminist visual and marketing culture described by scholars, but worth noting nonetheless, that there are marked similarities in these "hot and hostile" images to feminist visual and performance art critiquing the male gaze. Rebecca Schneider describes how in the performances of Annie Sprinkle and other explicit-body female artists, as well as in the work of visual artists such as Barbara Kruger (Kruger, 1981), these artists "interrupt" their own acts with the presence of their viewing eyes (Schneider, 1997, p. 86). According to Schneider, their own eyes, as distinct from a third party director or creator, are made visible as a constructing agent within the logic of their performances, and as witnesses to the "show" of feminine desirability playing out across the stage of their own bodies (1997, p. 86). Feminist discourses of discontent may sometimes be reflected here, in heterosexy SNS profile decorations, in strange and unpredictable ways.

Viewed through a premise of self-production, it is important, I suggest, to also account for the potential function of "hot and hostile images" in signalling an acknowledgment of, and perhaps dissatisfaction with, the masculinized and sexualizing gaze. A particularly important function of such images in a premise of young women's self-production may be to challenge the presumption that a profile owner who engages with heterosexy images, or even codes herself visually in explicitly sexual ways, is *sexually available to viewers.* "Hot and hostile" images may be of use for young women in signaling a self that is "hot" and aligned with ideals of femininity, but not necessarily "up for it." Images of heterosexy female bodies that "look back" aggressively at the camera, or pose in ways which emphasize or explicitly reference their own situation of being gazed upon, construct sexual objects who are positioned as seeing themselves being seen, and perhaps also signify some discontent with the weight of the gaze. As Boler, Harris, and Jacobson note of the emergence of female vlogging culture, "We witness a historical moment when women continue to battle the patriarchally tolerated visual and material violence against women, yet are fortressed with newly gained access to the 'gaze' via means of production" (Boler, Harris, and Jacobson, forthcoming, p. 6). These authors suggest that emergent forms of culture "inevitably carry the equivalent of handheld-camera queasiness as we negotiate the contradictions, pitfalls, and mires faced in the challenge of disrupting the profound historical weight of something like the 'male gaze'" (p. 6).

Heterosexy Self-Imagery

Several of the profiles examined contained heterosexy "selfie"-style images of the profile owners, most often alone, and posed for the camera. The young women's eyes are directed toward viewers in the majority of these shots. Their gazes suggest "camera seduction" and reciprocity of a viewer's potential desire in the way that Thornham has suggested images of women do in much advertising and pinup girl photography (2007, p. 37). Other conventions of advertisements and pornography are also visible in such shots. Lips and mouths are often emphasized, posed pouted, slightly open, or puckered in a kiss shape, now commonly referred to as "duck face" photos on social media. Some young women photograph their own torsos and midriffs in swimwear or other flesh-revealing clothes, and some pose in Playboy bunny t-shirts or wearing bunny ears. In one such series of images, for example, Micki (accessed 17/09/07) poses kneeling on what appears to be her bedroom floor, her Playboy singlet rolled up to her chest, with her knees apart, pulling at, and then unzipping the fly of her short denim shorts. This is a common photographic sequence seen in soft pornography magazines, as well as on pornographic websites and amateur cam sites (Dobson, 2008).

Many fears have been raised by journalists and scholars about the Internet as a "paradise" for stalkers and would-be sexual criminals, and about young women's employment of SNSs for this kind of sexualized self-presentation and display of sexual behavior, as documented by Thiel-Stern (2009, 2014), Shade (2007), and Edwards (2005). Sexual representation on SNSs is often framed by media commentators as risky, licentious, or deviant. It seems to me that the automatic linking of online sexual self-representation to risk of predation, abuse, and violent crime that occurs in media commentary about young women's use of SNSs, as well as in some academic research (Moreno et al., 2009; Moreno, Swanson, Royer, and Roberts, 2011; Moreno, Brockman, Wasserheit, and Christakis, 2012) is akin to the kind of victim blaming that goes on in relation to other sex crimes, where the victims' clothing choices and behaviors are assessed and judged in terms of their ability to "provoke" violence from men. We see this victim-blaming mentality continued most recently into digital realms around the issue of youth sexting, discussed in the following chapter. Almost all of the educational campaigns that have sought to address gendered harms that sometimes emerge around certain sexting practices have adopted an approach that targets the behavior of teenage girls sending sexual images of themselves in confidence to a male partner or desired partner. As I discuss further in the following chapter, educational films addressing sexting depict the supposedly "unavoidable" outcome of girls' images being circulated publicly by peers, followed by bullying and abuse of the female subject of the image (Albury and Crawford, 2012; Karaian, 2012; Hasinoff, 2013; Dobson and Ringrose, 2015). It is important not to assume in commentary about young women's heterosexy self-representation that such self-representation signifies sexual availability to an entire networked public.

It is also worth noting that this kind of *self*-imagery was not ubiquitous on the SNS profiles I examined. In my study it was the least common kind of *self-imagery* found on the profiles in relation to other types of *self*-imagery posted. Heterosexy decorations and porn-themed page-layouts were commonly employed by profile owners (e.g., Playboy bunny-themed page layouts). Of the profiles I analyzed, 15 of the 45 profile owners posted heterosexy photos that were apparently of themselves—that is, photos featuring their face or body which employ the kind of "sexy selfie" conventions described earlier. By way of comparison, 40 out of the 45 profile owners posted photos of themselves laughing, playing, and posing with their (primarily female) friends. That heterosexy photos of the self *do not* constitute a category of self-imagery engaged in ubiquitously may be significant, considering the selection criteria for my study of SNS profiles.[4] I looked specifically at profiles that projected mainstream feminine aesthetics, which, many journalists and scholars have argued, is heavily grounded in "pornified" aesthetics (Paul, 2005), and sexualized female performativity (Rush and La Nauze, 2006;

American Psychological Association, 2007; Gill, 2008; Oppliger, 2008; Durham, 2009; Ringrose, 2010). It is worth keeping in mind that even in a supposedly pornified postfeminist Western cultural context, and even among young women who project a normative young feminine identity, many young women do not engage in heterosexy self-imaging for various reasons. Sexualized bodily exposure may be perceived as too risky—socially, mentally, or physically—because of the prominence of risk discourses, reputational fear, or a perceived inability to physically meet the very narrow cultural and racialized standards of heterosexy bodies (Leage and Chalmers, 2010; Renold and Ringrose, 2011; Albury and Crawford, 2012; Jackson, Vares, and Gill, 2013). As Ringrose (2010) has suggested, many girls and young women defer instead to more abstracted icons, images, and texts to signify heterosexiness, such as the cartoon figures, images of celebrities, and hot and hostile female body images I have discussed. The young women who did post heterosexy selfies met normative standards of feminine attractiveness as couched in whiteness, slimness, and typically feminine and Anglophone facial features. In the next chapter we see how even very gender-normative forms of sexual self-representation in networked publics are heavily policed and often shamed through pedagogical messages to youth and by young people themselves, in a way that reinforces gendered victim-blaming messages about sex, and strongly contradicts postfeminist cultural discourses of empowerment through sexual subjectification.

* * *

Branding the digital self through animated female cartoon-like heterosexy figures, images of couples engaged in sexual acts, heterosexy images of female celebrities, "hot and hostile" female body images, and seductive self-images may be experienced as fun, exciting, even liberating for some young women, as such visualizations can serve to code the digital self as cool, legibly feminine, and sexually and culturally knowledgeable. Such digital self-branding may serve young women in the complex and potentially laborious process of visually and textually negotiating a postfeminist feminine self; a self who appears visually complicit with current standards of active, up-for-it, girl-powered femininity, without overtly evidencing sexual desires or sexual activity that might render her vulnerable to slut-shaming (Renold and Ringrose, 2011; Ringrose, 2010). Through heterosexy self-representations online, young women are negotiating complex a priori cultural calls to postfeminist sexual subjectification (Gill,

2003; Stokes, 2010) on the one hand, and imperatives on the other from peers, adults, and via media discourses, to manage their sexual reputations (Leage and Chalmers, 2010; Ringrose, 2010; Stokes, 2010; Albury and Crawford, 2012; Dobson and Ringrose, 2015), as I discuss further in the following chapter.

Heterosexy Representations and Binary Disruption: Citing the Object's Eye?

In these final sections I consider some broader political and socio-cultural functions of heterosexy material posted by young women on SNSs. I provide a political reading of this material in relation to Rebecca Schneider's theories of object–subject binary disruption by female performance artists. Schneider offers analysis of performance by female artists working with the "explicit body," mostly their own explicit bodies. The performances she discusses are largely personal and self-representational rather than fictional. Hence, I suggest there are aspects of this feminist analysis that can be usefully applied to my inquiry of heterosexy self-representation by young women on SNSs.

Previously, I briefly explained the term "commodity dreamgirls" as out-of-reach objects which have come to hold and symbolize the most potent displaced desires of viewers in visual culture (Schneider, 1997, p. 92). In advertising, this is often precisely the way in which images of women's bodies are used. Schneider has argued that this kind of distancing and fetishization of the female body in representation relies on constructing the female object as metaphorically "blind": she is unable to see out of the "dreamscape" and into the realm of viewers, and is seemingly unaware that she is being *seen*, as well as desired. For this reason, the dreamgirl is also unable to communicate and interact with her viewers. According to Schneider, feminist representation should not just be about creating different, diverse kinds of female subjectivities. Rather, she argues that a central project of feminist representation should involve a more fundamental disruption and questioning of object–subject binaries themselves. The "problem" of female objectification, Schneider notes, cannot simply be fixed by attempts to "de-objectify" women in representation (1997, p. 57), and make them known as "real subjects." This is because the representation and constitution of a "real woman" is a concept so fraught with possibilities of fixity, exclusion, and essentialism that many feminists have abandoned the notion in favor of a questioning of the binary thinking that locates objects and subjects as opposite positions (Case, 1988; de Lauretis, 1989; Schneider, 1997; Coleman, 2009).

According to Schneider, representations of women that helpfully question such binary modes of thinking are ones where, within the logic or premise of the performance, female sexual objects are constructed as "objects" that are also simultaneously authorial, "creative eyes." Viewers must somehow be made aware that the object of representation has a perspective on her own desirability as an object, and an ability to *see herself being seen* (Schneider, 1997, p. 100). The eye of the object must be cited in performance. When the objects of visual representation can literally or metaphorically be seen gazing out of their own dreamscapes, and perhaps taking pleasure from *seeing their viewers see them*, the clear-cut object–subject binary is thrown into confusion. Schneider writes about performance scenarios created by female artists in which:

> The "seen" takes on an agency of her own and wields the unnerving potential of a subversive reciprocity of vision, an explicit complicity, or mutual recognition between seer and seen, who become seer and seer, subject and subject, object and object in the scene of viewing. (1997, p. 86)

Self-representations on SNSs are not conventionally understood or contextualized by their viewers as "art," as explicitly or intentionally creative or political self-representations. But, I suggest in chapter 1, such self-representations are viewed and contextualized through a premise of self-production, whereby viewers conventionally assume a high degree of conscious intent, choice-making, and intrinsic motivation in the construction of SNS profile self-representational texts. This is different to how commercial media representations of women are conventionally understood. It is different, again, to how we conventionally interpret presentations of self in face-to-face interactions, which are generally understood to be molded to fit the given social context (Goffman, 1969), but are not understood as *bounded, reflectively constructed texts* (Thumin, 2012, p. 6) in the way mediated self-representations are. Perhaps, when viewed through this premise of self-production, the kind of heterosexy self-representations discussed in this chapter could function to "return the gaze." Perhaps they signal a potentially disruptive pleasure on the part of the profile producer in being seen. Perhaps heterosexy self-representation, in particular, functions as a kind of "citing of the object's eye."

Complications of the object–subject binary in representation have accompanied the rise of social media, and young women's heavy participation in it. I suggest, along with other feminist scholars, that a cultural shift has occurred with new media technologies whereby we can, and in many ways need to, position large groups of young women as cultural producers themselves (Molyneaux, O'Donnell, Gibson, and Singer, 2008; Senft, 2008; Keller, 2012; Szostak, 2013; Boler, Harris, and Jacobson, forthcoming). I am not suggesting that SNS self-representations should be read necessarily as artistic, creative, or intentionally political. But I do think it is important to point out that in panicking over young women's sexual self-representations on SNSs we assume a *lack of reflectiveness and conscious intent,* as well as a lack of creative or political intent that cannot necessarily be judged from representations alone. The profile owners who employ various kinds of heterosexy imagery in their self-representations regularly negotiate complex spaces and overlaps between the "real" and "unreal"; between playful and parodic versus "authentic" modes of self-representation; between "essential" and "fixed" aspects of self, and unfixed, mutable aspects of self. This degree and particular type of reflection and negotiation around everyday identity performativity is, in many ways, something that people who have not *grown up* with social media—that is, with mediated communication and expression in networked publics as a feature of everyday life for many—may never fully comprehend (Robards, 2014).

Heterosexy SNS self-representations, in particular, force the question of where and how to draw up boundary lines between self-representation seen as political, disruptive, or subversive, and self-representation seen as *re*-productive, repetitive, regressive, or "falsely conscious" gender performativity. This is not a new question. In the 1990s Linda Williams (1993), for example, raised this question in her analysis of Annie Sprinkle's porn/performances.[5] Digital technologies do, however, force us to ask the question in a new context. Object–subject representational binaries are certainly complicated in and by social media in ways that could not have been predicted by feminists 20 years ago. Heterosexy self-representation, following Schneider, may reveal "the object's eye" in a way that allows both young women and their viewers to enter into double positions of seer and seen simultaneously. I think it is less clear that such "challenges" and "disruptions" function as such—as politically and socially significant in postfeminist digital cultures. As Thumin (2012) notes, increasingly all of those with access to digital technologies and means of digital media production are called toward self-representation. In this techno-social context, we have to ask: what does it mean to call attention to one's ability to self-represent, to produce the self as a sexual object/subject? Is this a politically productive project for feminism in this context, or more about surveillance and regulation (Kanai, 2015a)? Digital self-representational practices such as those discussed in this chapter thus perhaps force a critical reevaluation of the larger political project of object–subject binary disruption in representation.

Negotiating Postfeminist Digital Cultures

The level of sophistication and literacy with the portrayal of identity, with "the gaze," and with sex, popular culture, and mediation that I have pointed to in this chapter is also one of the aspects of feminine self-representational practices and heterosexy self-branding in postfeminist digital cultures that I am most ambivalent about. This is because of the *work*, and also the potential *exclusion from gender legibility* of those unable to perform such work, required to construct cool and gender-normative self-representations. What I want to highlight and problematize in conclusion is the way in which postfeminist representational sensibilities, as they translate into a visual, self-representational context, appear to call upon young women to construct themselves as highly sophisticated and media literate sexual subjects. In order to differentiate the feminine self from older, weaker versions of femininity, and construct the self as sufficiently *postfeminist*, girls and young women are required not only to engage with heterosexy and pornographic visual tropes, but to also knowingly and "playfully" engage with complex binaries of sexual object and subjecthood, sexual desire and satiation, complicity with a masculinized sexual gaze and refusal/noncompliance. And they must appear to do so in the spirit of "fun" and "lightheartedness" that characterizes postfeminist sensibilities, rather than being too "serious" or "earnest" in relation to sexual and gendered self-representation.

Jessica Ringrose has established the difficulties that young teenage girls face in negotiating appropriate performances of sexuality (Ringrose, 2010, 2013). Her research on girls' negotiations of sexual self-presentation on SNSs illuminates the consequences girls face if they fail to get this contemporary feminine sexual performativity "right." Such consequences include peer aggression, conflict, ostracizing, and labelling, especially if girls fail to take into account their position as raced and classed subjects, as these differences alter significantly the rules and boundaries around presentations of one's sexual self. In short, a lot of effort may be required in the construction of postfeminist heterosexy digital feminine identities.

The representational literacy and sophistication required potentially adds to the *work* of gender for young women, to the labor that needs to be done to visually and textually construct normative, legible, and cool femininity.

In this chapter I have drawn on representational theories, and raised possible readings of this material as expressing sexual desire, challenging gaze relations and assumptions about self-representation and sexual availability, and "citing the object's eye" in representation. I have done this not as a way of uncritically celebrating young women's participation in sexualized postfeminist digital cultures, but in the hope of slowing down judgment, and allowing some cooling of the heat generated around young women, media, and sex. It is unhelpful and too simplistic, I have suggested, to position girls and young women who engage with and produce heterosexy imagery in their self-representation as "victims" of sexualization. The premise of self-production adds a layer of complexity to interpreting heterosexy self-representation that feminists, academics, parents, and other commentators need to acknowledge when seeking to understand this kind of material. Heterosexy self-representation on SNSs may potentially provoke an uncomfortable disjuncture between the commodity dreamgirl and the specificity of the material self/body represented and constituted here. Schneider's work articulates some of the political power potentially available to female artists who use pornographic tropes and their own explicit bodies in representation in ways that complicate neat object–subject divides. We must consider whether such powers are available to and sometimes intentionally utilized by young women in practices of representing the self on social media.

At the same time, we need to acknowledge the complex social and cultural pressures young women are under, and the amount of media literacy and identity-negotiation work potentially required of them to participate in postfeminist digital cultures in gender-normative ways. The heterosexy self-representation I have examined here provides some insight into the complexities young women face in navigating the challenges of everyday mediation and self-representation in postfeminist digital cultures. Albeit in limited and heteronormative ways, sometimes these young women may be expressing desire, and/or speaking back to a gendered system of gaze relations that equates heterosexy aesthetics and self-representation *a priori* with sexual availability. As I have suggested, we need to find ways of discussing this kind of material, and young women's engagement with it, which foregrounds, and is careful not to marginalize, the possibility of female desire and sexual expression via social media. We need to avoid the temptation to simply dismay over that which we do not understand.

* * *

I have mentioned in brief in this chapter that the requirement to differentiate the feminine self from older, weaker femininity, by presenting a sophisticated and sexually knowing self, may contradict other requirements firmly in place in many girls and young women's social lives to keep their sexual reputations in check, and not appear as excessively sexually active or desiring. I explore further in the following chapter the situation teenage girls describe in research into youth sexting and cybersafety, in relation to self-produced female body images, where significations of female sexual agency and activity appear to remain heavily condemned by both peers and adults.

Chapter 4

Girls, Sexting, and Gender Politics

Introduction

In the previous chapter I provided a close reading of some common heterosexy profile decorations and images used by young women in a context of feminine self-representation on social network sites (SNSs). The dominant discourse perpetuated about such imagery in public debate, news media, and some scholarship is that such images equate to physically and mentally risky "self-sexualization" or "self-objectification" (Hall, West, and McIntyre, 2012), and thus serve as evidence of young women's vulnerability to negative media influence in sexualized postfeminist media cultures. This dominant discourse about sexual self-representations and their meaning for young women as indicators of vulnerability and psychopathology is currently most evident in debates and panic about youth sexting. This chapter examines the issue of youth sexting. Dominant pedagogical messages about youth sexting, and young people's own framing of the gender politics of digital sexual self-representation, highlight a key contradiction in postfeminist cultures between the positioning of girls and young women as empowered and powerful postfeminist sexual subjects, and the positioning of girls as "at risk" and vulnerable to the harms of cultural sexualization. I argue here that scholars, stakeholders, and activists concerned with the well-being of young people need to *slow down* (Henderson, 2008) when it comes to sexting, and reconsider the way it is currently approached. The work of this chapter is to show why it is so important that we find a way to assume and discursively position girls as *sexual agents* in our approaches to youth sexting, and make space for experiences other than those of girls' victimization and damage in relation to sexting, while addressing current gendered power imbalances in relation to the circulation of sexual and bodily images.

I start by outlining what available research tells us about the prevalence and gender dynamics of youth sexting. I then discuss the way youth sexting has been approached in media prevention messages aimed at young people in Anglophone Western countries, before charting how young people themselves perceive the gender dynamics of digital sexual communication in my own qualitative research.[1] Sexual shame discourses and messages of self-responsibilization, self-protection, and "self-respect" are the prominent terms that frame communication to youth about sexting, and serve to position girls as psychically, socially, and physically vulnerable to harms, as well as to blame for such harms, if they express or visually produce themselves sexually via digital means. In our focus-group conversations with girls and boys in years ten and eleven in two Australian public high schools, I suggest "three C's" that can be identified as framing these discussions about sexting, gender, and cybersafety discursively and affectively: "consequences," "consternation," and "culpability." In this chapter I discuss data from the two focus groups conducted with mainly female participants. Girls use discourses and affects of consequences, consternation, and culpability to produce themselves as "agents through abstinence" (Hasinoff, 2015) in relation to sexting. Positions and articulations of sexual agency and desire are *present* in these conversations, but remain confusing, illegible, and largely inaccessible to the girls with whom we spoke. Sexual agency and desire for girls, in short, remains socially illegitimate.

As I discussed in chapter 2, we are regularly invited in postfeminist media and visual culture to assume young women's sexual empowerment. It has been observed by scholars of postfeminist media culture that popular media images and discourses such as those we find in advertising, music videos, and celebrity media coverage regularly position sexuality as a source of power for young, heterosexy women, often their primary source of power (Gill, 2007). The sexual objectification of women's bodies is something relatively *unremarkable* in postfeminist media culture: we are conditioned to see it as normative, not necessarily politically meaningful or worth fighting about in a context where women in Western democracies are positioned as having already won so many other (implicitly more meaningful) gains (McRobbie, 2004, 2009; Douglas, 2010; Gill, 2011). And yet, we still question the agency and well-being of women and girls ardently and vigorously when it comes to matters of sexuality. As Amy Hasinoff explains, visual signs of self-sexualization for girls and young women continue to be normatively associated in everyday life contexts not with power but with sexual violence. Hasinoff suggests that, for instance, "People who see a preteen [girl] wearing a crop-top in the mall might cringe or sigh—such powerful affective responses come from the connection these observers make between this girl's self-sexualization and the problems with a culture that objectifies women and tacitly authorizes sexual violence" (Hasinoff, 2014, p. 114). If sexual violence were not the pervasive and gendered issue it is, she suggests, concerns over girls' self-sexualization may not be so prevalent. We still assume that sexual self-representation constitutes risky or deviant behavior that evidences a girl's "low self-esteem" and makes girls and young women vulnerable to violence; that instead of empowerment, sexual self-representation signals a girl's or young woman's status as a victim of *damaging* (not empowering) cultural influence. This is one of the obvious contradictions of postfeminist cultural conditions, and of assumptions about women's status in society in the Anglophone West, and yet it is one that still often remains obscured from view. The issue of youth sexting throws light onto this contradiction.

The Prevalence of Youth Sexting

To date international research with teenagers and young people has focused largely on the prevalence of sexting practices. Rates of reported participation in sexting among youth vary significantly, due largely to different ideas about the media practices that should be defined as "sexting," and differing sampling and surveying methods. Some studies include sexual text messages, for instance, while others define sexting as the sending, receiving, or circulation of nude or seminude self-produced images or videos. Some studies have measured participation in these various media practices only via SNSs, and others only via mobile phones. Some surveys on sexting have reported that young people are sharing sexually explicit images or videos *of themselves* quite commonly, and this has generated significant public panic about sexting in media and educational spheres. For example, a United Kingdom survey study finds 40 percent of high school-age teenagers report that *they know of friends* sharing sexually explicit self-images, 53 percent report knowledge of sexts being circulated beyond the intended recipients, and 27 percent say sexting happens regularly or "all the time" (Phippen, 2009, p. 2). While these high rates refer to measures of what young people *think their peers are doing* rather than what *they themselves* are doing, they have been taken up widely as indicators of the prevalence of sexting. A survey of 1,416 young people from across Australia, aged mostly between 13 and 18, reports an overall rate of 49 percent for youth who report having sent a sexual image or video of themselves (Crofts, Lee, McGovern, and Milivojevic, 2015), however, the authors note that their sample may consist disproportionately of young people who have participated in sexting because of the way it was promoted.

Other studies asking young people about their first-hand experiences of sexting media practices in the United States (Lenhart, 2009; Mitchell, Finkelhor, Jones, and Wolak, 2012), Europe (Livingstone, Haddon, Gorzig, and Olafsson, 2011), and Australia (Joint Select Committee on Cyber-Safety, 2011; Tallon et al., 2012) have reported much lower rates of youth under the age of 18 who claim to have been directly involved in sexting through either sending, receiving, or being requested to send sexual self-images. However, concerns about *underreporting* in these studies have been raised. For example, Mitchell and colleagues (2012) conducted phone surveys with 1,560 youth who were between the age of 10 and 17, and found that only 2.5 percent reported creating, or appearing in a "nude or nearly nude picture or video" of themselves or another minor, and 7.1 percent reported receiving such an image (Mitchell et al., 2012, p. 16). This low figure has been reported in academic literature—less so in news media. However, 2.5 percent has been suggested as an underestimate because the researchers conducted a phone survey for which parents had to be present in the home and give consent to enable their child's participation (Strassberg et al., 2013, p. 16). Also, Mitchell and colleagues only surveyed households with landlines, which are thought to be more conservative, and have higher socioeconomic status and less ethnic diversity than households with no landline (Temple et al., 2012, p. 829), thus making their sample less representative.

Recently, some studies that focus primarily on *older* teenagers, and use anonymous surveys administered at school, have reported more plausible "middle-ground" rates of sexting. In the United States, Strassberg and colleagues (2013, p. 15) find nearly 20 percent of teens aged between 15 and 17 report having *sent* an image of their breasts, buttocks, or genitals; almost twice as many have received such an image; and 25 percent report forwarding a sext they have received. Temple and colleagues (2012, p. 829) find that 27 percent of teens aged between 14 and 19 report having sent a naked picture of themselves. An Australian survey conducted in schools around the country and involving over 2,000 youth echoes these rates for *nonsexually active* teens: the authors find that 26 percent of Australian youth in years ten to twelve (aged between 15 and 18) have sent a sexually explicit image of themselves (Mitchell et al., 2014, p. 63). They report higher rates of sexting among *sexually active* teens: 50 percent of the sexually active teens they surveyed had sent an explicit self-image (2014, pp. 63–64).

Despite the fact that participation rates vary in quantitative research on sexting, as more studies become available a clearer picture is emerging about youth sexting. We can garner from the available research that sexting is *not* a ubiquitous practice among young people, and unsurprisingly, sexting becomes more common with age and is more common among sexually active young people. In extant research the reported prevalence of all the sexting media practices usually measured—sending, receiving, and being asked for images—increases with age and with sexual activity (Lenhart, 2009; Phippen, 2009; Green et al., 2011; Livingstone et al., 2011; Mitchell et al., 2012; Drouin, Vogel, Surbey, and Stills, 2013; Campbell and Park, 2014; Mitchell et al., 2014). For example Tallon and colleagues (2012, p. 34) found 16–17 year olds were more than three times as likely to report sexting as 12–13 year olds. Mitchell and colleagues (2012, p. 16) found that 72 percent of those who had appeared in, or created, a sext in their survey were aged 16 or 17, and that both the rates of creating and receiving sexts increased with age, with 31 percent of 17 year olds either having created, appeared in, or received nude or nearly nude images or videos (2012, p. 15). Among university aged young adults in the United States and Spain, *sending* sexually explicit self-images or videos has been reported at rates of between 30 percent and 67 percent, with higher figures reported for receiving such images (Agustina and Gomez-Duran, 2012; Drouin et al., 2013; Gordon-Messer, Bauermeister, Grodzinski, and Zimmerman, 2013).

The Gender Dynamics of Youth Sexting

In the research literature on youth sexting it is stressed that participating in sexting does not commonly cause problems for young people, especially if sexting is defined broadly (as it usually is) as the production and circulation of sexual, nude, or seminude images via personal media devices. In their qualitative research with young people about how they understand sexting, Kath Albury and colleagues (Albury, Crawford, Byron, and Mathews, 2013) find that seminude and explicit body images may be taken and shared by youth in several different contexts, not all of which are sexual, and most of which are inoffensive and benign in their impacts in young people's lives. Much of the time, sexting goes on among young people consensually and without incident, and some studies suggest it goes on most commonly between young adults in committed relationships

(Drouin et al., 2013). But when sexting involves pressure, nonconsensual image distribution, bullying, and abuse, this appears to happen along clearly gendered lines. In most of the studies mentioned so far, boys and girls do not appear to be sending sexual images of themselves at markedly different rates. However, it appears that girls are significantly more likely than boys to report being *asked* for sexts, while boys are more likely to report asking for sexts (Tallon et al., 2012, p. 29; Temple et al., 2012, p. 829; Strassberg et al., 2013, p. 18). Girls more commonly report being bothered by receiving sexual messages online (Green et al., 2011, p. 35), or by being asked for sexts (Temple et al., 2012, p. 829; Salter, forthcoming). Girls appear to be more vulnerable than boys to having their sexts shown or sent beyond the intended recipient (Temple et al., 2012; Salter, Crofts, and Lee, 2013; Strassberg et al., 2013; Salter, forthcoming). More boys than girls report sending on a sexually explicit image of someone else (Mitchell et al., 2014, p. 63), in some cases without the person's knowledge that they were taking the image (Strassberg et al., 2013, p.18). More boys also report being shown or sent explicit images not meant for them (Tallon et al., 2012; Mitchell et al., 2014, p. 63).

Sexting is criminalized for young people under 18 via various laws governing the production and distribution of child pornography in several countries, including Australia. Many legal scholars and activists have put forth cogent arguments about why the laws in this area need to change, and change is slowly occurring.[2] But currently, in the gendered social context in which sexting media practices occur, boys and young men are the ones most likely to engage in abusive or harassing sexting media practices, and are also most vulnerable to criminalization in relation to sexting. The criminal cases that have emerged nationally and internationally largely involve boys' circulating images of girls (Salter et al., 2013, p. 304), although it should be noted that in many legal contexts both girls and boys are at risk of serious legal penalties, even for possessing private and consensually produced and/or shared self-images on personal media devices. In 2011, sexting was added as a new concern category for the phone and Internet based counseling service ChildLine UK. They report that 66 percent of counseling sessions where sexting was mentioned were with girls, 7 percent with boys, and in 27 percent gender was unknown (ChildLine UK, 2012). In troubling sexting incidents reported to the service by young people, boy acquaintances were named as the top perpetrators by both girls and boys. Several incidences of suicide of teenage girls in the United States, Canada, and Australia have reportedly followed the nonconsensual circulation of sexual images created by girls, and related intensive bullying by peers on and offline (see May, 2013a).

Reflecting long-standing gendered double standards around sexuality and body display or exposure, the research on sexting indicates a scenario whereby boys and men are seen as, and expected to be, interested in pictures of girls' and women's bodies, and sometimes pressure girls via text messages and SNSs to take and send sexually explicit self-images or videos. Qualitative researchers also suggest that girls who participate in various sexting practices are vulnerable to social exclusion, bullying, abuse, and related psychological harm as a result of sexually explicit messages or images being circulated in networked publics (Ringrose, Gill, Livingstone, and Harvey, 2012; Salter et al., 2013; Walker, Sanci, and Temple-Smith, 2013; Salter, forthcoming). This research illuminates the kind of gendered social context in which sexting becomes linked to social shame and psychological distress for girls, and criminalization for boys.

Walker and colleagues (2013) conducted semi-structured interviews with 33 young people, aged between 15 and 20, from suburban Melbourne. Participants in their study report the use of technology for sexual interactions as relationship maintenance, and some young people also say that participation in behavior seen as "risky" is part of the appeal of sexting. Some young men in their study report social pressure to "request and show each other images of girls" as part of their social lives (2013, pp. 699–700). They suggest that many girls feel "coerced, threatened, or bribed by boys to produce and send images," and note that sometimes sext images are "saved as a form of blackmail or revenge or posted on social networking sites" (pp. 699–701). Young people also reported anecdotes of sexual videos and images of girls being circulated around their networked peer communities. As Powell (2010) points out in relation to unauthorized sexual images—that is, explicit images taken or shared without the subject's consent or, sometimes, knowledge—the circulation of such images between peers is precluded by a culture that frames images of girls and women's bodies as *highly valuable* social currency, as sought-after, and fetishized. In his focus groups about sexting with Sydney youth aged between 18 and 20, Salter (forthcoming) finds reports from girls of sexual harassment behaviors, such as being pestered for explicit body images after a break up with a boy by *other boys* they had considered platonic friends. Some describe being sent explicit images of boy's genitals repeatedly and unwantedly. Salter notes that sexting may usually be a "private" practice between young people, and that it only becomes publicly known when a breach of trust occurs in some way. The breaches of trust Salter describes are, again, shaped by longstanding gender dynamics.

In their report on sexting culture in schools in the United Kingdom, Ringrose and colleagues (2012) draw on focus groups, interviews, and online observations conducted in two schools in London with 35 teens aged between 13 and 15. Their work elucidates that broader sociocultural gendered power dynamics centrally shape practices of digitally mediated sexual communication. For instance, they note that harassment and objectification of young women is often accepted in school cultures, and occurs both online and offline, through comments about appearance and sexuality, bodily appraisal, and pressure for girls to display themselves sexually via postfeminist popular media and cultural messages more broadly (Ringrose, Harvey, Gill, and Livingstone, 2013). They find use of the screenshot feature on mobile phones, where, for instance, boys "jokingly" ask girls repeatedly for sex acts via text message, and take a screen-shot of a girl's response for further circulation if she consents to the act (Ringrose et al., 2012, pp. 40–42). They suggest that self-produced images of girls' bodies are a new form of social currency for boys, and some boys brag about their "collections," and their ability to procure such images (Ringrose et al., 2013, p. 312). They also suggest that, for girls, being asked for sexual images, while sometimes felt as a pressure, also signals one's feminine desirability and *value* (2013, p. 311).

Pedagogies of Sexting: Agency through Abstinence

Stakeholders and governments in Australia and internationally have had to respond quickly to the highly publicized possibilities of extreme legal, social, and psychological consequences for youth involved in sexting, and have been highly proactive in doing so, developing several educational films, marketing campaigns, and fact sheets to warn youth of the various legal and social risks of sexting. The predominant approach taken in educational and government campaigns has been to try to prevent youth sexting by warning young people of the current risks and dangers. The pedagogical film and poster campaigns I have viewed and analyzed from Australia, the United Kingdom, the United States, and Canada try to address the gender-imbalances of sexual communication in networked publics described earlier through scare tactics aimed squarely at girls. Thus, the risks highlighted in these campaigns are mainly psychosocial, rather than legal. This is in a context where sexting is criminalized under child pornography laws, as said, and both boys and girls have suffered harsh *legal* punishments for producing or sharing sexual self-images (Calvert and Richards, 2009; Funnell, 2011; Karaian, 2012; Crofts and Lee, 2013; Hasinoff, 2015).

Some scholarly literature addresses sexism within public pedagogical discourses, and educational interventions into sexting, which have been criticized for foreclosing on the possibility of youth sexual agency and competency, as well as for generating shame around teenage sexuality (Angelides, 2013; Simpson, 2013). It has been suggested that some of the most popular educational film resources on cybersafety promote victim-blaming responses to technology-facilitated sexual harassment and violence against girls and women. Albury and Crawford (2012), for example, argue that Australian government attempts to educate and intervene in youth sexting practices have perpetuated the idea that girls themselves should be held accountable for the negative, highly gendered consequences of a sext gone viral. Ultimate responsibility and blame is placed on individual teenage girls to police and control their images and self-representation vigilantly, in ways which have obvious parallels with sexual violence victim-blaming discourses (see also Bailey and Hanna, 2011; Karaian, 2014; Dobson and Ringrose, 2015). The pedagogically intended narratives of many of the films that address sexting position girls as "inherently at risk of sexual violence" (Albury and Crawford, 2012, p. 465), and as victims in danger of "sexual self-exploitation" (Karaian, 2012). Amy Hasinoff suggests that pedagogical sexting discourses currently proceed from the assumption that "girls who sext do so because they have low self-esteem," and thus, girls' agency is narrowly defined in messages about sexting as *sexual refusal.* As Hasinoff argues, educational sexting interventions idealize "the psychological health of extremely cautious teenage girls who abstain from all sexual activity" (2015). I have argued with Jessica Ringrose that current pedagogical messages about sexting also further naturalize cultural gendered dynamics whereby girls' and not boys' sexual images are marked as both more highly valued/fetishized *and* more shameful than boys' (Dobson and Ringrose, 2015). In advocating control of the self by young women, the ethics of men and boy's behavior remains largely unremarked upon in these campaigns. Through such a lack of remark, male sexuality is further naturalized as brutal and uncontrollable. Meanwhile, women's role as the moral and sexual gatekeepers of society is also further naturalized.

Scholars have called for harm-minimization rather than "abstinence" responses to sexting, and suggested the need for campaigns that help youth unpack the underlying gender dynamics that obviously structure the circulation of sexual images in networked publics. In the context of these debates about youth sexting and the efficacy of pedagogical interventions addressing it, we wanted to find out in our research how high school students themselves understand these messages, and how they negotiate gender roles around digital technologies and sexual communication in networked publics. We used the film *Tagged*[3] as a basis for focus group discussions with 24 young people in rural Victoria, aged between 15 and 17. These groups were friendship-based and largely gender-divided. We asked young people about their views on the sexting incident portrayed in the film, and the gendered roles they perceived around mobile and digital technology use among peers.

Most of the young people we spoke to about their views on sexting and technology use expressed incomprehension that other people, girls in particular, would circulate or share a sexual self-image, either publicly via SNSs, or via private digital and phone message platforms to a trusted peer. In what follows I discuss the three Cs that were prevalent in our focus group discussions with mainly girls, both discursively and affectively: consequences, consternation, and culpability. I argue that sexual agency and desire for girls remains illegible and illegitimate in the context of prominent pedagogical messages about gendered psychosocial risks and consequences. In this social context, the teenage girls with whom we spoke worked to avoid association with the position of sexualized girl or "dumb slut," and cultivated a sense of *agency through abstinence*, following Hasinoff, via discursive and affective expressions of consternation around sexting. Sexual agency for girls was discursively framed largely in terms of "attention seeking," and was seen to make a girl culpable for resulting harassment, bullying, and abuse, which was framed as "inevitable." Girls' sexual agency was thus confusing and ambiguous in these discussions: it was present, but largely illegible and not available to be easily taken up. These conversations with young people thus make clear the limits of postfeminist popular media discourses and representations that position and address women as sexually empowered in Western democracies. Women are positioned in postfeminist popular cultural representations as freely choosing sexual subjects, or agents whose sexual desirability stems at least *in part* from their agency and desire, rather than stemming purely from bodily conformity with the narrow norms of heterosexiness. These conversations illuminate why it is so important that pedagogical messages seek to question, rather than reinforce, broader postfeminist discourses and assumptions about gender and sexual reputation, risk, and desire.

Consequences: Girls Need to Know Them

In the cybersafety film we showed in the two schools, the lead character, Kate, had privately sent a sexually explicit self-image to Jack, with whom she was in a relationship at the time. After they broke up, Jack circulated Kate's image among his friends in revenge for an online fight video involving him that Kate reposted from YouTube. Speaking of the sexting incident depicted, a year ten girl commented about the character Kate:

> *Skye*: She kind of let it happen, she let the photo happen, she let the photo be taken.
> *Amy*: She let the photo be taken?
> *Skye*: It's a different thing to not know [that the photo was being taken].
> [...]
> *Amy*: Is there anything wrong I suppose then, do you think, of sending a sexy image of yourself, just in and of itself? If people didn't find out about that, is there anything wrong with that?
> *Violet*: I think that you should know the consequences of it. Some people will do it knowing that they did it, and then the next day be like "Why am I getting bullied?" This is what makes people *kill themselves* and stuff but they put themselves in that situation. And they obviously knew that if they posted a photo... Like, some people would actually post a photo of themselves because they think it's funny, or they post it to people that they know are going to tell other people, but then, the next day they act like the victim when they're the person that put themselves in the situation, like *they knew* that would happen.

Violet considered this question carefully before answering, and although she and the other girls in this focus group spoke in quite disparaging terms of girls who might seek sexual attention (as I discuss later), she was careful not to claim forthrightly that sexting was morally wrong or bad. For Violet, as for many of the teenagers we spoke to, sexting was seen as something that was not wrong in and of itself, but was particularly risky and thus stupid for girls in the context of perceived social, psychological, and potentially legal heavy consequences.

Sexting for girls is seen as connected to getting bullied and "people killing themselves and stuff." It is seen as inevitable that a sexually suggestive or explicit image of a girl's body would be circulated in the networked public of the school beyond its intended audience; so much so that Violet suggests some girls take advantage of the viral potentiality of networked publics to covertly gain publicity and attention. This is a possibility I return to at the end of the chapter. In the statement "they're the person that put themselves in the situation, like *they knew* that would happen," Violet makes clear the lines of responsibility for victimization that are seen as tied to any form of sexual self-image production for girls in the context of the perceived inevitability of this.

In a group of four year eleven girls and one boy with whom they were friends, the young people articulated more explicitly this distinction between seeing intentional mediated sexual communication as something morally wrong, and seeing it as simply too risky for girls to rationalize in the context of "consequences" for all involved. In the following exchange, I was trying to clarify what seemed like a contradictory position taken by Lianah, who expressed keen and articulate awareness and dismay regarding sexual double standards for young people. Lianah was concerned that the film *Tagged* did not make the perceived "life-changing" consequences of sexting clear enough. The end of the film depicts Kate moving to a new school because of the bullying she faced after her sext was circulated. However, her reputation follows her and she still faces sexual taunts and graffiti on her locker at the new school (see Dobson and Ringrose, 2015). (I thought the film was quite severe in its suggested consequences for Kate, and so did some of the other young people with whom we spoke.) Lianah was adamant that the film sent the "wrong message" to young people in the end, because in the last scene, one girl comes up to offer Kate friendship and assure her that her sext will be soon forgotten. Lianah, perceptively, saw this final scene as contradictory to the overall message of the film, and also the wrong message to send to girls about "sending their tits around":

Amy: When you say that, you say it quite disparagingly, about sending your tits around. So to you there is something wrong with that?
Lianah: Yes.
Amy: What is that?
Lianah: Well she shouldn't be sending the pictures around in the first place, but I don't like the message that the film gave, because it was just like people forget about it. Like, you can do it, because people will end up not caring.
Amy: So what's wrong with sending pictures of your tits around?
Danny: Well I don't really think there is. I think the only problem with it is kind of what you will—like the reason.
Lianah: What will happen to you.
Danny: Yeah, what will happen to you.
Amy: Who will judge you, and what might happen?

Lianah: It's not so much doing it that's the bad thing, it's the consequences that are the bad thing. Like if people want to send them around, okay, whatever, let them do what they want. People should just keep in mind that other people do have access to them, they can send them to other people, it can be spread, their social life can crumble, their careers can crumble if they end up on a Sexual Predators List. It's not doing it that's bad, it's the consequences.

Amy: So when you say they shouldn't do it, it's because of the consequences [. . .] not because you personally think it's a bad thing to do.

Lianah: No. Like, if they're comfortable with their body, and they want to show people, okay, that's their choice.

Amy: Would you all agree with that?

All: (nods) Yeah, it's the consequences.

Some participants adjusted initial assertions about the wrongness or distastefulness of this behavior, sometimes in response to our questioning, as well as to assertions by other group members that sexting is not "wrong" in itself but too risky, as Lianah does earlier. Some young people were hesitant to agree that the film was "realistic" in the social consequences it depicts for Kate, who must change schools because of sexting-related bullying, suggesting that in their own school communities, people would be more supporting if a girl was upset or embarrassed because of a sext circulated of her. But it was difficult for participants to sustain this criticality in response to the message of the film, and most fell back on to the position made most accessible by the film—that girls still should not sext because if they do they will face harsh psychosocial consequences. It would seem here that, in line with what scholars have suggested, narrative emphasis on gendered social and psychological consequences perhaps works to naturalize them for young people, and few possibilities arise to question how and why sexting *becomes associated* with the ruining of lives and careers, and "people killing themselves and stuff." Claims are made about it being a girls' free "choice" to show others her body if she wants to, and is "comfortable" doing so, but girls must normatively align themselves with an "abstinence stance" on sexting in order to appear rational, smart, and in control.

Consternation: A Key Affective and Discursive Reaction to Girls Who Sext

Girls who were seen to seek sexual attention through mediation, despite the risks, became positioned in our conversations as sources of consternation and bewilderment. Just the thought, the imagining, of a girl who would agentically produce a sexual or body-revealing self-image appeared to produce affective and discursive reactions of discomfort, shame for the imagined girl, and ***dismayed bewilderment***. Often this happened discursively through a comparison with real-life sexual activity in these conversations. As said, it was perceived as inevitable that a girl's digital sexual image would be circulated further than she may have intended. Thus, unmediated, "real" sexual interaction was framed as the more rational and respectable choice for young women, as the following conversation with the year elevens illustrates:

> *Myrtle*: I just don't understand why people do it. But like, you don't need to take a photo and show someone your body, like, just go to the beach with them! (Laughter.)
> [...]
> *Danny*: The real things better than a photo. (Laughter.) You want to show it off at its best, then a photo's probably not the best way to go about it.
> *Myrtle*: I don't know what I'm saying, but I just ***don't understand*** why they have to take a photo of themselves. [...] Like, even if you are in a relationship and your boyfriend asks for photos, you really shouldn't, because if you're in like a proper relationship, wouldn't he like, just come over and just see the real thing anyway?
> [...]
> *Erica*: Just taking photos is just like pretty much—I don't know how to put it, but just like putting yourself a bit down because they could just come over and see the real thing and stuff.
> *Amy*: So why is it putting yourself down more to have a picture than it is to show them? (laughter from all, and a long pause)
> *Erica*: I don't know really. I couldn't find the right words.

The group of year ten girls similarly positioned themselves as "abstaining agents" through suggesting that unmediated sexual interaction was the more "rational" choice, as no peers could be trusted in the techno-social context of easy media circulation among peers through digital and social networks:

> *Amy*: So you think people need to know the consequences of it?
> *Violet*: (nods) Common sense.
> *Jordan*: You think you know sending a naked photo's obviously going to get sent around.
> *Skye*: Even...
> *Jordan*: Even if to your boyfriend (group nods).

Skye: The friend will send it to themselves from, like, his [your boyfriend's] phone.
Isabelle: I find it so stupid.
Amy: What do you find stupid? When girls do it?
Isabelle: Yes.
Amy: Because they should just presume that it's going to be sent around?
Isabelle: Well, they should *know* that it will be, and if they want to—the guy that they're sending it to, why can't they just...Like, say it's your boyfriend or someone you've got a thing with or whatever, like, why can't you just, like, go see them? (laughter).
Amy: What about if you just want to—so what about if it's somebody you trust?
Violet: You're stupid.
Isabelle: You can't trust anyone.

Through joking and laughter about why the "real thing is better than a photo," about why sexters should just get together to see each other's bodies in person, and expressions of bewilderment ("I just don't understand" and "I find it so stupid") these young people position themselves as knowing agents, in control. The laughter and comparison with real-life sex and body exposure work to frame digitally mediated sexual interaction as "obviously" stupid, irrational behavior for girls, and thus a funny source of consternation and bewilderment among these social groups. While some young people considered sexting by boys to be silly or sleazy, it was not framed both discursively and affectively in the terms of incomprehension it was for girls. Sexting for boys was articulated as more of an understandable and predictable behavior, a source of "eye-rolling" reactions rather than excessive laughter and dismayed bewilderment. The digital mediation of sexuality was pointed to by Erica as more degrading or shameful than real-life sexual activity (putting yourself a bit down), but it was difficult for her to pinpoint the basis for this feeling. These discussion help illuminate the kind of affective reactions young women in particular are invited to perform in response to films like *Tagged*, to adults, and to each other, in order to avoid identification with the abject figure of the "sexualized girl" or the "stupid slut."

These expressions of consternation and comparisons with real-life sex also highlight the assumption that sexual attention or interaction is seen as the primary motivation for girls to produce a sexual self-image. Sexual or body images for girls appear to function chiefly as signals of a desire to initiate sexual interaction or gain sexual attention.

Significantly, this does not appear to be an a priori assumption made about boys' self-produced sexual or body images. As several other researchers have found, boys' self-produced images are perceived to be motivated by a wider range of possible intentions such as humor, mate-ship/bonding, or pranking (Albury et al., 2013; Albury, 2015; Ringrose and Harvey, 2015).

Culpability: Sexual Attention Seeking

I have mentioned in brief the claim made by Lianah that sexting is a girls' "choice" to make if she is comfortable with her body. This was a claim made by young people in several of our discussions, but, I suggest, it was one of the more contradictory and ambivalent assertions in these conversations. Several young people positioned sexting in terms of "body confidence" and agentic choice for girls, as Albury et al. (2013) also found, at the same time as they spoke of such behavior in disparaging and "othering" terms, discursively framing it as negative "attention seeking." "Attention seeking" appears to be the most accessible way to explain the motivations of girls who intentionally represent themselves in heterosexy ways, or show their bodies either via SNS profiles or in private message interactions. In both of these contexts, sexual or body-revealing self-representation was explained by young people for girls in terms of attention-seeking behavior. Seeking attention was perceived in a negative light, and girls who were seen to seek attention via either publicly posted *or privately shared* body or heterosexy self-images were also perceived as *culpable* for any harassment or bullying that eventuated from the misuse of their images by others. The affective tones of disapproval apparent around attention seeking clearly troubled the sentiments expressed by young people at other points in these conversations that sexters should be allowed to "do what they want," and that sexting might be an expression of "body confidence." I would suggest this ambivalence gestures toward a tension between the simultaneous positioning of girls as *sexual agents and victims* that remains unresolved in the broader cultural and social context (Hasinoff, 2014).

Discussing the idea of posting heterosexy self-images on SNSs, participants in the year eleven group commented:

> *Myrtle*: I don't have the confidence to do it. But like, I don't want to see some chick like in her bra and undies on Facebook. Like if she was going to do that, no. Like I don't particularly want to see it.

Erica: That's what most of the younger generation does. Like kids from around about year ten and under take pictures explicitly, even on Facebook.

Danny: A lot of the time it's just probably to get attention. Because they want attention. But then they get too much and they complain. It's like "Well you did this to get attention, and now you're getting attention."

In the year ten group, Jordan explained how "some people" post heterosexy photos on SNSs for attention, rather than creating them for a specific person:

Jordan: As well, some people would only do it for attention, not *for* anyone specifically, younger people. There was a girl that did post a photo of herself on her own Facebook and ever since then she just loves the fact that she's known so well for it, she doesn't care about it, and other people are getting in trouble for saving it because it's like child pornography, or something. But she's the one that posted it on her own Facebook, it was no one that sent it around. She posed for it as well, like she knew it was taken.

Affective and discursive reactions of consternation, and also the culpability associated with sexual attention seeking for girls, highlight contradictions in postfeminist media culture more broadly. As feminist scholars have argued, we are regularly asked to assume women's sexual empowerment in visual culture, advertising, and marketing to women, and invited to believe that in the postfeminist era visual symbols and signifiers of women's *sexual agency and desire* now constitute a significant part of feminine heterosexiness, rather than *only* the body, and the racialized, classed, markers of bodily discipline and servitude of male desires that have long constituted female heterosexiness in representations of women. At the same time, sexual self-production for girls and young women is still most commonly constructed via pedagogical discourses as the result of "low self-esteem" (Hasinoff, 2015). These contradictions in cultural representations of, and address to, girls and young women perhaps help to explain some of the contradictions and tensions in our data. Young people position girls who engage in sexual self-production through digital media simultaneously as choice-making, responsibilized agents, and as "stupid," "irrational," and "attention seekers," driven by low self-esteem. Sexual agency and desire was most often *othered* by the young women with whom we spoke: it was positioned as a choice that was fine for "some people" to make, but not one that was intelligible, or easily taken up.

In several of these discussions with young people, we could note distinctions between "culpability" and "sympathy" being made. Culpability applied to girls who might consciously and purposefully send a sexual image of themselves to someone, or post one online. Sympathy, it was explained to us by several young people, might be given by peers to girls whose images have been taken without permission, who were thought to have been coerced in some way, or were not considered fully culpable because of intoxication. Erica articulated the lines of responsibilization seen to go along with sexual agency for girls in the following comment:

> *Erica*: If a girl just got bored and just sent pictures around for attention, like people would have a bad opinion on her. While if she was drunk and somebody else took the pictures, then that's different, because like you know, she doesn't really have control over it.

Erica summates a view that we heard often in these focus groups: if girls are thought to have been tricked (while drunk) or pressured into producing or sending a sexual self-image, or victimized by someone capturing their image nonconsensually, young people suggest, this is *understandable*, and they expressed the need for sympathy and peer support for girls in this situation. However, if a girl is seen to be *agentically* producing and sharing images, that is, of her own accord and not apparently under pressure or influence, this is framed as much less *understandable* and less deserving of sympathy, and instead, deserving of the "slut" label. Sexual agency or desirous intent is inscribed onto a girl's bodily image that is perceived to have been taken consensually, no matter whom for, where posted/sent, and in what context. As Skye comments of Kate in the film "She *let* the photo be taken. [. . .] It's a different thing to not *know* [that the image was being taken]."

These young people were all, however, largely critical of the actions of boys who broke a girl's trust by sending around an image of a girl shared privately with them. The group of year ten girls clearly expressed that they thought Jack's actions in the film were wrong, and they would think badly of a boy who did that. However, some girls in this group disagreed with my suggestion, in trying to summarize their views, that it was not fair that Kate was the one who was socially shamed in *Tagged* because of her sext, when it was Jack who broke her trust by sharing the image:

> *Isabelle*: To some extent I don't [agree] because she did it.
> *Amy*: You're looking ambiguous Jordan, or unsure?

Jordan: Well, I don't know, I think when you send a photo you know, everyone knows, that it's going to be sent around so when it does be sent around you can blame yourself and be "Well I did that to myself."

Isabelle: In the film she was blaming other people, she was putting it on him, tried to put it on everyone else when it was came down to the fact that she sent it and she knew that.

[...]

Amy: You don't think it's so unfair then because you think it should be up to the girl to police herself?

All: Yes.

Jordan: It's just common sense.

While they perceive Jack's actions as clearly morally wrong, their sympathies for Kate only go so far; the assumption being that a girl should "know" the kind of negative attention and "consequences" she will encounter if she engages consensually and intentionally in sexual self-mediation, even at the request of a partner in the context of a promise of trust and privacy. This is "common sense." Distinctions are made between girls who are perceived to be sexual agents, and are thus seen as responsible for the negative consequences they face from sexual self-mediation, and girls perceived as victims of coercion or force, via this appeal to common sense. Only where covert and unauthorized filming of a girls' body has occurred is a girl whose image has been circulated in a networked public seen as "innocent," and thus deserving of sympathy. The assumption of risk, and of culpability for abuse, harassment, and violence for girls is pervasive and largely unquestioned in these conversations, as it is in many of the cybersafety messages directed toward young people. And it is this discursive and affective *surety* and "common sense" around risk and culpability that highlights the limits and contradictions of discourses and representations positioning sexual agency and desire as "empowerment," and as a central part of "heterosexiness" for young women in postfeminist popular media cultures.

Legitimizing Sexual Agency and Desire

I want to further unpack the importance of legitimating sexual agency and desire for girls in these final sections. I return here to Violet's suggestions, quoted earlier, to help me do so. In explaining that girls need to know the "consequences" of sexting, Violet says that "some people would actually post a photo of themselves because they think it's funny, or they post it to people that they know are going to tell other people, but then, the next day they act like the victim when they're the person that put themselves in the situation, like *they knew* that would happen." It is pertinent to unpack the media practices and social process condensed in this statement by pointing out that Violet means to suggest that after a girl has created and then either publicly posted a sexual self-image via SNS *or* shared an image of herself via private messaging with selected peers, it will be circulated further and drawn attention to via digitally networked groups of peers, and girls will then get teased or bullied on and offline as a result of this. Violet's comments illuminate the confusion and contradictions around how girls' sexual agency is normatively understood and articulated in postfeminist cultural conditions. Sexual agency and desire is gestured to here, and it is the perception or attribution of sexual agency and desire to girls' self-produced images that is seen to make girls culpable for abuse and harassment. But desire is still ultimately missing as *legitimate* for girls—it is not a position girls can legitimately or easily take up (Fine, 1988; Tolman, 2002; McClelland and Fine, 2008). Disguised, secret, or hidden means of seeking sexual attention are perhaps the only socially legitimized means for girls. Violet's assertions suggest the possibility that some girls are discovering covert strategies for gaining sexual attention or expressing desire within these difficult conditions, where the procuring of sexual currency is not sanctioned by peers.

On the one hand, we must acknowledge here the troubling possibility many girls who take or publicly post sexualized self-images do not predict or calculate the extent of their sexual image circulation and associated harassment in the way Violet's comments imply. But her comments also raise a vital question: to what extent is there space for girls to adopt subject positions and affects in relation to sexting *other* than those associated with victimization and psychosocial damage? We need to *slow down* in approaching youth sexting, and ask before proceeding to intervene: how can we make it possible for young people to *socially legitimize sexual attention seeking as an intention* of certain media practices and self-representations? If seeking sexual attention were legitimate, perhaps the position of "victim" of peer harassment would become less socially *necessary* for girls to assume or claim, and also perhaps less potent as an experience, even when an unethical breach of trust has been perpetrated against them. To explicate this a little further, I draw on the ideas of feminist criminologist Jo Woodiwiss.

Woodiwiss (2014) has argued for the need for "more than one story" about childhood sexual abuse. I find her arguments to be productive for thinking about sexting and the legitimate positions available for girls who produce sexual self-images. Woodiwiss argues that we need to distinguish between "wrongfulness" and "harm" in understanding childhood sexual abuse (CSA). In conflating these two things, she suggests, only one story, and one associated subject position, is currently available to victims of CSA, and this is one of debilitating harm and lifelong psychological damage. As she suggests, victims of CSA are "confronted with a framework within which to makes sense of their experiences that not only directs them to see themselves as helpless, passive and sexually innocent in order to avoid the risk of being held, or holding themselves, responsible for their abuse, but also tells them of ruined childhoods and lost innocence" (Woodiwiss, 2014, p. 144). Internalized negative messages, she suggests, easily become self-fulfilling prophecies, and further so when victims see this framework of harm and psychological damage reflected back at them from those caring for them.

It seems to me that there are similar issues at stake in our approaches to youth sexting. Via a range of social actors and forces including teachers, parents, and peers, girls are being conditioned to see themselves as *normatively damaged* by the wider circulation of their sexts in networked publics. This position and the normative associated affects of victimhood and damage have been socially legitimated and made legible for girls. Victimhood in relation to sexuality is somewhat understood and accepted by both youth and adults for teenagers; agency and desire, perhaps less so (Rasmussen, 2006). Current educational discourses about sexting perpetuate this discourse about girls as inherently "damaged" by the publicisation of their sexual images in a way that boys are not. We have conflated the wrongfulness of breaks of trust, and sometimes of intentional sexual harassment and abuse via digital means, with the harms possible here. In the process we have legitimated only one story for girls who engage in sexual self-production via digital media. We risk discursively and materially producing *further* harms for girls, I suggest, if we continue to legitimate through representation, policy response, and public discourse, only one sexting story for girls: a story about damage and how sexting leads to bullying and "people killing themselves and stuff." Hence the import of making space for, and perhaps even assuming, girls' agency and sexual desire in our approaches to sexting.

Conclusion

The conversations with young people make clear the constitutive limits, ambiguities, and contradictions of postfeminist discourses and representations that position women as sexually empowered in Western democracies, freely choosing sexual subjects, or agents whose sexual desirability stems at least in a sizable part from significations of this agency in representation, rather than only from the narrow raced and classed bodily markers that constitute heterosexiness. Notions of "consequences" and "culpability" circulate in our conversations with young people, as well as affective responses of consternation, bewilderment, shame, and dismay. I suggest that these are commonly invited reactions to the imagined figure of the girl who is seen to use digital media to produce herself in sexual ways. In defining sexting for girls as stupid and irrational, and also in their affective responses of consternation around agentic sexual image production or circulation, the young women with whom we spoke clearly do not see or experience sexuality as an uncomplicated source of power. Even when the images in question are of young women whose bodies fit within narrow categories of feminine heterosexiness in terms of size, racial features, and normative feminine attributes (as does the character of Kate in *Tagged*), sexual self-production is still articulated as more of a risk than a power.

In the previous chapter I suggested that in a viewing premise of self-production our interpretation of sexual images is and should be complex for a few reasons. Feminist performance artists have been engaged in explicit female body representation prominently since the 1970s, often with political intent. Feminist artists and scholars have opened up questions around where, how, and to what end we draw up binaries and boundaries between art and pornography or sex work, and between the "agentic artist" and the "nonartist"/sex worker/victim (Williams, 1993; Schneider, 1997; Gibson, 2004; Willson, 2008; Dennis, 2009). Is explicit body representation necessarily a kind of "sex work"? Is pornography *never* "art"? Does our assumption that a woman was centrally involved in choosing the specifics of her self-representation (the premise of self-production) change the way we interpret its meaning and her social status? I suggested that similar questions need to be applied to young women's own heterosexy self-productions on SNSs, lest we risk redrawing simplistic binaries between political and nonpolitical representation, agency and victimhood, "resistant" acts of representation versus "nonresistant" acts. This does not currently appear to be happening in relation to sexting, where concerns about girls' and young women's well-being are sometimes justified, but, I suggest, pedagogical expressions of concern are currently serving to perpetuate further harm against them.

In a sense, by pointing to sexual agency as a risk for girls, sexting education films such as *Tagged* can be seen as calling out the illusory aspects of postfeminist cultural messages about power for girls and young women as based on sex and attractiveness. But if, as much of the available research on sexting suggests, girls are regularly experiencing and perpetuating "slut shaming" in various forms, from male and female peers at school and elsewhere (Ringrose et al., 2012, 2013; Walker et al., 2013; Harris et al., 2013) as well as teachers who surveill them (Albury, 2015), it would seem counterproductive to reinforce and normalize messages of shame and risk around sexual self-production for girls. Research into youth sexting makes it clear that long-standing sexual double standards and beliefs about male and female sexuality are still the basis for harassment and abuse. Symbolic and discursive acts that disempower girls and women and implicitly authorize violence against them are perpetrated too in pedagogical messages and current popular cybersafety campaigns that assume women and girls' victimhood status and act to "protect them" from expressing sexuality to avoid assumed social victimization and psychological damage.

The question becomes one of finding ways to speak back to strong postfeminist cultural messages about the power available in, and allure of, mediated sexual subjectification (Gill, 2003) that contradict girls' and women's current social experiences, while not reinforcing and constituting further risks and harms in our own discursive and affective responses to girls, sexting, and gender politics. We need to make space for positions, experiences, and affective reactions *other* than just those of victimization and damage, even when wrongs have been perpetrated against girls and women in relation to sexting. Adults concerned with girls' well-being need to lead the way in legitimizing girls' and young women's *sexual attention seeking*, desires, and sexual agency, outside the narrow and fetishistic terms by which these are legitimated in postfeminist popular culture.

Part II

Valuable and Devalued Selves

Chapter 5

Postfeminist Self-Making: Textual Self-Representation and the Performance of "Authentic" Young Femininity on Social Network Sites

CRAZY............................SILLY..............................
FUNNY..............................CUTE..........................
BRAVE..............................SWEET.........OUTGOING
..............................OPINIONATED.......................
ANNOYING................BLONDE................................
FUN...................STUPID.......................................

(Laaanni, accessed 05/03/08)

I'm mean, funny, caring, rude, friendly, easy going, fun, loud, annoying, loving, jealous, spoilt and impatient! If I come across as a total bitch, I'm not! i just dont like you!!!!

(Robbi, accessed 03/09/07)

♥I AM♥
VERY FUKIN ANGRY
A Pornstar
A bit of a crunchie
Honest
Loud
Annoying
Faithful

Trustworthy
Generous
Bitchy
Open minded
Angry
Bad tempered
Lovable
Helpful
Silly
Crazy
Spontaneous
Fried
Loving
♥♥♥♥♥♥

(Bitch Cunt/Janine, accessed 04/09/07)

In this chapter I discuss some of the common features of the decorative textual "mottos" and self-descriptions posted on the social network site (SNS) profiles I analyzed. These were public profiles owned by Australian women aged between 18 and 21 at the time of my study.[1] Self-representations constructed through text on SNSs are updated, edited, and rewritten fairly frequently, as the self is reflected upon and revised for one's audience of peers and strangers in the networked public. Such texts are themselves ephemeral and fluid, and also constructed to present identities that are fluid, in flux, and subject to change and revision. Yet there were common themes that appeared repeatedly and shaped the contours of the textual self-representations in my study. First, self-creation, and notions of DIY self-making are prominent in these texts. The mottos commonly displayed by young women on these SNS profiles advocate active choice-making vis-à-vis the self, and responsibility for one's own self, life, and emotions. These textual self-representations construct the profile owner's identity as an ongoing project, available for constant monitoring and revision, in line with theories of individualization in late modernity (Giddens, 1991; Beck, 1992). And yet, a somewhat paradoxical notion persists that one's self-representation should reveal an "interior" self that is "truthful" and "authentic," as I discuss. The self and identity is then positioned not as something *wholly* chosen and created, but also as a hidden interior, the "truth" of which must be told and made "transparent," I suggest, in line with shifting ideas about morality and value(s) in late modernity.

It was common on the profiles I examined for young women to describe likes, dislikes, and personality traits in stream of consciousness style self-descriptive lists. These lists are constructed as "random," and thus, I suggest, implied as "authentic." As such, authenticity is constructed in these textual self-representations as the ability to publicly articulate a random interiority made up of whims, desires, preferences, aversions, and emotions. These lists of random attributes are highly gendered in terms of the common preferences and aversions claimed. In these self-descriptions, common echoes of a "therapeutic narrative" (Illouz, 2007) of self-actualization as achieved through self-expression can also be identified. Notably, the self-descriptive texts commonly highlight the writer's perceived flaws, weaknesses, and sources of suffering, along with more positive attributes. Similarly, young women's own participation in social activities and behaviors such as drinking and partying are framed in these texts as "excessive," wild, and risky. These self-representational practices performatively signal one's ability to "reveal interiority," to be "transparently" available to one's viewers in a networked public. The texts work overall to foster a sense of confidence and self-acceptance—two highly valued traits of postfeminist femininity. Such self-representational practices, I suggest, perhaps enable young women to negotiate conflicting demands of digital self-representation to construct a self that is fluid and open to revision, and yet also "authentically" youthful and feminine, and stable in its gendered attributes.

I also discuss the pedagogical tones that can be identified in many of the aphorisms and self-descriptive texts in my study, particularly those texts communicating messages of self-acceptance. Looking back a few decades to a time when feminist psychologists were bemoaning girls' "loss of voice" in adolescence and their inability to stand up for themselves while enacting and embodying normative femininity (Orenstein, 1994; Pipher, 1994), the propensity for confident, and also often *pedagogical*, self-representational texts on young women's public SNS profiles seems striking. As I discuss, in a context of self-production by young women, such texts need to be seen in conversation with feminist interventions into educational spheres, particularly since the 1980s and 1990s, which sought to encourage girls' confident public self-expression. Self-representational texts signaling (gendered) authenticity, transparency, and also self-confidence and acceptance are thus significant, and also somewhat overdetermined, I argue, for young women.

Last, I discuss the way these digital self-representations are defended against the assumed negative judgments of viewers in these texts in uncompromising tones. Some of the texts displayed by young women explicitly instruct/warn viewers "not to judge," and dare viewers to test them on this warning. The textual mottos and self-descriptions by young women discussed in this chapter perhaps indicate both the value and sociocultural currency of confident, self-assured, youthful feminine self-representations, as well as the harshness and hostility experienced by many young women in postfeminist digital cultures as sites of "incited judgment" (Nurka, 2014).

Individualization and DIY Self-Making

Scholars such as Ulrich Beck (1992), Anthony Giddens (1991), and Zygmunt Bauman (1995, 2001) have outlined the ways in which the collapse of industrialization in the West, the rise of globalization, and the breakdown of cultural traditions have profoundly affected individuals' life trajectories and sense of identity. These shifts and processes as they relate to notions of self and identity have been broadly termed "individualization." Individualization is seen to be occurring in relation to politics, society, and culture. In the Anglophone West in particular, it has been argued that social class, gender, race, ethnicity, and geographic location, previously seen as major determinants of an individual's public identity and life trajectory, no longer necessarily determine one's available choices, biography, and sense of identity (Beck, 1992). Beck, for instance, argues that in late-modern society individuals have come to be seen as, and for better or worse, often must be, entirely responsible for their own life chances and biography. He writes, "The proportion of life opportunities which are fundamentally closed to decision-making is decreasing and the proportion of the biography which is open and must be constructed personally is increasing" (1992, p. 135). As such, the focus is on someone's personal responsibility for their own failures, problems, and individual limitations, as well as their own successes, achievements, and personal merits. Further, it is suggested that factors such as one's class, one's trade or profession, as well as cultural institutions like religion can no longer be assumed to be central in the way individuals articulate a sense of identity and define their moral worth and values. Scholars have suggested that the late-modern world is characterized by, and understood in terms of, unpredictability and risk. Individual subjects are required to adopt "entrepreneurial subjectivities" (Harris, 2004; Hearn, 2008; Marwick, 2013) to navigate such conditions, and demonstrate a capacity for self-dependency, flexibility, and self-invention and reinvention as necessary. Sociologists interested in identity, subjectivity, and social constructs of the self argue that the self is now seen as an ongoing "project." Public identity is seen as a pliable, ever-changing mask, available, through skilled consumption and image management, for constant update and reinvention (Hopkins, 2002; Harris, 2004; Elliott and Lemert, 2006). As Anthony Elliott writes, "In contemporary social conditions, durable selfhood is replaced by a kind of supermarket identity—an assemblage of scraps, random desires, chance encounters, the accidental and the fleeting" (Elliott, 2001, p. 131).

Many scholars, and feminists in particular, have critiqued the individualization thesis for a lack of attendance to the ways in which gender, sexuality, social class, race, ethnicity, geography, and other factors of both individual embodiment and social life are still major determinants of one's available choices for most of the worlds' population (Walkerdine, Lucey, and Melody, 2001; Harris, 2004; McRobbie, 2009; Skeggs and Wood, 2012). Opportunities via individualization have opened up for only a minority of already privileged citizens, largely in the Anglophone West, feminists have suggested. Such critiques of the individualization thesis are valid, but the work of Beck and others in this area also helps to explicate how broad-ranging social discourses and processes of personal responsibilization and de-traditionalism function to invisibilize difference and social stratification along long-standing lines of inequality. As Beck notes, individualization processes have not made social and global inequalities disappear. Rather, in neoliberal and late-modern societies they are "increasingly perceived in terms of psychological dispositions: personal inadequacies, guilt feelings, anxieties, conflicts, and neuroses" (Beck, 1992, p. 100).

Some key aspects of individualization discourses are reflected, I suggest, in the mottos and self-descriptions discussed in this chapter. Reading the self-descriptions of these young women provides a sense of the way in which self-making, autonomy, and self-reliance are seen as necessary in this sociocultural climate. Young women commonly posted mottos along the lines of Kristy's: "Sometimes you gotta get fucked up to feel sober, cry to see clear, and fall one hundred times to learn how to pick yourself back up" (accessed 05/03/08). Anna writes in her self-description, "I am unattached, free as a bird. I don't depend on nobody and nobody depends on me. My life's my own." (accessed 20/02/08). Mz_Princess states in her self-description (shown in full later): "I believe that confidence is the best accessory

[...] I ALSO BELIEVE: That if life gives you lemons, you should make lemonade...And try to find somebody whose life has given them vodka, and have a party." A sense of ultimate self-reliance and personal responsibility is communicated in these statements.

A quote appearing on the profile of BitchCunt/Janine exemplifies the way in which discourses of self-making and self-creation frame identity performance on the profiles I analyzed. BitchCunt/Janine displays in capitals, in very large font, prominently on her profile the aphorism "LIFE ISN'T ABOUT FINDING YOURSELF IT'S ABOUT CREATING YOURSELF" (Bitch Cunt/Janine accessed 04/09/07). This statement neatly summates a key shift noted by generation researcher Jean Twenge (2006), from an ethos of spiritualized self-discovery embraced by the baby boomer generation, to an ethos of entrepreneurial self-invention and reinvention to suit fluid and shifting needs and purposes that pervades in the cultural landscape of the 1980s and beyond. Katy/Kuntastic Bitch describes herself as a "walking contradiction," distancing herself from ideals of coherency and consistency in the following self-description. Katy aligns herself with constant change that, she writes, makes it impossible to apprehend her and "figure her out":

> I am the complete opposite of everything that is the same, two extremes revoking each other, a walking contradiction.
> My mind is constantly ticking.
> You will never understand me because when you think you have me all figured out I am already changing.
> Just keep that in mind
>
> (Katy/Kuntastic Bitch, accessed 18/03/08)

The self is often constructed in these texts not as something "inbuilt" and fixed, but rather, available for assemblage, and like an SNS profile, also for constant updating, reflection, and improvement. There is a sense in which the self must now be *performed*, and is created, not "discovered," through its performance (Illouz, 2007, p. 55).

Sometimes the necessity of autonomy and the responsibility of DIY self-making are communicated in less celebratory tones. Individualization and responsibilization come across in these texts as tenets that are not always pleasant to live, but admirable and respectable. One of the popular decorative textual mottos circulating at the time of my study, seen on the profiles of both SheZzaCat and Laaanni states: "Nothing lasts forever, so live it up, drink it down, laugh it off, avoid the bullshit, take chances, and never have regrets, because at one point, everything you did was exactly what you wanted." (SheZzaCat, accessed 06/12/07; and Laaanni, accessed 30/10/08). Another aphorism circulating, seen on the profile of Sugarfrog/ Crazybitch states: "Someday everything will all make perfect sense. So for now, laugh at the confusion, smile through the tears, and keep reminding yourself that everything happens for a reason." (accessed 04/09/07). Fee posts the statement prominently on her profile: "every 60 seconds you spend angry or upset is a minute of happiness you'll never get back" (accessed 29/10/07). Many of the popular mottos and aphorisms young women use to decorate their profiles similarly communicate that if nothing makes sense, if one is confused, hurt or disappointed by the circumstances in which they find themselves, one should remember that it's one's own *choices* that have led to this point. It is the individual who is seen as primarily responsible for their own happiness and success. This is to be achieved through dedicated self-reflection, conscious effort, and self-reinvention when necessary.

Postfeminist Self-Making

Structural and social factors that may impose upon an individual's chances for emotional stability, happiness, and success are minimized in such expressions, as other scholars have found in research with girls and young women on their attitudes toward feminism. In her study of young English women's relationship with feminism, Shelley Budgeon found in her interviews that the suggestion of life choices and opportunities being limited by social or structural factors was met with "very strong expressions of individualism" and expressions of "the principal of upholding individual rights and responsibilities" (2001, p. 14). Budgeon also found a disavowal of social and structural inequalities expressed by young women in phrases such as "Don't let anyone tell you what to do" and "You just have to do what you want," given in response to the interviewer's suggestion that structural factors might effectively limit an individual's opportunities (2001, p. 14). Similarly, Christina Scharff (2012) suggests that feminism is repudiated by many young European women as a position aligned with the acknowledgment of structural disadvantages. Her participants' awareness of gendered social inequalities did not translate into support for feminism, as many young women "believe that structural inequalities can be solved individually," and are not keen to align themselves with what is seen as a position of accepted victimhood and lack of personal responsibility (Scharff, 2012; see also, Bail, 1996; Bulbeck, 2001; Rich, 2005; Baker, 2010).

The self-description of Blondebaby helps to illuminate the idealization of a confident "can do" feminine subjectivity in the postfeminist, late-modern neoliberal context (Harris, 2004) as commonly expressed in these texts. Blondebaby writes:

> I'VE JUST HAD A MASSIVE REVELATION IN LIFE, I turn 22 in June. I have a very loud voice and although I'm a strong willed person I'm pretty lazy. I live in Blondebaby world where everything moves fast; most situations are over dramatized, pretty things sparkle like diamonds and nothing is un-achievable. I wont like you if you don't speak, or if you own a ute. I've had my fair share in loser boyfriends...I try to see the good in everyone but I believe that karma is a bitch. I'm a hard worker and usually get everything I want because of that. Yesterday I worked in a talent agency putting talented people in TV commercials...Tomorrow I'll be a dance teacher. I only listen to what I want to hear. I'm very outgoing but choose my friends wisely. My favorite quote is "Life is either a daring adventure or nothing at all". I live by that everyday.
>
> (Blondebaby, accessed 30/10/07)

Like many of the self-descriptions posted by young women, Blondebaby's self-description speaks to notions of confident self-belief and meritocracy; that is, success as achieved through ambition, determination, and hard work. In this text, Blondebaby highlights her ability to reinvent herself, and communicates a sense of excitement about her future. She ends her self-description with an aphorism about life she tells viewers she "lives by everyday," that "Life is either a daring adventure or nothing at all." This aphorism exemplifies a common discursive construct of both late-modernity and youthfulness itself as risk-focused and thrilling.

Young women are perceived as being among the main beneficiaries of the rapid social and structural changes that have occurred in the latter half of the twentieth century (McRobbie, 2007, p. 722). They are perceived as the beneficiaries of a postindustrial, casualized, and service-based "feminized" workforce (Walkerdine, Lucey, and Melody, 2001, pp. 3–5). As Anita Harris summarizes the situation, new possibilities have opened up for young women via feminist achievements in the spheres of work, as well as changed economic conditions in late modernity, and "new ideologies about individual responsibility and choices also dovetail with some broad feminist notions about opportunity for young women, making them the most likely candidates for performing a new kind of self-made subjectivity" (2004, p. 6). It is also young women who are seen as most skilled in the tasks of consumption and image-management, and thus, Harris argues, young women have become idealized as the subjects "par excellence" of an individualized and meritocratic neoliberal society in which self-invention and reinvention, and *the performance of such*, have become life-determining skills. Harris details the specific image of a self-reliant, ambitious, materialistic, and highly *visible* "can do girl" hailed as a symbol of late-modern adaption and success. These are traits that, I suggest, many young women are keen to align themselves with in their digital self-representations in order to construct a publicly valued postfeminist feminine self. The work of feminist scholars helps to contextualize these self-representations of young women on SNSs, which are commonly aligned with discourses of individualization and meritocratic self-making. Feminist scholars have described the prominent place of young women in visual cultures as newly moneyed, "conspicuous consumers," due primarily to the expansion of the job market for women. As Harris suggests, current social, political, and economic conditions have been somewhat glamorized by government institutions and in popular culture, where white middle-class young women are hailed as confident, self-reliant, ambitious, and industrious "can do" girls—models of ideal citizenship for *all girls* to aspire to despite the intensification of social stratification along long-standing axes of inequality.

Gendered Randomness As "Authenticity"

As I now discuss, many of the self-descriptions I analyzed on young women's SNS profiles are constructed to foster, through text, a sense of "authenticity" and individual "uniqueness," in line with the genre of self-representational media as outlined by Nancy Thumin (2012). These texts also help to construct the "premise of self-production," which I suggest defines a subgenre of self-representational texts that are conventionally understood by viewers as intrinsically motivated and produced for primarily social and expressive rather than commercial self-promotional purposes (see chapter 1). Authenticity and uniqueness as qualities take common shapes and forms for young women on SNSs. Many of the self-descriptions I viewed are made up of long, often very long, lists that describe in stream of consciousness style the preferences and aversions of profiles owners on everything from food to entertainment to personality traits and qualities in people. The profile owners also list their own perceived personality traits and qualities, values, favorite quotes, sayings, and so on. These self-descriptions often constituted a creative appropriation of the MySpace profile format users were prompted to complete at the time of my study, where they were asked to provide a brief paragraph on likes and dislikes, including favorite TV shows, music and movies. Some examples of these texts follow.

> I have tried to live my life so that my family would love me and my friends would respect me. As for the others, they can do whatever the hell they please. Love all types of random shit. Anything random gets a laugh outta me. Love meeting new peeps, its always fun and im always out for a good time. I live for the nights I cannot remember and for the people I will never forget. I believe that Monday is an awful way to spend 1/7th of your life, I believe that confidence is the best accessory, I believe that "Jack & Jills are Mickey Mouse," but who doesnt??? And...I ALSO BELIEVE: That if life gives you lemons, you should make lemonade...And try to find somebody whose life has given them vodka, and have a party...Got a sister Sarah who's just a straight up champion—We're like tighter than a Nun's......! I'll leave it there. Haha
>
> (Mz_Princess, accessed 18/03/08)

> I'LL TRY ANYTHING TWICE...JUST TO MAKE SURE. I'M LOUD, CHILLED, CRAZY, QUIET...ANYTHING I WANT TO BE. I LOVE MY MATES TO DEATH. I LAUGH AT MY OWN JOKES. I LOVE AN ICE COLD DRINK ON A WARM DAY. I'M THE BEST FRIEND YOU'LL EVER HAVE UNLESS YOU PISS ME OFF & I PUNCH YOU IN THE FACE! I'M A SINNER. I DON'T LIKE RULES. I HAVE MORE CLOTHES THAN I CAN WEAR...I STUDY JOURNALISM & ASPIRE TO BE FILTHY RICH. MWAH HA HA. MY MUM IS MY BEST FRIEND & I DON'T KNOW WHAT I'D DO WITHOUT HER. I'M UNIQUE. I WISH I COULD DANCE SEXY BUT I DON'T KNOW WHAT TO DO WITH MY ARMS. I LOVE LAZY SUNDAYS. I SING IN THE SHOWER. I DANCE IN THE RAIN. I DONT LET PEOPLE THAT MEAN FUCK ALL TO ME BRING ME DOWN. I HAVE 12 PIERCINGS & 4 TATTOOS. I HAVE TO MEET SOMEONE 5 TIMES BEFORE I REMEMBER WHO THEY ARE. I LOVE TO DRINK, DANCE, PARTY & GET MESSY UNTIL THE SUN COMES UP. I LOVE DOLLING UP. BUT I'D CAMP IF I HAD TO. I LIVE FOR THE WEEKEND & THE WEEKEND LIVES FOR ME. I'LL SLEEP WHEN I'M DEAD COZ I DON'T WANT TO MISS ANYTHING. NOTHING BEATS FOOTY & A PIE. HIGH FIVES FOR BEACH, SUN, SURF, 24HOUR MACCAS, THE FIRST PASH, FRIENDS, FAMILY & MINIATURE PONIES.
>
> (Rochelle, accessed 30/10/07)

> So for everyone that doesnt already know it...i go to uni & im in 2nd year...studying to be a jnr primary/primary school teacher so one day u can all send your kids to me!!! what else?! Umm...im always late. never get around to calling people back...sorry!! im easily side-tract. Talk a little TOO much. Love laughing and having fun and misbehaving and partying too much...LOVE summer at the beach, sunbaking and surfing and fish & chips. Love shopping for bathers, and pointless things "just cos..." Love girly magazines, DIAMONDS. shoes. accessories. lip gloss. sunglasses. perfume. massages. day spas. pretty places. 7 star hotels. camping. camp fires. trackies & thongs. and desperately want a jet ski!!! LOVE randomness. honesty and bluntness. outgoing people who can party all night. Taylor! and Rick...him too...dont really like smoking. definately hate hangovers. AND people that tail gate me. ph calls in the middle of the night. cucumber and melons! that's it :) XxX XxX XxX XxX XxX
>
> (SuzeXO, accessed 20/02/08)

"Random" is a term found often in these self-descriptions, and randomness is described as a qualitative preference by several profile producers. Mz_Princess says she loves "all types of random shit. Anything random gets a laugh outta me." SuzeXO states with emphasis that she *loves* randomness. These writers construct themselves as being random through the self-descriptions and long lists of often paradoxical likes and dislikes, juxtaposed in a stream of consciousness order. Unpredictability and incoherence are, I suggest, carefully inserted into these lists of preferences, and help to signal one's authenticity, possibly, as Hugo Liu (2007) posits, to mask the pretense of the act of digital self-description. In his research on SNSs as "taste performances," following Erving Goffman's theories of performance of the self, Liu observed that people sometimes include what he calls "mistakes" to make their expressions of what they like seem more genuine and less constructed. He writes:

> Sometimes, including a mistake or flaw can enhance a perfectly coherent expression. These "disingenuous mistakes" (Davis, 1992) manipulate the sense of authenticity associated with Goffmanian (1959) "expression given off."'[...] With respect to a SNP [social network profile], one can imagine that a perfectly coherent declaration of interests [...] can only be made more perfect by scattering a few deliberately errant (but not destructive) tokens throughout in order to mask the pretension of the act. (Liu, 2007, p. 258)

A sense of randomness is inserted into these young women's self-descriptions by introducing preferences or descriptive sentences that seem inconsistent with other preferences or character traits listed, or unrelated to those around them. This fosters the impression that the writing is "transparent" and reflective of the current temporal, ephemeral, "interior" thoughts, desires, and whims of the profile owner. The randomness and authenticity produced in such texts is also gendered. Key expressions of femininity are given off in these self-descriptions, and usually combined with other traditionally unfeminine preferences, activities, and traits. Aligning one's preferences with feminized interests seen as pleasurable, such as shopping and fashion, while also including more contemporary feminine attributes and gender-subversive interests, is key to constructing the self here. Representing the self as aligned with key notions and values of youthful femininity, yet also as predominantly random, may be a way for young women to negotiate the conflicting demands of self-representation in networked publics, where fluidity and self-reinvention are required and built into these techno-social systems, while a strong sense of authenticity and a self at least somewhat fixed around certain aspects of youthful femininity remains highly valued.

For example, Rochelle signals her femininity when she tells viewers that she has more clothes than she can wear and loves "dolling up." She repudiates the weakness and demureness associated with more traditional, "prefeminist" notions of femininity by also letting viewers know that "nothing beats footy and a pie," and that she will punch you in the face if you piss her off. This gendered contrast perhaps serves to make her self-description and self-alignment with the consumption and fashion-oriented aspects of femininity appear authentic and natural. Her preferences (high fives) include "sun, surf, 24 hour Maccas (McDonald's restaurants), the first pash [kiss], friends, family and miniature ponies." This list further fosters a sense of individuality, uniqueness, and randomness by juxtaposing weather, food, romance, family, and animals. Similarly, SuzeXO contrasts a love of the traditionally masculine preferences of "surfing and fish & chips," with shopping, "girly magazines, DIAMONDS. shoes. accessories. lip gloss. sunglasses. perfume. massages. day spas." to construct a self that is multidimensional. She then lists "people that tail gate me. ph calls in the middle of the night. cucumber and melons" as quirky, personalized dislikes. In her self-description quoted in brief earlier, Blondebaby writes under "likes": "karaoke, necklaces, being loved, tiled floors, jeans, Jessica Simpson."

Under dislikes she writes: "liars, bourbon, babies, muddy feet, spew, macaroni and cheese, having your glasses smashed." Blondebaby's mention of babies as a dislike, along with liars, bourbon, spew, and muddy feet, positions her as focused on what are seen as the "fun" aspects of youthful femininity, rather than caregiving and domesticity. This exemplifies the way that in many of these texts key aspects of traditional femininity are repudiated, while those aspects of femininity tied to fashion, style, celebrity, and consumption are confirmed as pleasurable (Zaslow, 2009).

Further, the self-descriptions are peppered with affirmations of uniqueness and individuality through odd or quirky revelations that, I suggest, most often reaffirm this normative and socially valued postfeminist construct of youthful femininity. Mz_Princess's statement of personalized beliefs (quoted previously) exemplifies the gendered nature of the "randomness" presented. She writes: "I believe that Monday is an awful way to spend 1/7th of your life, I believe that confidence is the best accessory, I believe that 'Jack & Jills are Mickey Mouse,' but who doesnt???" Confidence is feminized as the best *accessory*—something fashionable, and something that one "puts on" to add style to one's embodiment and self-presentation. This statement about confidence is followed by a cryptic, likely personal, in-joke that remains undecipherable to unknown viewers. A feminized and fashionable confidence and randomness are positioned together as key values for Mz_Princess. Similarly, several young women describe themselves on their profiles as "random laughers," as follows:

> I'm the type of person to randomly burst out laughing at something that happened yesterday (Harriet, accessed 09/10/07)
> I'm the girl who laughs out loud in the middle of silence at something that happened the day before (Georgie, accessed 20/2/08)
> I'm the type of girl who will burst out laughing in dead silence at something that happened yesterday (SheZzaCat, accessed 06/012/07)

Through these statements, young women signal a sense of eccentricity, girlish innocence, fun, and also a *transparency of interiority*. In drawing attention to their inability to control their impulse to laugh despite the temporal and social context, these young women are also signaling the highly valued ability to *perform a sense of interiority for an audience*—one constructed as truthful and authentic in the sense that it performs an obliviousness to the demands of social context.

Psychologization Discourses: The Value of an "Interior" Revealed

The construct of gendered randomness as authenticity I have highlighted brings us to a central contradiction at play in these digital self-representations. At the same time as notions of identity as something available for creation and reinvention have become popular, scholars of digital culture have noted shifts toward moralizing discourses of fixed and "truthful" identity performance online (Bollmer, 2012; Cover, 2012a; van Zoonen, 2013). Bollmer (2012), for instance, argues that concerns about the ability to hide or disguise identity in digital spaces have resulted in demands for online identities to be "truthful," "transparent," and "fixed," requiring individuals to internalize notions of offline bodies and identities as such. Sociologists of subjectivity and selfhood in late modernity have suggested that morality is tied strongly to notions of showing "authenticity" in a world where traditional influences on belief are less certain. Moral and ethical selves, as Skeggs and Wood (2012) outline, are perhaps less defined by the state, religious authorities, or patriarchal families in late modernity and more by one's ability to *tell* the self as a source of moral good. According to Skeggs and Wood (2012), one's ability to engage in the revelation of interiority has become a measure of moral worth and value. They suggest that the "opening out of the self to public judgment" has become a way in which personhood is evaluated (Skeggs and Wood, 2012, p. 11). As these authors surmise, in the twentieth and twenty-first centuries we have seen an increased focus on the self as a concept defined by, or strongly related to, the revelation of interiority, individual uniqueness, and "performance" as a means of telling, and *through telling, producing* these qualities (2012, p. 72).

Several scholars have noted the influence of psychology as a discipline that has grown immensely in size, popularity, and industry value over the course of the twentieth century (Taylor, 1989; Rose, 1996; Butler, 2005; Illouz, 2007, 2008; Skeggs and Wood, 2012). In late modernity, selves are thought of as things that need to be externally expressed or "revealed" as part of a relatively contemporary quest toward psychological "self-actualization," even though, as Butler (2005) has argued, the self can perhaps never be *fully* known, fully told, or narrated comprehensively or coherently. These key ideas help in understanding the style of textual self-description encountered on young women's SNS profiles, particularly the stream of consciousness lists of character traits, likes, dislikes, and "random" proclivities that I have suggested are commonly employed to foster a sense of authenticity and transparency of interiority. The popularization of psychological discourse also helps to understand the propensity for young women to highlight their perceived flaws, sources of suffering, and to frame their socializing and partying as "excessive" in their self-descriptions, as I discuss further.

The work of Nikolas Rose (1996) follows a Foucauldian line of inquiry, and charts the way in which power and governance can be seen to operate through processes of "subjectification." Subjects governed by neoliberal means, Rose suggests, are not regulated by external state powers but through the internalization of power. In the ideal workings of neoliberal governance, "rational" and "healthy" choices in relation to consumption, lifestyle, work, family, and so on are internalized as personally fulfilling and "self-actualizing" choices. Rose suggests the psy-disciplines, or what Foucault calls "technologies of the soul" (Foucault, 1991, p. 178), play a vital role in such processes through the encouragement of certain desires and subjectivities and the regulation and disciplining of others. As Rose astutely notes, humans are in constant movement and exposed to different practices that subjectify them in different ways, and are thus not, in practice, "the unified subjects of some coherent government regime" (Rose, 1996, p. 35), while still being subjected to forms of power and discipline that can easily remain obscured. As Valerie Walkerdine and colleagues surmise, psychologizing and individualizing discourses and services "combine with people's desire to make something of their lives." (Walkerdine, Lucey, and Melody, 2001, pp. 2–3).

Eva Illouz argues that we can trace the popularization of a "therapeutic narrative" that has had an immense cultural impact on notions of the self across the twentieth century. A therapeutic narrative, she suggests, "makes one understand one's life as a generalized dysfunction, in order precisely to overcome it" (Illouz, 2007, p. 52). Performative expressions of suffering and psychological complexity become constitutive of identity in the shoring up of therapeutic narratives for telling the self. Conceptualizations of "self-help" as a meritocratic ideal that individuals are responsible for their own success and happiness and can better themselves through educative practices and tools of self-development have become inextricably tied to psychoanalytic narratives of selves as "suffering" (2007, p. 42) and in need of "authentication" and "liberation" *via narration*, she suggests. Performative practices, such as support groups, confessional television talk shows, Internet blogging, and so on, Illouz suggests, serve to reorganize experiences into "therapeutic narratives" (2007, p. 55). The telling of therapeutic narratives both *produces and enacts* the psychic suffering and healing that constitute this narrative in a circular fashion. As Illouz notes, there is ongoing work involved now in not only having a "unique self," but also *performing* it (p. 48). Being capable of expressing the self "authentically" and "transparently" to others is seen as key to the late-modern goals of psychological health, self-esteem, and self-actualization.

In summary, identities have come to be seen as unstable, context-dependent, and available for constant updating and remaking. At the same time, notions of a unique, authentic, interior self that exists to be performatively excavated, revealed, and "accounted for" (Butler, 2005) have become widely accepted. Such notions inform discourses about the self across a range of cultural institutions and media representations. Further, morality and ethicality are tied to the performative revelation of interiority, to one's ability to "show and tell" interiority to others. Thus, the textual narration and performative construction of youthful feminine selves online that can be judged by a potentially wide audience as plausibly "authentic," "self-produced" representations become entangled with judgments about moral worth and value.

Highlighting Flaws and "Excesses"

Personality traits are listed in many of the self-descriptions I viewed that contradict somewhat, including Rochelle's description of herself as loud and quiet, chilled and crazy, "anything she wants to be"; Robbi's description of herself as "mean, funny, caring, rude, friendly, easy going, fun, loud, annoying, loving, jealous, spoilt and impatient"; and BitchCunt/Janine's description of herself as trustworthy and bitchy, bad tempered and loveable (shown at the start of the chapter). Describing the self with contradicting traits, and in particular, including *negative* character traits too, as I now discuss, may help to further signal through text "authenticity" and "interiority." This practice also helps signal the confidence and esteem that is so key to the social and material value of young femininity. Through stating flaws and weaknesses, these young women foster a sense of psychological complexity and demonstrate their ability to publicly perform a self that is *confident enough to be transparent*, open, and multiplicitous, rather than one-dimensionally "good/likable."

According to generational researcher Jean Twenge, Generation Y, that is, those born roughly after 1981, and from whom my data is collected, claim that "being true to themselves" (meaning saying, wearing, and doing what they want, acting how they want, and expressing how they feel) is much more important to them than being liked by others or accepted by society in general (Twenge, 2006, p. 39). I question the degree to which social acceptance is qualitatively less important to this generation, and suggest instead that perhaps it is the case that social acceptance is now heavily contingent upon the internalization and everyday performance of a sense of strong personal acceptance, autonomy, and self-esteem. Some further examples of self-descriptive texts from young women's SNS profiles follow in which we can note the way the writer's perceived flaws, weaknesses, inadequacies, and sources of suffering are highlighted for viewers, along with proclamations of confidence, strength, and self-acceptance. Such multiplicitous descriptions serve to construct the self as confident, as well as morally and socially acceptable, by demonstrating one's capacity for a seemingly "transparent" performance of interiority.

> shopping.....friends.....dancing all night till my feet hurt.....Chuck (my dog).....music.......[name of club removed].....cigarettes........... alcohol.......clothes.....ebay.....myspace.....pink(the color)........... playboy.......sunglasses.......Leg warmers......high boots......... jewelry.......partying with jacki.......IM CRAZY.................. SILLY...........................FUNNY............................. CUTE...........................BRAVE............................. SWEET.........................OUTGOING......................... OPINIONATED..........................ANNOYING............. BLONDE............................ FUN........................... STUPID..........GIVE ME A DANCE FLOOR I'LL DANCE TO ANYTHING....... ALWAYS MAKE A SCENE...................HATE DRAMA........................... WHEN IM DRUNK I WANT EVERY BOY IN THE ROOM.....I WILL DANCE ON TABLES................I DONT REGRET ANYTHING...................HATE IT WHEN MY HAIR GETS WET......................I HOLD GRUDGES.............DANCE TILL MY FEET HURT.......................DRINK TILL IM BLIND............... NOT THE BRIGHEST CRAYON IN THE BOX.......LOVE GIVING PEOPLE SHIT.........................I LAUGH TILL MY STOMACH HURTS.............IM RANDOM...
>
> (Laaanni, accessed 05/03/08)

I AM GORGIEGEORGIE♥
I Love I Laugh I Cry I Bitch
I hold Grudges
Im extreamly Stubborn
I Cheat to win
I ♥ getting my own way
I Hate Fakes and Plastics
Ill Never change
I fall for the ones i Cant have
I do Judge people
I live for the ones who tell me they Love me
I Drink way to much
I Trust people to easily
I ♥ my Kittens
I dont look like the girls in the Magazines
I am a Snuggler
I Lie to get what i want
I fall asleep to the sound of Rain
This is who I AM and this is my Life
You are WELCOME to it.....

(Georgie, accessed 03/10/07)

18 Year's Old
brunette, But Natuality Blonde
Star Sign—Aqurius
Love's Alli, Marcus
& The Girl's
[...]
Family means everything in the worldd
Best Friend Is Michelle,
Love's her Forever!!
Love's confrontation
Is a BITCH and not affraid to show it.
Can never seem to stay out of trouble
HATE'S ppl Telling her what to do...
Can Never talk about the way she Feel's
Or Wat she is Thinking bout
Bottle's everything up...
Live's for the weekend
Love's Getting Fu*kedd up
Love's been immature
Has a very different Personality,
Hate me Or Love me, See what i caree...
Love's chillin with Marcus & Alex
Love's the weekends with the [...] boyyz
Live's in her own Little LaLa Land,

wishes Life was pefect
Is a princess in her own Special wayy
Will Live Life To The Fullest,
Does'nt understand why alot of things happen
Will do anything for the people she love
If you respect me, Ill respect you back,
Be Mean to my Babi GurlAlli,
& I Promise you'll Regret It...
Forgive's, But never forgets
Is in LOVEE with the T.V show Buffy The vampire Slayer
Love's The Little Mermaid
Unpredictable
Very Immpatient
Does'nt like to be alone,
make's me depressed
Will always stand up for myself
& wat I belive is right
Loves to eat cheesebuger's
No Pickles, No onions & Extra Cheese
Love's the Summer
Has an un-normal obsession with buying Sunnies (13 Pairs)
Remembers But Never Regrets
(Sugarfrog/CrazyBitch, accessed 06/01/08)

Among other things, these excerpts exemplify the way in which the young women whose profiles I analyzed commonly list and describe traits and proclivities normatively understood as flaws or weaknesses. Cinderella writes: "I will forget your name, I will forget your birthday, and I will forget your phone number, but don't use this against me, because I will get shitty and never talk to you again." Rochelle tells her viewers "I have to meet someone 5 times before I remember who they are." SuzeXO reveals that she is "always late. never get around to calling people back...sorry!! im easily side-tract. Talk a little TOO much." Penny Darling lets viewers know that she "Hates waiting, shes very impatient" and also hates "being told NO. Hates not getting exactly what she wants, when she wants." Sugarfrog/CrazyBitch describes herself as unpredictable and "very impatient." And Laaanni and Georgie both describe themselves as people who "hold grudges." Laaanni also writes that she is "not the brightest crayon in the box." Georgie mentions her extreme stubbornness, and confesses to her viewers that she lies to get what she wants, and trusts people too easily. But, she states, signaling a degree of acceptance, if not pride, she will "never change." Similarly, in the excerpts from some of these self-descriptive lists provided at the start of this chapter, all three profile owners quoted describe themselves as "annoying," and list qualities such as loudness, silliness, being jealous, bitchy, bad-tempered, rude, and impatient, along with being loving, caring, generous, fun, friendly, and loyal.

Young women also commonly note psychological disorders they have been diagnosed with, or have self-diagnosed. For example, in her self-description, Harriet reveals to viewers that she has a borderline personality disorder and that some days she hates herself and her life. She sums herself up as "complicated." Anna tells us she "suffers from insomnia," and is also "a Smartass why not?...you will learn to love it." Cinderella describes herself as an "undiagnosed ADHD kid." Sugarfrog/CrazyBitch confesses that she can "never stay out of trouble," cannot talk about the way she feels and "bottles everything up," and that she doesn't like to be alone because it makes her "depressed." These selves are represented to viewers as imperfect and in need of ongoing work. They must be contextualized within a framework of the continuous change and flux associated with writing the self digitally, and also within late-modern discourses of continuous self-reinvention and improvement. Psychological complexity is signaled in these texts. So too is signaled the capacity and *confidence* to disclose psychological flaws and complexities to a networked public of peers and potentially other unknown viewers.

Further, on the young women's profiles I analyzed, preferences, practices, and ambitions that might be deemed controversial, "excessive," or "risky" in some way were also highlighted for viewers. For example, it is common for young women to list favorite alcohol and cigarette brands, and many young women explicitly defend their drinking, smoking, and sometimes illicit drug-taking practices explicitly as part of "who they are." Harriet states in her self-description, "I do have the occasional alcoholic drink and cigarette, if you're going to judge me or hate me for it then I guess there's not much I can do. I'm not going to change for anyone." Cinderella similarly tells her viewers "I live my life my way. I'm not straight edge, but have respect of it, but if you preach to me or don't like me because I choose to drink and smoke then your not worth my time." Several young women describe their partying and drinking practices in terms that highlight such practices as excessive. For example, SuzeXO tells viewers she loves "having fun and misbehaving and partying *too much*." Laaanni writes that she drinks until she is *blind*, and dances until *her feet hurt*; Georgie, that she drinks "way *too much*"; Rochelle that she likes to "get *messy* until the sun comes up"; and Sugarfrog/CrazyBitch tells viewers she "Love's Getting Fu*kedd up" and "Love's been immature."

Weekend partying, drinking, and spontaneous, "wild," "excessive" social behavior with close and valued friends were highlighted on almost all of the profiles I analyzed, as I have discussed in more detail elsewhere (Dobson, 2011, 2014a). This aspect of self-representation aligns with broader notions of youthfulness, and such alignment may further help to position these performances as authentic expressions of interiority for young women. As Fleur Gabriel notes, social media activities "reveal the way that youth has always been a discursive construction and a social performance" (2014, p. 109). In performing identities aligned with risk-taking and excessive partying online Gabriel suggests that "young people are performatively constituting the meaning of youth as transgressive, as at risk, as lacking foresight, as in need of protection, and as creative, capable, reflexive and self-aware" (p. 109). Online self-representation by young people perhaps demonstrates some of "the effects of existing assumptions about youth development" in ways not previously visible (p. 109). Gabriel's point is that in order to fit with dominant developmental and socially normative expectations around youthfulness, young people *must* represent themselves online as "risk-takers" and thrill-seekers. This point resonates strongly when reading these self-descriptions in which partying, heavy drinking (getting "fucked up," "messy," "wasted," and so on) and various other controversial activities, character traits, and preferences are highlighted for viewers. My point here is that such references to partying and excessive drinking also serve to bolster the performative construct of a self that is *confident enough* to highlight its own social "excesses" in a networked public.

Textual descriptions of flaws, weaknesses, and sometimes pathologies and other sources of suffering on SNSs, along with prominent disclosures of youthful social and drinking-related excess, are perhaps part of the project of signaling the self as "authentic" and "transparent," and as confident to "show and tell" interiority (Skeggs and Wood, 2012) to an audience. Illouz astutely notes that "at the same time that the discourse of triumphant self-reliant individualism has never been so pervasive and hegemonic, the demand to express and perform one's suffering whether in support groups, talk shows, therapy, legal courts, and intimate relations has never been as strident." (Illouz, 2007, p. 57). SNSs perhaps become another key vehicle for the culturally valued performance of interior complexity and suffering, as well as confidence and self-esteem, for an audience of both peers and strangers.

Pedagogical Tones, Feminism, and Self-Esteem

The final element of textual self-representations on young women's SNS profiles I discuss here are the pedagogical tones that, I suggest, are evident in much of these mottos and self-descriptive texts. For example, in the section on "Individualization and DIY self-making" I discussed several decorative textual mottos and aphorisms that communicate pedagogical messages about the value of self-making and the need for autonomy, self-responsibility, and self-reliance. Examples from young women's profile decorations, self-descriptions, and public blog posts, I suggest, communicate pedagogical messages to viewers primarily about self-acceptance and staying "true" to the self regardless of external social and relational conflicts or pressures. Autonomy and independence are strongly advocated.

> Dani <u>BELEIVES</u> in DOING what makes you HAPPY, BEING with who makes you SMILE, LAUGHING as much as you BREATHE, and LOVING as long as you LIVE!!!
>
> (Danirocks's self-description, accessed 05/03/08)

> I'm not a perfect girl.
> My hair doesn't always stay in place & I spill things a lot.
> I'm pretty clumsy and sometimes I have a broken heart.
> My friends & I sometimes fight &
> Maybe some days nothing goes right.
> But when I think about it & take a step back
> I remember how amazing life truly is
> & that maybe. Just maybe. I like being
> Unperfect...
>
> (BitchenDiva, decorative profile motto, accessed 3/3/08)

> **Bitchology**
> Being a Bitch means...
> I stand up for myself and my beliefs
> I stand up for those I love
> I speak my mind, think my own thoughts
> or do things my way
> I won't compromise what's in my heart
> I live my life MY way
> I won't allow anyone to step on me
> I refuse to tolerate injustice
> It means I have the courage &
> strength to allow myself to be me
> So try to stomp on me, douse my inner flame,
> Squash every ounce of beauty I hold within

> You won't succeed
> And if that makes me a Bitch, so be it
> I embrace the title and I'm proud to be a Bitch!
> (Sugarfrog/Crazybitch, decorative profile motto, accessed 04/09/07)

> **Judge Me**
> & i'll prove you wrong
> **tell me what to do,**
> **& i'll tell you off.**
> say i'm not worth it & watch where i end up.
> **call me a *bitch* & i'll show you one.**
> fuck me over & i'll do it to you twice as bad.
> **call me crazy**
> but you really have no idea =)~
> (Micki, decorative profile motto, accessed 17/09/07)

> Standing your ground
>
> It's hard to stand your ground and not change for someone. Once that person sees that they got you wrapped, they take advantage of you. No matter what, you should always be yourself and know that if it's not good enough for someone then say GOODBYE! You should always be true to yourself no matter what. It may be hard but in the end you wont be hurt as bad...
>
> (Lorena, blog post, accessed 06/12/07)

> Dear Katy
>
> Stop fighting, this is who you are, you will never be good enough regardless of what you do. I know the dream of a close family shall now fade, but you can rectify that in the future when you have your own. This is who you are, if they cant accept it then its their choice, never change for anyone else's approval. Live for yourself.
>
> Love Katy
>
> (Katy/Kuntastic Bitch, blog post, accessed 18/03/08)

These posts, I suggest, can be read not only as proclamations of one's own capacity for authenticity and "being true to yourself," but also as statements *addressed to others somewhat instructively*. Through the practice of explicitly declaring one's own self-acceptance in a networked public, an example of the morality of "authenticity" and self-acceptance is made for viewers. In relation to such public declarations by young women, it is worth recalling that as recently as the mid-1990s feminist authors such as Peggy Orenstein (1994) and Mary Pipher (1994) were expressing concern for the silenced voices of girls. Concerns regarding what these authors saw as a loss of confidence, "true self," and "voice" that occurs in early puberty for girls have contributed to the notion that public expression of "voice/self" is key to girls' and young women's empowerment and self-actualization in particular (Harris, 2004). In Australia, educational policies directed toward nourishing girls' self-esteem were formulated in the 1980s following several dire reports released on the issue (Tsolidis, 1986; Kenway and Willis, 1990). These textual expressions exemplify self-esteem discourses which have, since the second-wave feminist movement, and more specifically, since the perceived "girl-confidence crisis" which came to a head in the early 1990s, been directed specifically toward girls and young women. While Twenge suggests that self-esteem rhetoric has now been widely popularized via educational and media discourses aimed at young people (Twenge, 2006), girls and young women in particular have been the subject of pedagogical encouragement to develop voices and opinions of their own and to make them loud and public (Harris, 2004). Echoes sound here of feminist-driven calls for girls to "stand up for themselves" and express themselves loudly and clearly. These expressions position the ideal young feminine self as confident, psychologically strong, and direct. They promote self-acceptance and esteem to their viewers as highly valued traits.

It is important to note, then, that these kind of pedagogical validations of "being true to the self," and particularly the discursive emphasis on not bending to suit the needs of others, have particular cultural and historical significance for girls and women. Some media and scholarly commentators concerned with the "narcissism" of young people as apparently evidenced through social media fail to acknowledge this. Many second-wave feminists were critical of the ways in which girls and women socialized to put the needs and desires of their families before their own (de Beauvoir, 1949/1972; Greer, 1970; Brownmiller, 1984). Pipher (1994), writing of her US-based psychology practice in the early 1990s, perceived in the raising of girls a primary focus on pleasing others and being and appearing "nice." Girls are indoctrinated, she argued, to at least *appear* happy and be nice to others (Pipher, 1994, p. 39) even when they might not be feeling that way. The second-wave feminist movement therefore emphasized the need to teach proceeding generations of girls to stand up for themselves, get in touch with their own desires, and go after what they want, rather than selflessly supporting the professional goals of men and the needs of children. Encouraging women to put their own needs and careers first is an ongoing project in some contemporary strands of feminism, as Catherine Rottenberg (2014) suggests, and it is still an issue with much public purchase, as the popularity of books such as Sheryl Sandberg's (2013) *Lean In* attests to.

In an effort to teach girls to better express their emotions, desires, and ambitions to others with whom such expressions may cause conflict, traits previously undervalued and discouraged in young women such as stubbornness, determination, ambition, anger, and even aggression are now culturally lauded as a kind of postfeminist "authenticity" for girls and women. According to Twenge, personality testing data reflects a generational shift toward such traits, which have been traditionally categorized as "masculine," for *both* sexes. Twenge found that over 50 percent of young women in the 1990s scored as masculine by identifying with traits such as assertiveness, self-reliance, ambition, and forcefulness, as compared to the average of 20 percent of women who scored this way in the 1970s (Twenge, 2006, p. 193). We can see such traits reflected in the ways in which the young women in my study commonly describe themselves as loud, opinionated, angry, brave, and uncompromising. As I have suggested so far, "authentically" being yourself appears to take a particularly self-assured form in the digital textual self-representations I viewed.

As Anita Harris suggests, attempts to address concerns about the self-esteem of girls via practices in schools, and discourses in media and government policy, amount to pressure on girls and young women to express opinions, feelings, and interior selves publicly (Harris, 2004, p. 125). Having perhaps been raised on cultural messages about the need to make one's voice loud and public, young women do represent themselves through text in digitally networked publics confidently, boldly, and "loudly." We must keep in mind the possibility that young women are still now, as suggested by psychologists in earlier decades, expressing in networked publics what they think others (peers, teachers, parents, and strangers) wish to hear—that is, expressions of high confidence, autonomy, and self-esteem. In the postfeminist context, young women are called upon to distinguish themselves from older, weaker, and less autonomous versions of femininity that were more prominent and socially valued prior to the cultural, social, and economic changes the second wave of feminism heralded in the West. The kind of textual expressions discussed in this chapter allow them to do so.

The texts I have discussed communicate a forthright sense of self-acceptance, and sometimes fierce self-reliance. They communicate that the profile owners do not care what viewers think, even as the act of detailed self-representation in a networked public seems to betray an investment in being seen and accepted by others. But youthful, post-feminist feminine self-representations carved out around what might be described as various excesses—of confidence, loudness, hedonism, drinking, partying, and so on—are still regulated, disciplined, and pathologized for girls and young women at the same time as they are called forth. This happens most obviously as feminine selves and bodies intersect with classed and racialized selves and bodies, and bodies sexualized on the basis of nonheterosexual desires and young motherhood, as several other scholars have documented (Driver, 2007; Thompson, Kehily, Hadfield, and Sharpe, 2011; Koffman, 2013). As I suggest in conclusion, we might also find strong proclamations of confidence and autonomy troubling for what such expressions possibly suggest about the harshness of the postfeminist digital terrain, a harshness likely stepped along long-standing lines of social difference.

The Judgment of Digital Feminine Selves

On several young women's profiles in my study there were explicit provocations for viewers to "judge" the profile owners. This is exemplified by the textual decoration "Judge Me" displayed on Micki's profile: "Judge me and I'll prove you wrong, tell me what to do, and I'll tell you off. Say I'm not worth it and watch where I end up. Call me a bitch and I'll show you one. Fuck me over and I'll do it to you twice as bad. Call me crazy but you really have no idea." This decorative text was seen on the profiles of several other young women while browsing MySpace, not included in my study. Laaanni too displayed a profile decoration prominently on her page with the words "Judge Me" written in large, bold font. These words were written across a photograph by the well-known American photographer Sally Mann entitled *Candy Cigarette* (1989). The photograph depicts a young, pretty, white girl in a white dress with blonde hair, who appears to be smoking a cigarette and looking directly into the camera, appearing non-pulsed. In its use on young women's SNS profiles, the image was appropriated with the text "Judge Me" added to it prominently. This appropriated version of the photo was also seen on several other MySpace profiles not included in this study, and still appears in Google image searches for the text "judge me." Mann's photograph was controversial upon its original exhibition, as part of her *Immediate Family* series. The girl pictured is Mann's young daughter. In its appropriated use as a profile decoration, the title of the image is, significantly, lost. Along with it is also lost the statement that signals the cigarette in Mann's daughter's hand as a fake one. "Judge Me" appears in this appropriation to signify the voice of the young girl pictured apparently smoking. I would suggest that in its use by young women on their SNS profiles, the image signals a kind of "performative shamelessness" (Dobson, 2014a, b). With this text added, the girl in the image is signaled as confident in her autonomy, able to disavow social approval of her actions, provoke criticism, and defend herself against it.

These two provocations to viewers to "judge" the profile owners are instructive for what they reveal about the social media landscape in which they are produced, and performing ideal youthful femininity within it. Perhaps textual performances of self-acceptance and confidence function as self-protective measures for young women. Expressions of adamant confidence and self-acceptance found on young women's SNS profiles might be seen as layers of discursive armor donned for the purposes of public online self-representation. As we can see in this chapter, and as I have noted elsewhere, a high level of self-revelation is normalized in youth social media cultures. Participation involves "literal self-exposure in terms of the information presented about one's self, the amount of digital communication required to maintain social circles and friendships, and also in terms of the amount of photographs of the self and of one's social life" (Dobson, 2014b, p. 108). As Bollmer puts it, "network citizens" must embrace "the demand to *connect* and *expose oneself*, maintaining flows of information to others" (2012, p. 8). Young women are incited to "discourse and display" (Harris, 2004) themselves in very public ways, and before gazes that may be understood or experienced as heavily scrutinizing and often sexualizing. The profile owners in my study, as I have suggested, signal confidence and dismiss the need for social approval through their textual self-representations. But strong claims of "I don't care what you think" and provocations to "judge me" also perhaps suggest an emphatic request to the viewers *not to judge*. Such a demand, in other words, would appear to betray a great deal of investment in the judgments of others, perhaps from both the immediate peer-defined and broader social worlds.

These constructions of young feminine selves on SNSs need to be understood as performances created in relation and response to the assumption of a judging and judgmental gaze from peers and others. Camille Nurka (2014) argues that an "incitement to judgment" is central to postfeminist digital cultures. Polls, rating systems, forums, and pages dedicated to "democratic" evaluation and judgment of female bodies have proliferated in recent years, she suggests. A "judging public" is solicited in these various online spaces "whose political agency, indeed *right*, is grounded in the aesthetic spectacle" of judging female bodies (Nurka, 2014, p. 486). Performative alignment with discourses of self-making, randomness, confidence, and self-acceptance may help to shield the self somewhat from the potential "heat" of exposure in networked publics. For young women who engage in the kind of out-there, excessive and confident forms of public self-expression discussed in this chapter as well as chapter 3, "shamelessness" must perhaps be preemptively signaled; the judging gaze must be performatively disavowed within the self-representation. This may be especially important for girls and young women who experience added weights of judgment on the basis of bodies and lives marked by social differences such as race, class, and sexuality.[2] We do not yet really know the ways in which performing this new postfeminist brand of youthful femininity in networked publics impacts young women differently on the basis of social and bodily difference and inequality. Social rewards may be attained for some, while others face judgment and exclusion. Rewards for young women may be plentiful at certain times of life, while translating into disadvantage or penalty at other times in the life course, such as when entering into tertiary education, full-time labor markets, or upon entering motherhood. It may be that middle-class women, and women with social and cultural capital, have the resources needed to either continue, justify, transcend, or contain digitized postfeminist "youthful" and "excessive" performativity in other life phases. This may prove more difficult for women whose bodies are a priori marked by difference, for those who have historically been, and still are, subject to judgment on the basis of "excesses" and "improprieties" as perceived by others.

I have discussed some examples of the ways in which young women performatively incorporate and construct norms of postfeminist femininity as self-made, random, excessive, confident, and autonomous into their digital self-representation through the use of certain kinds of mottos and stylistic conventions for textual self-description. I have discussed the moral and social value placed on the capacity of individuals to signal notions of interiority and "transparency" performatively for others, and I argue that for girls and young women there are added imperatives and pressures around the display of a self that can be judged as "authentic" in this regard. Such imperatives and pressures at least partially determine the kind of textual self-representations seen on young women's SNS profiles. The telling of young feminine selves in ways that produce them as authentic is tied up with notions of self-actualization, self-esteem, and self-acceptance, and thus with social and moral worth. How these imperatives and pressures toward the specific kind of postfeminist self-representation called forth in digitally networked publics plays out for girls and young women remains to be seen.

Chapter 6

Digital Girls in Crisis? Seeking Feedback and Representing Pain in Postfeminist Networked Publics

Introduction

In the last chapter I explored textual mottos and self-descriptions from young women's social network site (SNS) profiles. These texts, written by young women for display on public profiles, communicate a sense of the young feminine self as strongly confident, and as "true" to herself in that she sticks to her own beliefs, wishes, and desires, and does not compromise to suit the needs of others or gain social approval. The writers of these texts performatively construct a sense of self-reliance and "shamelessness." This is a brand of young feminine subjectivity that has come to be seen as ideal, and is highly valued by governments, corporations, and educational institutions in postfeminist and post-girl power societies and cultures (Harris, 2004; Zaslow, 2009; Banet-Weiser, 2012; Ringrose, 2013; Harris and Dobson, 2015). For girls and young women who are able to internalize, embody, and perform this postfeminist brand of femininity, that is, those for whom such subjectivities are physically and psychically available, legible, and desirable, the social rewards may be great. In this chapter I explore what might be seen as the opposite of postfeminist, girl-powered performative digital subjectivities. While the mottos and self-descriptive texts employed by young women on the SNS profiles I viewed and analyzed represent and construct "can do" girls, the girl media producers explored in this chapter, who seek attention overtly and publicly by asking for appearance-related feedback or narrating and mediating pain through social media, represent "at risk" girls (Harris, 2004). Or rather, the girl figures discussed here are seen as no longer just at risk, but "in crisis." We can see boundaries hardening around this digital girl in crisis, giving her shape and contours in several different digital cultural phenomena over the last ten years, from the cam girls of the early 2000s who were quickly labelled "attention whores" with low self-esteem for broadcasting scenes from their bedrooms via webcam and asking for gifts in return (Dobson, 2008; Senft, 2008), through to online communities of girls living or struggling with anorexia and other eating disorders (Ferreday, 2003; Day and Keys, 2008; Boero and Pascoe, 2012), self-injury and "cutting" blogs and Tumblr pages (Adler and Adler, 2011; Johansson, 2014), and the largely feminized and youth-oriented online shoplifting communities and image blogs (e.g., google "lift haul").

In this chapter I discuss two examples of girl figures who I suggest are positioned as fitting within this broader rubric of "digital girls in crisis," but between whom there are important differences as well as commonalities I seek to unpack. First, I discuss girls seeking appearance-related feedback in networked publics; and second, girls narrating and mediating pain more overtly in networked publics. My discussion of girls seeking appearance feedback explores the "Am I Pretty or Ugly" videos, which first ignited news media panic in 2012 when several videos posted by young girls in the United States addressing this question to the networked public of YouTube went viral. These videos came into the global media spotlight again in 2014 when a UK performance artist posed online as a teenage girl to generate feedback from viewers on her appearance for her theatre show that explores the phenomenon and aims to draw public attention to this particular digital "girl in crisis." I then discuss videos made by teenage girls on YouTube narrating experiences of emotional pain and suffering often tied to bullying, depression, and various practices of self-harm including self-injury, cutting, and eating disorders. Such videos came to my attention after the highly publicized death of 15-year-old Amanda Todd, whose YouTube video, posted just weeks before her suicide in Canada, went viral. In describing these "girls in crisis" as representing a kind of femininity opposed to that projected in the self-representations discussed in the previous chapter, I do not mean to suggest that young women who construct confident, autonomous, and self-assured performances of self on their profiles *do not* seek attention, social approval, or external validation of worth. Young women who mediate emphatically confident identities via SNSs may or may not themselves feel or enact "confidence" regularly in their daily lives. What I have suggested is that currently lauded young femininity and digital self-representation is tied to the qualities and traits of confidence, autonomy, self-reliance, and to notions of individualism. In contrast, girls whose digital self-representations explicitly address a networked community requesting feedback, attention, or support are positioned as "in crisis" and their media practices are "spectacularized" (Projansky, 2014) as evidence of such.

In this chapter I am concerned with the self-representations of these two different "girl in crisis" figures, but also with the public discourses and affects that circulate around them. That is, I am interested in exploring what is commonly being represented and communicated by these girl media producers, as well as the question of what can be learnt from the discursive and affective reactions of public commentators called forth here—largely adult journalists, scholars, health professionals, and educators. As a feminist scholar I include myself in this particular public called forth, made up of those who hold an investment in young people's well-being and in girls' in particular. I draw much here from Beverley Skegg's work on gender, class, and value. Although class is not central to my analysis here, as my concern is primarily with representations rather than lived identities, her contentions about the deep relationship between *value* and *values* (Skeggs, 2014) are of great use in furthering our understanding of the digital production and circulation of young feminine subjectivities in contemporary postfeminist mediascapes. I argue that discursive and affective responses to girls seeking appearance feedback publicly suggests a concern about the *value* and *values* of these girls, who seem to be judged as either having a *lack* of self-esteem, or an *excess* of self-focus, and thus, little value. Girls who narrate and mediate pain publicly are positioned slightly differently, as already fully pathological subjects, and thus a key concern about their digital self-representations appears to be that their pathologies and emotions will spread virally and contagiously (Kramer, Guillory, and Hancock, 2014) and infect or "trigger" other girls in networked publics. Public responses to both girl figures, I argue, suggest a broader gendered devaluation, and increasing pathologization, of media practices of seeking feedback, connectivity, and relationality.

Systems of economic exchange within late modernity, especially as they are increasingly digitized and visually mediated, have been theorized as "affective" and "scopic." Emotions themselves, as some scholars have suggested, have become commodified in late-modern neoliberal societies, and hold exchange value (Hochschild, 1979; Ahmed, 2004; Illouz, 2007). Sara Ahmed argues that emotions can "accumulate over time as a form of affective value" (Ahmed, 2004, p. 11), and objects of emotion gain value through their circulation (Ahmed, 2004, p. 11).

On SNSs, the textual expression of positive emotion generates immense value for the owners of these sites. The circulation of emotion has been suggested as the primary source of capital for leading social media corporations such as Facebook (van Ryn and Fordyce, 2014; Young, 2014), and participation in social media has been theorized as a form of affective and immaterial labor (Andrejevic, 2011; Banet-Weiser, 2012; Carah, 2014). It also appears that Facebook routinely manipulates the content of posts that appear in users' newsfeeds in the process of determining and promoting content that spreads and generates engagement at the highest levels, as was revealed in a recent experiment testing "emotional contagion" via Facebook (Kramer, Guillory, and Hancock, 2014)[1]. Value and worth are also strongly tied to the visual in late-modern digitally networked societies—to images and their circulation, and to visual objects which can garner the gazes, attention, and engagement of viewers (Skeggs, 2005, 2014; Hearn, 2008; Banet-Weiser, 2012; Ringrose, Harvey, Gill, and Livingstone, 2013; Carah, 2014). In affective and scopic economies, "confidence" as an affect and also girls' circulation of self-images that signal confidence and self-worth through smiles, bodily display, and sociality has exchange value (Banet-Weiser, 2012; Koffman, Gill, and Orgad, 2015). Girls seeking appearance feedback overtly and publicly, and girls narrating and mediating pain, I suggest, are positioned as holding little exchange value in their current affective states.

Skeggs and several other feminist scholars have charted the way working-class women, and especially single mothers, are pathologized and cast as morally deficient and worthless subjects, suggesting that the lack of capital value dependent feminine subjects are seen to hold contributes to their pathologization in the neoliberal, post-social context (Skeggs, 2004; see also Ringrose and Walkerdine, 2008; Thomson, Kehily, Hadfield, and Sharpe, 2011; Skeggs and Wood, 2012; Egan, 2013). In examining the discourses and affects that circulate, shape, and define the boundaries around the two digital "girls in crisis" figures I discuss here, we can see how the mostly white and middle-class girls and young women who seek feedback through their media practices, and whose self-representations make explicit a desire for relationality, connectivity, and attention from others in networked publics are also devalued, and increasingly pathologized as lacking value and values. While self-reliance is lauded in the neoliberal context, dependence and the need for approval, attention, and care is seen as the height of "crisis" for girls and young women. The less one performs one's own worth through signaling affective confidence and *invulnerability*, the less value one has.

"Am I Pretty or Ugly?" Discursive and Affective Responses to Girls Seeking Feedback in Networked Publics

Since roughly 2009, and increasingly, it appears, young women in the Anglophone West have been posting videos on YouTube posing the question publicly to viewers "Am I Pretty or Ugly?"[2] There are around 16,000 videos that come up from a search for the phrase on YouTube. Although, it must be noted, many of these are now parody videos of the phenomenon, discussions of responses to it, and so on. In early 2012 the American news media featured several stories on this phenomenon, and a handful of these videos were shown on television news programs around the world (Banet-Weiser, 2014). In these videos, girls who appear to be between the ages of 10 and 14 speak into webcams in their bedrooms, and ask viewers to tell them honestly whether they think they are pretty or ugly, stating that they receive conflicting opinions about this from friends and peers at school, that they see themselves as "fat" and/or "ugly," but their friends dispute this, and they want to know "the truth." Some state that they have been bullied at school and called fat or ugly. Some show photo montages of themselves in different states of dress and makeup. Some diversity in racial features and skin tone is represented among the handful of the most highly viewed of these videos, but all these girl video producers are typically feminine in their features and appearance, and thus could be considered conventionally "pretty" by Western cultural standards, if quite young and child-like in appearance. Many of the videos from the 2012 news coverage have now been viewed hundreds of thousands of times, and have tens of thousands of comments left by viewers. More recent videos from 2014 onward have been viewed somewhere between one thousand and one hundred thousand times, and have comments left by viewers numbering well into the thousands. A handful of academic journal articles have now been written about the videos, with arguments made about the psychological impact and significance of this kind of publicization and public commentary and judgment of girls' and women's bodies (Nurka, 2014), the gendered marketization of self-esteem in relation to the videos (Banet-Weiser, 2014), and the kinds of "feedback" called forth in response to such videos in a postfeminist cultural context (Rossie, 2015). The videos have been positioned in news media commentary as part of a broader, ongoing, and constantly reformulated/reconfigured "crisis of girlhood," and evidence of the low self-esteem of girls in the Anglophone West, where concern most visibly and prominently focuses on middle-class white girls. The phenomenon is tied to what is seen as the sexualized, appearance-focused and youth-obsessed postfeminist media culture that is thought to intensify girls' "natural" body insecurities at the same time as many girls have at their disposal the tools for receiving feedback and judgment from a public of networked strangers (Banet-Weiser, 2011; Nurka, 2014).

Circulating "Horror" and "Dismay" Over Girls Seeking Appearance Feedback

In mid-2014 media coverage of the phenomenon was sparked again because of a performance piece based on the phenomenon by UK-based artist Louise Orwin. Interviewed on Australia's morning news/variety show *Sunrise*, Orwin, when asked why she made the show, describes her reaction to first encountering the videos as one of "genuine horror." As part of the research for her show, Orwin posed as a teenage girl online and created a fake profile for herself in order to solicit comments about her appearance. She told *Sunrise* that after one of her videos went viral, the comments she received on her looks were "devastating" to her as an adult performer, despite her sense of perceived distance from her "fake" profile and videos. She expresses fear and dismay about how such comments regarding, for instance, the distance between one's eyes or the shape of one's nose, might affect younger girls, who are assumed to be making such videos out of a more genuine desire for appearance-based feedback. Such girls are also assumed to be more vulnerable to negative comments than young adults and professional artists such as Orwin. The hosts Samantha Armytage and David Koch grimace and shake their heads about "pretty or ugly" videos, which are described in the onscreen headline as a "*dangerous* trend" and "the *dangerous* question teen girls are asking." Armytage ends the segment by stating, "Your *heart just breaks* for these girls," and Koch reiterates, "It is *so heartbreaking*" (Sunrise, 2014).

In an article in the New York Post, Elisha Maldonado describes her view that what is "disconcerting" about these videos is that they are made by girls who are too young to "know who they are as individuals," and are thus thought to be "insecure" and in need of validation from others. Further, Maldonado suggests, they seek validation "even by those they don't know," and to be "validated in a way that has no substance" (Maldonado, 2013). Scholars and various different experts have also expressed dismay and great concern over these videos which document young girls' media practices of seeking appearance-based feedback from the public of digitally networked strangers. As Banet-Weiser notes, some health professionals have called for their censorship or removal from YouTube (2014, p. 84). Asked to comment on the videos by the Associated Press for an article that appeared in various papers around the world, communications scholar Emilie Zaslow suggests that the videos "could be read as a new form of self-mutilation in line with cutting and eating disorders" (Zaslow quoted in Italie, 2012). Behavioral science professor Nadine Kaslow, quoted in the same article, confirms that similar kinds of negative impacts on girl video producers are thought to be possible (to self-mutilation and eating disorders), suggesting that in seeking such feedback publicly, girls may be shamed and humiliated as they become "public objects instead of being your own person" (Italie, 2012).

Feminist scholar Camille Nurka fleshes out this argument about the psychologically damaging effects of what is understood as a kind of public self-objectification. She describes the videos as "ritualized performances of disintegration" (Nurka, 2014, p. 6), and suggests that girls who make them suffer "vertiginous disorientation as they turn their bodies toward an indeterminate number and configuration of anonymous judges" (2014, p. 7). Nurka suggests that what is of concern from a feminist and psychological perspective is not only the confinement of these feminine identities to the "objectifying aestheticized binary" of "pretty or ugly" as a judgment by viewers, but also an "impeded developmental process of individuation" because of the way in which these girls seek clarification of their value and identity on the basis of "ultimately unsatisfying criteria" (2014, p. 6). Nurka's psychological reading of the phenomenon assumes a developmentalist model to suggest that these video creators are seeking a sense of wholeness, individuation, and bodily "coordination." This performance on YouTube, she suggests, will ultimately damage or disorient the self, because authentication from judges is being sought in a mediated public sphere "before a rudimentary and coherent body image [. . .] has been developed" (p. 6). The videos are problematic, she suggests, in their revelation of a "paralyzing dependence upon the other as the embodied self is sucked into the other's gaze" (p. 7). Such a reading communicates a kind of discursive and scholarly equivalent of Armytage's affective grimace and cries of heartbreaking pity for the girls.

Let me be clear: I had a similar kind of immediate, bodily, and affective reaction upon first viewing these videos. I pulled away from the screen in a grimace, shutting my eyes to them. I am not suggesting that such affective and discursive reactions of "horror" and "dismay" are the "wrong" responses to have to these videos. But I am curious about how and why such affective responses appear to be called forth by these videos from adult stakeholders in the current cultural, social, political, and economic climate and circulate prominently. I agree with Adrienne Evans and Sarah Riley (2014), who have argued in relation to cultural sexualization, that questioning our own reactions to cultural phenomena we find problematic or cause for dismay is one of the key tasks for scholars of culture. What can we learn from interrogating discursive and affective responses of horror and dismay that appear to be produced here as effects of recirculating and remediating the "Am I Pretty or Ugly" girl figures?

Valuable or Devalued Girls?

Sarah Banet-Weiser's ideas help in answering this question. Banet-Weiser offers us a useful way to understand this phenomenon, and the discourses and affective responses that circulate around it, as part of broader processes of "marketizing self-esteem," as well as "empowerment," as products and investments for girls (Banet-Weiser, 2014, 2015). In contextualizing the "Am I Pretty or Ugly" phenomenon and the gendered market for self-esteem, Banet-Weiser describes the sociocultural history of self-help in the United States, the production of "inner happiness, personal security, and a healthy psyche" as goals for self-made citizens, and the idea that "self-esteem" was a thing that would benefit "both the individual and society in general" (Banet-Weiser, 2014, p. 92). She describes the individualization of the self-esteem industry over the twentieth century that has resulted in current and relatively new understandings of "self-determination" as a capitalist industry (2014, p. 93), and the marketization of self-esteem for girls in particular that has occurred in postfeminist culture. Importantly, she points out that the framing of these videos as "simply an issue of girls' self-esteem" obscures law and policy battles through which women's bodily rights are being stripped back (2014, p. 97) at the same time as women are responsibilized—charged with managing and procuring their own self-esteem and empowerment. Banet-Weiser suggests that digital self-mediation provides these female video producers with an "illusion of agency" that does not and cannot fully cash out in this context (2014, p. 95).

The vulnerability of the girl, publicly mediated in this way, as Banet-Weiser suggests, functions as a kind of currency that can potentially be exchanged for attention, for feedback, and sometimes for "empowerment." Importantly, this exchange happens now not just in isolated physical locations such as schools or neighborhoods, but with a large and global audience through the digitally networked public of YouTube. It may be that vulnerability functions for some, primarily white middle-class girls, as a kind of currency, that self-representations seeking attention such as these can be exchanged for feedback on the self and thus hold some value for girls, and the promise of a kind of empowerment. But it seems to me important to point out that girls who are judged as having "low self-esteem," as the girls of "Am I Pretty or Ugly" videos most often are in commentary, are not considered objects of value to society, and thus their media practices calling for appearance-related feedback are actively disciplined and pathologized by media commentators, and also by many commenters on YouTube offering them direct "feedback." Girls whose bodies are marked with difference on the basis of race, class, size, and physical ability are particularly abject in postfeminist neoliberal systems of affective and scopic value and exchange and are subject to harsher forms of disciplinary "feedback" from commenters on this basis (Rossie, 2015). Media hype and concern from both professionals and scholars generated by this phenomenon of girls asking for validation of their specular worth in a premise of self-production online speaks to a particular investment in "can-do" girl subjectivities in contemporary society. Can-do girls have come to be instrumental to neoliberal economies as subjects who are, ideally, conspicuous consumers, entrepreneurial, confident, self-reliant, and highly self-assured (Harris, 2004). Going to YouTube to overtly seek validation externally of one's worth and scopic value appears to define one of the current boundaries, or constitutive limits (Skeggs, 2005), of young femininity. It appears to render girls and young women "worthless," perhaps because they are considered too insecure to perform the kind of confident entrepreneurial subjectivity seen as necessary to survive, thrive, and be of value to society.

Seeking Feedback in Networked Publics

Amanda Rossie (2015) argues that the act of producing "Am I Pretty or Ugly" videos needs to be conceptualized specifically as "seeking feedback," and that responses to the videos should be framed as forms of feedback rather than simply as "comments." Rossie charts the kind of feedback received by some young girl producers through an analysis of the textual feedback provided on three of the most frequently viewed of these videos from 2012, and in so doing, helps to chart some of the contours of the postfeminist digital landscape of YouTube. She finds feedback that gives friendly yet disciplinary advice to the girls on care of the feminine self and body, providing the girls with compliments about their looks before making detailed suggestions about hair and makeup styles that viewers think would further enhance the appearance of the girl producers. She finds feedback that sexually objectifies the girls, and rates them on their appearance on the basis of whether or not sexual desire is provoked for the viewer—their "fuckability." Much feedback judges the girl producers as "sluts" and "attention whores" for making such a video: seeking appearance-based feedback in a networked public is equated by many viewers with sexual promiscuity and sexual self-objectification. As Michael Salter (2013) notes, this kind of sexual objectification and harassment has long been faced by women who enter the historically masculinized public sphere, and thus is perhaps unsurprising. I would add to Rossie's analysis that much of the feedback girls receive here equates such public calls for attention and evaluation from others as signaling a lack of moral worth and respectable and ethical "personhood." For example, one of the viewers Rossie cites tells the video producer she should "eat some makeup" so she will be pretty on the inside (Rossie, 2015, p. 17). Another category of feedback draws from religious and multiculturalist discourses to suggest that "everyone" is or can choose to see themselves as "pretty," and as precious and valued, through adopting a view aligned with either the celebration of human diversity, or the perspective that in God's eyes "we are all beautiful."

What I think needs to be further articulated here is the way in which much of this feedback *simply answers the question* posed by the girls, without further judgment or abuse. That is, much of this feedback indicates the willingness of the online public called forth here to participate by responding to the request of these girls to help them assess their scopic worth. A scroll through comments on some of the most highly viewed of these videos reveals many *brief* positive answers to the question posed by the girls, such as "pretty" or "very pretty," as well as what appears to be only the odd answer of "ugly." I decided to try to quantify this observation by doing an analysis of the most recent hundred comments left on three of the most highly viewed of these videos.[3] It would appear that the majority of these comments are indeed simply, short, positive answers to the question posed by the girls. What I discovered was that negative comments, while not indicative of the general tone of feedback left on the videos, do appear most prominently as "top comments" on these videos because negative comments garner the most number of *replies*. Most of the replies to negative comments chastise the rudeness of the commenter, and reassure the girls of their prettiness. Thus, a quick browse of these videos can give an inaccurate impression of the weight of negative comments. Out of a total of 300 of the most recent comments on the three videos, the vast majority of comments answer the question in brief and simple terms. I counted 228 comments providing positive feedback to the girls. Out of these positive comments, 153 are *brief, simple,* positive answers, and another 75 comments offer a positive reply with added commentary about the import of "self-esteem," and/or paternalistic advice about using the Internet "more safely" in future. That is, some viewers tell the girls they are pretty, but they need to "beware" and not post such questions because of all of the "other" cruel people on the Internet who will "tear up your self-esteem," as one piece of feedback advises. Some viewers also respond empathetically by telling the girl producers that they are indeed pretty, and that their need for validation of this is relatable and understandable. Overall I counted 54 clearly negative comments out of the 300. Of these 54 negative comments, half provide a brief and simple negative answer to the question posed, while the other half expand with more vulgar and offensive details. Thus, from my analysis of 300 comments, most simply answer the question, and do so in positive terms, and *warnings* about cruelty and abuse from others appear to be more prevalent than negative or abusive responses themselves.

A key feature of our notion of "the public" according to Michael Warner (2002), is that it is made up of individuals who are not typically known to one another—strangers brought together primarily through their naming, or interpellation, as a "public." One of the things media and scholarly commentary about these videos has missed is the way in which there are publics called forth regularly online, made up of individuals who are most often strangers to each other, and yet, who often appear willing to be mobilized and to participate when asked to offer help in a wide variety of ways (Thomas, Waldram, and Walker, 2014). This is more obviously evident in trends such as crowd-sourced funding of arts and charity projects and political activism via social media (Castells, 2012; Gerbaudo, 2012). In a small but, I would suggest, important way, relationality, and the mobilization of a public of who respond with feedback when asked to do so, is a part of what is happening here.

Questioning Assumptions About Girls, Media, and Feedback from Networked Publics

What do we immediately assume about these girls, their intentions in producing such digital self-representations, the reactions of a "judging public" (Nurka, 2014), and the effects of receiving public judgment, all at once and immediately, in order to produce discursive and affective reactions of horror and dismay? Women are often encouraged toward and celebrated for entrepreneurial practices that rely on self-branding, attention seeking, and commodification of one's own body (Banet-Weiser, 2012), and particularly toward entrepreneurial practices centering around fashion and beauty (Harris, 2004). Yet, these particular media practices of explicitly seeking attention and scopic validation from others are dominantly positioned in terms of a lack of confidence, self-esteem, and moral values that must be disciplined. I contend that this is because these self-representations are viewed through a *premise of self-production*: they are seen as psychosocially and intrinsically motivated rather than as an entrepreneurial practice of self-branding or creativity. I want to note and unpack several assumptions in the public discursive and affective responses to these videos. First, a key assumption in much of the public commentary around the videos is that only girls who are already "vulnerable," who do not yet know "themselves" or their own "self-worth" would ask for appearance feedback publicly. This seems like a curious notion to me. It is also worth keeping in mind that the kind of self-knowledge and "self-esteem" suggested through such commentary is a relatively recent requirement of subjectivity, and the call to this kind of deep self-knowledge has generated whole disciplines and industries of psy-sciences and "self-help" (Rose, 1996; Illouz, 2008). It is worth considering the ways in which horror and dismay around this particular digital "girl in crisis" figure help to generate and maintain a market for self-esteem and self-actualization (Banet-Weiser, 2014), rather than positioning "self-worth" as an object or affect that these girls *lack*, as the publicized commentary about these videos tends to do.

Next, posting a video seeking appearance-based feedback is positioned as a "dangerous" media practice in the commentary that circulates around these videos, as well as in the comments left by viewers addressed directly to the girls, one that could potentially "destroy" the video maker psychologically. Professionals and scholars sought for comment about these videos appear to operate from the shared assumption that the public of strangers called forth is a nasty, abusive, and threatening one. A victim-blaming logic underlies cries of danger here similarly to the way in which I have suggested it operates in the framing of sexting as dangerous for girls (see chapter 4). Offensive feedback is assumed as an *inevitable* response to posting such videos in a networked public. We need to remember that it is abusive and sexist feedback that may potentially be harmful to girls, not the act of making a video asking for appearance feedback itself, or posting it in a networked public. When girls' practices of making and posting self-representational videos are labelled as "dangerous" or "risky," the possibility is obscured that such videos might generate any other kinds of responses from the networked public called forth. The "wrongfulness" of negative or abusive comments is also conflated with the "harm" potentially experienced by young girl video producers, as I have suggested about youth sexting, following Woodiwiss (2014). Thus, the possibility is also obscured that even abusive comments *might not* cause the mental breakdown, self-destruction, or "vertiginous disorientation" of the video producer herself. It is telling that several of the most highly circulated videos from 2012 have not been taken down yet by the girls who posted them, who continue to receive both positive and negative feedback from viewers.

Seeking public validation of one's looks is viewed as immoral by many commentators on this phenomenon. It is seen to demonstrate both a lack of self-worth and an excess of self-focus that has no value to society. Maldonado's (2013) article is a good example of this perspective. She writes of "Am I Pretty or Ugly" videos, "What these girls should be asking is not how they look to the rest of the world, but how they can give, out of their own unique abilities, to the world." The girl who publicly represents herself as not completely autonomous, self-reliant, and confident becomes positioned as *excessively self-focused* and narcissistic. In navigating heterosexy performativity, as discussed in chapter 3, girls must tread carefully to find a path between representing the self as "heterosexy" and not as excessively "sexualized." In performing the psychological traits of a confident, powerful, and valued femininity online (and perhaps in schools, job markets, and elsewhere) girls and young women perhaps walk a similarly fine line when trying to represent the self as confident and autonomously esteemed, but not overly self-focused or narcissistic. Banet-Weiser notes that the apparent forming of "online communities" around the production of such videos, through viewers interacting with the girls and each other, was reported as a particularly distressing and controversial aspect of this phenomenon in news media coverage (2014, p. 84). I think this is suggestive of a broader pathologization of digital spaces as places for community formation through relationality and exchange of feedback. Part of what becomes pathologized and abjected in the discursive and affective reactions to these videos is the young female feedback-seeking subject herself—a subject who is *not invulnerable*, but relational, not autonomous, but *heavily invested in and reliant upon feedback and attention from others*, and not just to increase her material wealth and value.

Last, it is important to note the way appearance-based feedback from strangers is assumed to be a particularly *meaningless*, but also *damaging*, form of feedback on the self. The assumption is that one's own specular worth is a faulty or inaccurate measure of self-value; as Nurka puts it, an "ultimately unsatisfying criteria upon which to map one's place in the world" (2014, p. 6). These videos make plain and obvious what often remains hidden in the logics of post-feminist culture: that for women especially, physical appearance is still strongly tied to one's social worth and exchange value. Female bodies that are judged as highly valued in terms of prettiness, hotness, and sexiness, are highly circulated through media, and are able to be exchanged for high material worth (as Hakim, 2011, and some other feminist theorists, problematically in my view, encourage women to "take advantage" of). Entrepreneurial self-branding and self-commodification is not, despite dominant neoliberal rhetoric to the contrary, a meritocratic route to material profit: it is not something that all individuals potentially profit from to the same degree regardless of bodily difference, race, class, and gender identity, by circulating the self-as-brand (Marwick, 2013). "Am I Pretty or Ugly," as a question in the postfeminist cultural context, is not so much a "misrecognition" of the self, I would suggest, but a recognition of the scopic economy where certain bodies and faces are indeed highly valued and seen as potential pathways for girls and women to "empowerment" and material success.

These videos thus make obvious the sexist standards that are often obscured by postfeminist discourses of "choice" and "empowerment" vis-à-vis fashion and beauty practices. Girls and women are encouraged by fashion and beauty industries to engage in laborious practices of self-discipline to meet narrow cultural standards of beauty. Feminist scholars have been documenting the workings of, and sexist practices within, the fashion and beauty industry for decades now. They have outlined the ways contemporary postfeminist culture, fashion, and beauty are marketed to women as "choices," as practices that women can choose to participate in for fun, personal pleasure, and "empowerment," despite the fact that women's social acceptance and worth is still heavily determined by whether or not they "choose" to participate in gender-normative bodily "care," and are able to meet narrow raced and classed standards of attractiveness (Faludi, 1992; Bordo, 1993; Wolf, 1991; Jeffreys, 2005; Gill, 2007; McRobbie, 2009; Gill and Scharff, 2011). These young girl video producers seem *earnest* in their desire for confirmation of worth from an other. They do not come across as confident or empowered, nor as "ironic," playful, or disinvested in the question. These self-produced self-representations thus undermine and clash with popularized ideals that, in postfeminist society, it is one's personal, "internal" feelings of beauty and worth that matter most.

I have been struck most not so much by the videos themselves, which are not particularly unusual or unique in a digital culture where rating sites have become popular for everything from school and university teachers, to landlords, to dating partners, casual sex partners, and paid sex workers (Walter, 2010; Nurka, 2014). Nor are these videos unique on YouTube, where thousands of girls of a similar age range also seek feedback from viewers on their singing and dancing abilities, fashion tastes, and so on. Search, for instance, "can I sing good" to see an astounding range of videos posted by girls who appear to be between the ages of 6 and 14, asking for feedback from the networked public about their talents and abilities. I am struck most by the responses produced in public commentary on these videos, as well as my own viewing reactions, which appear to be largely assemblages of affective and discursive horror and dismay, as I have outlined. Seeking appearance feedback publicly, this phenomenon suggests, has come to be framed as one of the constitutive limits of valued contemporary young femininity. While confidence, self-reliance, and self-assurance are called forth as key features of postfeminist femininity, as argued in the previous chapter, seeking appearance feedback publicly has become a boundary point which if crossed, young feminine subjects appear to be judged as *lacking* in self-worth, as *excessively* self-focused (narcissistic), and thus of no value to society.

Girls in Crisis: Seeking Help in Networked Publics

If girls seeking appearance feedback publicly mark a constitutive limit of postfeminist young femininity, representing the self as suffering and in need of help in networked publics moves one well past the boundaries of girl-powered postfeminist femininity and clearly into the realm of the "girl in crisis." I first became aware of a particular genre of video blog on YouTube after the death of 15-year-old Amanda Todd, who hanged herself in her bedroom in Canada on October 10, 2012. Just weeks before her death Todd posted a video on YouTube in which she tells her story of victimization and abuse that occurred both on and offline, and describes related drug and alcohol use, self-harm, anxiety, and suicide attempts. Todd uses hand-written flash cards, held up to show a sentence or two at a time, and an emotive music soundtrack to narrate her experiences of bullying, abuse, and also self-injury, depression, and anxiety. Approximately two years before her death Todd showed her breasts briefly to a man in his early twenties on a video chat website. After she did so, he blackmailed her for more images, and exposed Todd's privately sent picture to her peers online. Todd describes suffering anxiety and depression. She moved schools. A year after the original incident, the individual who blackmailed Todd created a Facebook profile using Todd's topless photograph as the profile picture, and contacted classmates at her new school. Todd moved and changed schools again, and continued to face bullying online and offline. She was assaulted during a physical fight with another girl over a boy with whom she had slept, and a suicide attempt followed this incident. Todd experienced bullying and abuse online and offline by a number of different people, related to a number of different incidents, over a period of several years. She practiced self-injury and attempted suicide during this time. In her final YouTube video she pleads directly with viewers for help. She tells viewers, "My anxiety is horrible now never went out this summer." She tells viewers that despite seeing a therapist and being on antidepressants she is "constantly cutting" and "really depressed."

YouTube videos surface that are algorithmically flagged as similar/related to Todd's video. These videos have several stylistic features in common, such as: the use of hand-written flash cards to tell a story while the subject remains mute; use of a black and white film setting; and an "emo" ballad soundtrack. Many such videos predate Todd's. Naming conventions also emerge: videos made in this style come up repeatedly under titles such as "my bullying story," "my self-harm story," "my secrets," "if you really knew me," and "hi my name is [. . .]." For example, a search for "my bullying story" brings up around 384,000 videos. A browse of the first 50 of these videos suggests that teenage girls feature in them most prominently. As Jen Gilbert notes (2015), this style of video has also been taken up by young men and women describing experiences of homophobia and homophobic bullying or harassment at school. These issues are shaped by gender and sexuality. Research indicates that rates of suicide and self-harm practices remain higher for nonheterosexual youth (Rasmussen, 2006; Cover, 2012b). Feminist scholars have also charted the cultural feminization of dieting and food deprivation practices (Bordo, 1993) and self-injury practices (Brickman, 2004). The videos featuring boys tend to convey experiences of homophobic abuse, although not all of the male subjects of such videos identify as gay, bisexual, transgender, or queer. The stories told by girls in this format prominently feature stories of self-harm of various kinds, anxiety, sexualized and homophobic bullying, slut shaming, and gender-based harassment on and offline. Many girls describe stories of the bullying they face or once faced at school and/or online, while others describe experiences of intense grief after the death of a parent or friend. Many describe a combination of self-injury, eating disorders, and drug and alcohol use as a source of pain and suffering itself, and as a way of coping with various painful experiences.

Narrative conventions can also be noted around the telling of these painful gendered stories in flash card style. For example, many of these videos begin with the producers writing to viewers: "Hi. My name is [. . .]. Most people know me as a happy person." They will often perform a deliberately affected "happy face" by smiling, before going on to describe this outward cheerfulness and strength as a front. The middle sections describe painful emotional states and associated stories. Inwardly, these video producers often admit, they are weak, depressed, anxious, and suffering. Girls admit to crying alone every night and describe feelings of pressure to live up to a "confident" and "happy" performativity that they can no longer bear, or that they feel is not authentic. A revelation is performed in such videos that the confidence and happiness usually communicated by these young female subjects in their everyday lives is a front. Sometimes there is a "happy ending," in which the video producers say they are better now. Some videos have a pedagogical message, telling viewers in the same situation to seek help and talk to someone, affirming that there will be *someone* who cares about them. But hope is not always communicated. Sometimes these stories end with explicit cries for help. Todd, for example, ends her video by describing a recent suicide attempt, and pleading with viewers for support, stating, "I have nobody. I need somebody." Such flash card style videos, especially those produced by girls, have become more visible since Todd's death. This particular style of narration has also now been somewhat institutionalized via its appropriation in a Canadian cybersafety campaign by The Children of the Street Foundation, designed to respond specifically to Todd's death.

Elsewhere I have discussed the political significance of girls' literal silence in this particular flash card format for narrating pain suffering on YouTube, terming these videos as "pain memes." I argue that the appropriation of this style in the Children of the Street cybersafety campaign does a kind of violence to Todd and to other girls who have been harassed and abused online, appropriating their representational conventions to connote a message of self-blame and responsibilization (Dobson, 2015). Here I want to frame such videos as part of a broader phenomenon of girls using digital networks to narrate and/or mediate their experiences of pain and suffering, build communities of support, and seek help.

Girls Narrating and Mediating Pain in Networked Publics

In addition to girls' and young women's YouTube videos describing stories of pain, Tumblr and Instagram blogs, and other online forums focused around the narration and mediation of experiences of pain and suffering, self-injury and cutting, and various eating disorders are another hotspot of concern for commentators and professionals invested in youth, and girls in particular. I describe these media practices, representations, and online communities under the rubric of girls "narrating" and "mediating" pain online. With the term *narrating* pain I wish to capture here the various ways in which girls and young women use online spaces to post expressions and stories of their experiences of living with, struggling to overcome, and/or recovery from, for instance, depression, self-cutting, and anorexia. With the term *mediating* pain I wish to capture the ways in which girls and young women also use such spaces to visually document or describe in vivid detail pain, and various kinds of practices that harm the self and body, in a more immediate sense: through, for example, posting images of one's fresh self-cuts, or posting descriptions of techniques for injuring one's body or depriving one's body of food.

Public responses to girls asking about their prettiness online reveal a concern with the state of "girls in the West today" more generally, a concern about the possibility that the confident, idealized figure of girl power may be a sham, lost, or under threat. Self-representations narrating or mediating experiences of pain produce feminine subjects that are more clearly seen as temporally "in crisis" rather than "at risk." Such representations are thought to be made by girls and young women who are already "diagnosable" in some way, subjects who are seen as possessing particular affects or symptoms that produce them as pathological. The concern with girls and young women who narrate and mediate experiences of pain in networked publics seems to be that pain, as both a bodily state and emotion (Scarry, 1985; Spelman, 1997; Ahmed, 2004; Pavlidis and Fullagar, 2014), is contagious and spreadable via digital networks; that through its circulation it will spread and infect girls in particular, who are seen as vulnerable (Johansson, 2014, p. 28). Indeed, the "contagious" nature of emotion is seen as a well-evidenced phenomena in the field of psychology, and recent research in this field claims to have found evidence suggesting that emotion is contagious (although not particularly contagious) via SNSs (Kramer, Guillory, and Hancock, 2014). These claims have, however, been hotly contested due to the very small effects found, the subjective nature of the "emotional language" scale used to measure positive and negative emotion on Facebook, and the inability to contextualize the emotive language used in posts and thus account for sarcasm and irony (van Ryn and Fordyce, 2014). The concern of pain spreading digitally, I would suggest, is not entirely unfounded, but perhaps fails to capture the complexity of how "affects are produced as effects of circulation" (Ahmed, 2004, p. 8), in the assumption of a simplistic model of direct media effects or psychological "triggering."

While there are important differences among various media practices such as expressing pain textually, narrating recovery from it, depicting/documenting it, and promoting or fetishizing it, the lines and boundaries between such practices are blurry, unstable, and in constant temporal flux, as are the emotions and experiences of media producers in pain. Distinguishing between "therapeutic" and "harmful/promotional" representations of pain and self-harm content involves making judgments about a poster's intent and a viewers' interpretation and experience of viewing, which are all highly variable and can be difficult to pinpoint. As scholars have suggested, this has tended to lead to blanket bans and censorship of any online content deemed to *potentially* promote various kinds of pain and self-harm (boyd, Ryan, and Leavitt, 2010; Johannson, 2014). As Anna Johansson charts, in 2012 Tumblr instituted a ban on blogs seen as promoting self-injury, and other photography-based SNSs and blog hosts have since followed suit (Johannson, 2014, p. 17). Johansson suggests that YouTube is seen as a particular site of risk, on which "it is the very display of and approach to bodily marks that puts a video at risk of being heavily criticized or even removed" (2014, p. 24). As Johansson notes, similar kinds of concern from media and health professionals has occurred around online sites seen to promote eating disorders, leading to censorship of content deemed "pro ana" by some Internet service providers (2014, p. 25). As I discuss in brief here, a small but growing body of research examines self-harm digital media practices and communities, which appear to predominantly involve girls and young women. We might summarize the hypothesis put forth by health professionals and media commentators that mediation and discussion of painful and self-harming practices in networked publics will "trigger" some viewers to experience pain or engage in self-harmful practices themselves (boyd et al., 2009; Johansson, 2014), and the research I discuss later seeks to investigate such claims.

I am interested in trying to understand what the public representation of such gendered narratives and mediations of pain does, provoked by Ahmed's question "what does pain do" (2004, p. 27). I want to know here: what does the representation of particular gendered forms of pain and suffering in networked publics do for girls and young women who produce them? If it is of concern that the digital narration and mediation of pain has caused or will cause more of it to spread, it seems pertinent to try to understand what it is girls are doing when they represent their pain publicly. What I want to first unpack in these final sections of the chapter is the way in which the figure of the "girl in pain" is called forth by postfeminist logics of representation, even as she is disavowed. She is a girl figure who demonstrates her compliance with femininity, while also demonstrating a kind of "postfeminist knowledge" that compliance with femininity is normatively painful and difficult. I also want to suggest that girls who narrate and mediate pain online cannot be thought of as completely "territorialized" (Colebrook, 2002) self-governing, self-responsibilized subjects. Their media practices of narrating and mediating pain via networked publics suggest, or speak explicitly to, desires for connection, relationality, and social support.[4] They appear also to mobilize "counter-publics" (Fraser, 1992; Warner, 2002) outside the boundaries of, and often in opposition to, authorized providers of help and support—outside of institutions and professionals who are socially sanctioned to monitor and manage girls in pain.

Demonstrating "Gender Awareness" via Painful Self-Representation

Angela McRobbie (2009) articulates the ways in which feminism has been "taken into account" and repudiated as no longer necessary in various cultural practices, discourses, and representations in the postfeminist sociocultural landscape. Part of this process of the acknowledgment and rejection of key tenets of feminism has involved acknowledging "gender troubles" or "female complaints" as normative, she suggests. Increasingly, experiences of pain, anxiety, self-esteem issues, and body-acceptance issues are framed as par for the course of growing up a girl. McRobbie argues that "Popular culture is asking young women to get used to *gender melancholia*, and to recognize themselves and each other within its terms" (2009, p. 115). As I discuss in chapter 2, she suggests that that signs of "gender distress" such as self-cutting, dieting, anorexia, and expressions of low self-esteem are being normalized for girls and young women in popular postfeminist media culture. Social media can be seen as also part of this normalization of "gender melancholia," as it provides young women with opportunities to publicly express and advertise their "pain, anxiety and self-loathing" (p. 116), she suggests. Such experiences and affects are also discursively positioned in this cultural landscape as "predictable and treatable, things to be managed medically rather than subjected to sustained social scrutiny" (2009, p. 112).

Perhaps then, the "girl in pain" figure—the girl who uses social media to speak or write publicly of her low self-esteem, depression, body-images issues, eating disorders, and self-injury habits—is called into being as a normative and accepted, if not always highly valued, feminine subject. She is a figure who legitimates femininity as a painful but desirable embodied state. Femininity has long been theorized by feminist scholars as a subject position and embodied state which can and frequently does result in depression, anxiety, and body-image obsession as one tries to achieve and maintain it (Brownmiller, 1984; Bordo, 1993; Brumberg, 1997). As McRobbie suggests, in the postfeminist era it has been more widely acknowledged in public discourse that being " 'culturally intelligible' as a girl makes one ill. But by today's standards, that is almost acceptable" (2009, p. 97). Via the public narration and mediation of experiences of pain and suffering that circulate around emotional states such as depression, anxiety, and grief, and the bodily practices involved in self-injury, anorexia, and bulimia, girls and young women are perhaps able to demonstrate their "knowledge" of feminine subjectivity and embodiment as both a desirable and a plagued condition. That is, public self-representations of pain online may do the double work of signaling a desire or attempt to achieve ideal youthful feminine subjectivity—to achieve a fit, skinny, and heterosexy body and an attitude of girl-powered self-confidence and happiness—while also demonstrating one's "gender awareness" that this subjectivity remains near impossible for most girls to live, and its pursuit can be deathly. Feminism, and feminist knowledge of the pain of femininity can perhaps be "taken into account" in such self-representations in a way that does not necessarily prompt or suggest the need for social or political action.

Following McRobbie's suggestions about the pathologization of femininity via the cultural logics of postfeminism, I suggest that the girls in pain depicted in "pain meme"-style YouTube videos are called forth in postfeminist digital cultures, not as figures of high social and economic value, but perhaps as figures of *low cost* both economically and politically. As McRobbie suggests, it may be better "to be an ill girl than a girl who gets up out of her sickbed and challenges the power of the heterosexual matrix" (2009, p. 96). The circulation of these girls in pain in digital networks produces affects of an individualized, psychopathologized feminine pain, a pain for which *the self* appears to be both the cause and the cure. But, as I argue, self-representations produced by girls and young women narrating and mediating pain cannot be theorized as completely "territorialized" by the post-social imperatives of self-responsibility and self-governmentality. Key here is that through the narration and mediation of pain online, these girls, like the girls of "Am I Pretty or Ugly," also publicly express desires for connection and relationality, and mobilize publics of "strangers" into "counter-publics" and communities of support. They *make public* the more painful aspects of contemporary femininity that, in the logics of postfeminism, are ideally supposed to be managed individually and privately.

Forming Counter-Publics through Pain

Self-injury, cutting, and suicide websites represent a particularly potent and literal manifestation of girls' and young women's narrations and mediations of pain online. Research into such sites tends to support the claim that these sites function to mobilize what I suggest can be thought of as "counter-publics" (Fraser, 1992) or alternative "communities of support" (Wehlage, 1989). The use of these sites has been investigated in an effort to assess the opportunities and risks for those who produce and consume self-harmful content online. Self-injury related sites, it is suggested, allow participants the possibility of connecting and interacting with others who self-injure or are suicidal (Murray and Fox, 2006; Adler and Adler, 2011; Lewis, Heath, Sornberger, and Arbuthnott, 2012; Rodham et al., 2013), and foster a sense of "belonging" to a community (Baker and Fortune, 2008, p. 120). Murray and Fox surveyed 102 self-injurers online, recruited from an online community, seeking to determine whether digital connectivity between participants alleviates or exacerbates the problem (Murray and Fox, 2006, p. 3). Of their participants, 95 were female and 6 were male. The majority of participants said there had been no change or a decrease in their behavior since using the site from which they were recruited, and 10 reported an increase (2006, p. 4). The authors conclude, still, that overall their data suggest "either no change or a reduction in the frequency and severity of self-harming behaviour" (2006, p. 7). Lewis and colleagues (2012) examined comments on popular YouTube videos depicting self-injury as a way of assessing the impact of such content on viewers. They find that most of the comments on such videos are posted by individuals sharing their own experiences of "non-suicidal self-injury" (NSSI) (Lewis et al., 2012, p. 383). Comments expressing messages of support were common, while hostile comments were much less frequent in their sample (2012, p. 383). Comments mentioning that the videos "triggered" the viewer to want to engage in NSSI were rare (2012, p. 384), and some viewers mentioned that seeing the video deterred them from feeling triggered. They conclude that discussing and viewing NSSI online presents an opportunity to "receive validation and connect with others who share similar experiences" (p. 384).

Rodham and colleagues (2013) describe five key motivations for posters from a thematic analysis they conducted of 423 posts about NSSI experiences on a popular website. Posting pictures and text about NSSI presented posters with an opportunity to "confess" without any expectation of interaction (Rodham et al., 2013, p. 176). They found that posters sometimes marked "turning points" such as resolutions to stop or changes in behavior (2013, p. 177); expressed a desire for their posts to deter others from self-harmful behavior (p. 177); and sought to dispel myths about those who engage in NSSI and raise awareness about the problem (p. 178). The authors suggest that for posters to the forum, the opportunity to give and receive support from peers outside the medical community was important. Medical professionals, they note, were often perceived as not genuine because they are paid to listen (2013, p. 179). Similarly, Baker and Fortune note how "markedly different" the accounts of their participants were to the accounts about self-harmful online content provided in news media and by health professionals (2008, p. 121). They interviewed users of self-injury and suicide websites about their motivations for doing so. All ten of their participants were between 18 and 30 and all but one was female. The authors summarize the opportunities of turning online in terms of "empathetic understanding," "community," and "coping" (2008, p. 119). Their participants described the value of such sites for receiving understanding from others going through similar experiences, feeling a sense of belonging to a community, and as a strategy for coping with daily emotions. Some participants felt such sites supported their recovery "better than any therapy could" (2008, p. 121). As they note, the prevalence of "antipsychiatric attitudes" on these sites has led to their condemnation as "dangerous" by health care authorities, rather than to a questioning of the effectiveness of current therapeutic approaches. They suggest that many young people who are depressed or suicidal and engaging in self-harmful bodily practices may find the interventions of medicos "inaccessible, ineffective or aversive to the extent that they prefer to turn to alternatives online" (Baker and Fortune, 2008, p. 121). "Help" from authorized professionals is, as Baker and Fortune have noted, perceived by many self-injurers as not just ineffective but threatening and sometimes abusive (2008, p. 121).

The Antithesis of Girl Power?

In a sociocultural context where girls and young women have been publicly and visibly encouraged to speak loudly and confidently, narrating and mediating pain online can be seen as a refusal to speak on the terms and to the audience encouraged. Girls and young women narrating and mediating pain online speak with uncertainty and affective vulnerability, if they speak at all. As I have noted, many hold up signs to tell their stories of pain, or communicate primarily via text and image blogs. Girls and young women who narrate and mediate pain online make the injuries of gender public and visible, sometimes quite literally in the case of those who mediate self-injury and cutting experiences. I would not suggest that narrating and mediating pain is always consciously or necessarily a "resistant" media practice, but that seeking help and support, and reciprocating this in the communities in which they participate, as Skeggs notes (2014), does itself speak against the dominant logic of *value* so privileged in postfeminist and neoliberal societies, whereby the creation of material worth is valued above all else and caring for others is devalued. It speaks against the self-assuredness, confidence, and autonomy of the highly valued postfeminist figure of girl power.

The use by young women of social media sites such as YouTube, Tumblr, and Instagram, positions this media as likely intended for an audience of peers and young people rather than adult authorities. Both the medium and the forms of expression employed in girls' pain meme videos are often not easily accessible to adult medical and healthcare authorities. The act of narrating and mediating pain in networked publics thus itself perhaps complicates a theorization of these media producers as "self-governed" "neoliberalized" subjects. Self-representations of girls in pain may perpetuate self-responsibilization as the solution to "gender troubles" at the same time as they contradict sharply the happiness and confidence promised by girl power, producing and circulating instead affects of discontent, sadness, anger, vulnerability, and dependence. At least in the case of online self-injury communities, participation appears to mobilize unauthorized communities of support. The connectivity through pain, the relationality, and community formation via negative emotions, as well as the rejection of professionally sanctioned forms of help, appear to be sources of fear and concern in media and professional discourses about self-harmful digital content. These media producers use the tools of digital connectivity to enlist support and care outside the boundaries of institutions and professionals authorized to survey and intervene—outside of what Foucault has called the "technologies of the soul" (Foucault, 1991, p. 178).

Conclusion

Rather than perform confidence and girl-powered autonomy, the girls discussed in this chapter mediate more explicitly practices of seeking attention, sociality, external validation, and support from others. When the need for social validation of worth, approval of the self, approval of one's face and body from others, and the seeking of relational support is made explicit via mediated public performances, this is seen to epitomize crisis. As Banet-Weiser has argued (2014, 2015), the "girl in crisis" figure generates a certain value herself in that she helps to create and sustain a market in "self-esteem" and whole industries dedicated to investing girls with "empowerment." A lack of self-worth is seen to demand intervention to invest the girl subject with a sense of her own value and values. In affective and scopic economies performing a sense of confidence in one's own worth publicly can make girls economically and morally valued subjects, and this value also potentially increases as the circulation of girls' own images increases. On the other hand, performative public mediations seeking "feedback" from others, and attention, help, and support, appear to be judged as practices that demonstrate the female subject's own lack of self-worth, her lack of value and values. The responses to "Am I Pretty or Ugly" videos, as well as to girls and young women who narrate and mediate pain in networked publics thus leads me to question the ways in which patterns of pathologization and medicalization may be expanding along gendered lines to encompass not just certain mental and psychological states, feelings, and desires, but also mediated practices of seeking feedback, attention, and relationality from "publics" who are not sanctioned to provide such.

Afterword

Notes on Visibility and Self-Exposure

In January 2015 Sport England launched its new promotional video *This Girl Can*.[1] Within a month the video had received over two and a half million views on YouTube. The video opens with a shot of a fleshy, slightly "jiggly" female body in a bikini, walking toward the edge of a pool. The camera follows her from behind and cuts to a close-up of her bottom as she adjusts her bikini, pulling the Lycra over her flesh with a "snap" sound. The brief one-and-a-half-minute video depicts both girls *and* women of various ages, body shapes, sizes, and skin colors running, dancing, boxing, riding exercise bikes, and playing sports. The footage, much of which is in slow motion, is accompanied by Missy Elliott's hit song *Get Ur Freak On*. The girls and women are depicted *in action*, kicking and throwing balls, punching boxing bags, and falling down "knackered." They are shown sweating profusely, and their flesh moves as they run and bounce up and down vigorously on dancefloors. Slogans are superimposed across the bodies of the women on screen, including "Sweating like a pig, feeling like a fox," "I jiggle, therefore I am," and "I kick balls. Deal with it." The tagline posted on YouTube about this video states: "*This Girl Can* celebrates the women who are doing their thing no matter how they do it, how they look, or even how sweaty they get. They're here to inspire us to wiggle, jiggle, move and prove that judgment is a barrier that can be overcome."[2]

To my mind, this video *incites* judgment by inviting us to *view* girls and women no matter what they are doing, where they are doing it, or how they look doing it. As Simone Fullagar and Jessica Francombe-Webb point out, the reference to women of all ages as "girls" will not be appreciated by all women. Nor is the kind of active, girl-powered, "can do" version of femininity offered up here by any means available to, or desired by, all women (Fullagar and Francombe-Webb, 2015).

Exposure and visibility is central to this kind of postfeminist femininity, as I suggest throughout this book, and this is a significant limitation of its appeal. The centrality of exposure and visibility to postfeminist femininity is significant to consider in relation to flows of power (Banet-Weiser, 2011, 2012). In *This Girl Can* the camera invites us to gaze at the bodies and moving flesh of girls and women in a way that, to me, feels quite voyeuristic and fetishistic; perhaps no less so than the male-directed film noir and Busby Berkeley films analyzed by Laura Mulvey in making her argument that the gaze of the camera in film is constructed as male[3] (and heterosexual) (Mulvey, 1975/1989). The girls' and women's bodies here connote, as Mulvey puts it, "to-be-looked-at-ness." They are depicted in public and private locations, and the camera appears to have no boundaries in its exploration of their bodies, focusing close-up on a hand touching a bottom, on breasts and thighs wobbling, and on chins dripping with sweat and saliva. Hence, perhaps, my feeling of voyeurism as a viewer. Other shots are more fetishistic. For example, several shots depict young female bodies together on a dancefloor, with breasts and bottoms shaking vigorously, marked by the words, "Sweating like a pig, feeling like a fox." Another close-up depicts a young, blonde, white woman's face. She is panting, dripping with sweat, and her face is moving up and down in slow motion as she bounces on an exercise bike. This shot is accompanied by the words "Damn right I look hot." It is hard to imagine male bodies being depicted in a similar way and claimed as a "celebration" and "empowering" to men.

This video is intended as an invitation to women to own their own bodies and to use them how they want to, regardless of the judgments of others. But at the same time, women are reminded that "others" are implicitly *authorized to view and judge female bodies.* The camera here surveys and exposes these women's bodies; it is women themselves who must deal with this by learning to "overcome" feelings of judgment. The cultural conditions that facilitate the everyday judgment of women's bodies, and the cultural assumption that women's bodies are *public objects* up for judgment (Nurka, 2014; Ringrose and Harvey, 2015; Salter, forthcoming), does need to be challenged. But I would suggest that this kind of spectacular display of female bodies reinforces, rather than challenges, these cultural conditions. The message also patronizingly assumes that fear of these conditions of *assumed and authorized public judgment* might stop girls and women from participating in exercise (rather than, say, care and work duties and other time-prohibitive activities). As Fullagar and Francombe-Webb (2015) suggest, such campaigns might instead focus on the physical, emotional, and relational benefits of exercise, and locate sport and exercise "outside the cult of body worship and display." Girls and women are made visible, and their bodies are exposed in quite intimate ways and settings, under a guise of empowerment and celebration. While a culture of judgment is acknowledged, girls and women are told that they can overcome feelings of judgment via continued participation and visibility.

This kind of self and body exposure and visibility, especially as it is tied to notions of power for girls and women, is a key feature of femininity in the postfeminist, girl-powered cultural context. Girls and young women are invited, and sometimes culturally required, to participate in intimate forms of self and body exposure online under similar promises of power and self-actualization. While the media for digital self-representation change frequently, this message of continual visibility and self and body exposure, and visibility as a source of or means to power and social and material value for girls and young women (Banet-Weiser, 2012), has remained consistent for some time now. Girls and young women are still positioned as having to define themselves in response to, and against, the perceived weakness, passivity, and *dependence* of traditional femininity. As Emilie Zaslow writes:

> Girl power media culture is both a point of production and a mode of expression that shifts the ways in which we conceptualize femininity. In this new model, some elements of traditional femininity (beauty, care, and sexiness) are retained while others (passivity, weakness, and dependence) are met with a feminist reimagining so that girls are repositioned as active, choice-making agents. (2009, p. 158).

Making one's self and body visible and exposed digitally can be seen as part of the project of defining and defending the postfeminist self against femininity as shyness, coyness, weakness, and passivity; as well as demonstrating self-alignment with notions of feminine heterosexiness through one's own body and/or aesthetic style. Throughout this book I have problematized the kind of idealized and popular femininity which structures and frames young women's engagements with digital media. I have made several key points I want to summarize here, about postfeminist femininity and its logics of value, especially as it is digitized and signaled visually.

First, I have questioned critically the degree of literacy and sophistication involved in visually signaling heterosexiness in postfeminist digital cultures. I suggested in chapter 3 that the kind of sexual representations I commonly encountered on young women's social network site (SNS) profiles were not ones that straightforwardly "objectified" the female bodies depicted. I suggest that the "premise of self-production" through which personal SNS profiles are framed as "authentic" and intrinsically motivated self-representations may serve to complicate the binary of object/subjecthood and foreground for viewers the profile owners' own desire, conscious, and perhaps creative, intent, her own "eye" as an object (Schneider, 1997), and her pleasure in being seen. I analyzed some images displayed by young women that could be read as confronting and highlighting gendered visual conventions around the gaze quite directly. There is much potential in social media as a means of sexual self-expression, creativity, and the representation of female sexual agency and desire in *everyday, mundane ways*, and this is very important, as I suggest later. But I remain most ambivalent about precisely these same sophisticated, potentially creative, *challenging* representations of sexuality; about the playful parody and significations of literacy around gendered gaze relations that are often apparent in the way heterosexiness is visually constructed on young women's SNS profiles. I am wary of the labor and resources potentially required for girls and young women to signify sexual agency and desire in postfeminist digital cultures in ways that are cool, legible, and heterosexy. As Gill suggests (Gill, 2003), sexual media representations of women have shifted to centrally include both subtle and not-so-subtle signals and references to desire, choice, and agency. What does it means for girls and young women who have access to digital technologies and whose social lives require them to represent the self digitally that heterosexiness now involves finding ways to gesture toward agency, to "play with" or challenge the masculinized gaze, and notions of sexual objecthood and subjecthood? I wonder about the subtle and unconscious kinds of cultural and social capital that come into play here, allowing some girls to navigate the task of digitally mediating heterosexiness more easily than others, as well as the potentially increased chances of getting cool heterosexiness "wrong" in postfeminist digital cultures. What subtle differences factor in when girls and young women are judged by peers or adults as more straightforwardly an object or a slut, as sexual but *unsophisticated*, a *victim* rather than an *agent* of sexualization? And how do such judgments intersect with embodied identities and experiences of socioeconomic status, race, ethnicity, sexuality, and physical ability?

The prevalence of postfeminist, girl-powered media discourses and representations of sexuality and "sexual subjectification" (Gill, 2003) as agentically chosen, fun, pleasurable, and empowering for women has not necessarily translated into obvious shifts in sexual double standards in the social lives of girls and women. And this construct potentially serves to make normative, legible sexual subjectification an even narrower field of possibilities for young women. Recent panics about girls and sexualization may also serve to further narrow accepted sexual subjectification for girls and young women through encouraging their heightened surveillance. Our conversations with young people about sexting and cybersafety, discussed in chapter 4, illustrate the point that producing a digital identity that can be judged by peers as heterosexy but not "slutty" or "sexualized" involves a great deal of work, strategy, and negotiation. We were surprised at just how prevalent the word "slut" was in our conversations with both boys and girls about gender and cybersafety; at the extent to which girls described feeling policed in their everyday behavior by boys using this label; and also at the extent to which girls' distanced themselves from any claims of sexual "attention seeking," of *sexual desire or agency*, by labeling the behavior of other girls seen to seek sexual attention as "slutty." In short, the kind of gender politics and social experiences described to us around digital sexual self-representation and sexuality do not match with the kind of messages about sexual liberation, empowerment, and agency that prevail in postfeminist popular media cultures.[4] Our discussions suggest that even rather tame sexually suggestive self-images posted on SNSs would not be easily accepted by peers, even for girls whose bodies meet narrow standards of attractive femininity, as any kind of digital self-representation that can be judged as intended to seek sexual attention still appears to be socially illegitimate for girls. Sexual agency and desire thus needs to remain at the forefront of discussions about girls' and young women's media practices and self-representations, as this needs to be legitimized outside the narrow and fetishistic ways it is in popular cultural representations of women. Adult stakeholders concerned with girls' and young women's well-being need to be careful not to complicate the task of femininity and sexual identity negotiation further by policing, regulating, and shaming girls' sexual expressions, digital or otherwise.

I have also indicated my ambivalence about the kind of confidence promoted as a key part of femininity in the postfeminist era, as girls and young women are called to embody feminine heterosexiness and also actively differentiate themselves from notions of feminine weakness, passivity, and dependence. The cultivation of confidence and self-esteem may be felt as a pressure by many girls and young women, particularly those subject to intensified forms of surveillance and discipline on the basis of social class, race, ethnicity, or sexuality. The social, cultural, and economic value attached to demonstrable self-esteem and confidence for girls and young women perhaps leads to a devaluing and pathologization of those whose media productions and practices are judged as indicating low self-esteem, low confidence, vulnerability, and *dependence on affirmation of the self from others*, as suggested in chapter 6. But further, I am wary of the level of transparency and self and body exposure that appears to be indicated and normalized in postfeminist models of femininity, especially as they are digitized and networked. The ways in which visibility, and self and body exposure are tied to notions of girls' and young women's self-actualization and empowerment, as Harris (2004) and Banet-Weiser (2012) suggest, are particularly questionable.

Feminist scholars have made some pertinent suggestions about the meaning of visibility and body exposure for women that provoke critical questions in relation to postfeminist femininity and the promise of power through social media visibility to young women. As Peggy Phelan argues, "fetishization of the image is the risk of representational visibility for women" (Phelan, 1993, p. 6). Phelan scrutinizes the assumption that "Increased visibility equals increased power" (1993, p. 7), arguing that, "If representational visibility equals power, then almost-naked young white women should be running Western culture" (1993, p. 10). Naomi Wolf (1991, p. 139) argues in relation to cultural inscriptions of flesh-revelation and nakedness that *exposure* has significant cultural politics and gendered power dynamics attached to it. In the West, revealing the flesh is culturally inscribed into feminine display and performativity, and girls and women are constantly reminded of this in visual culture. Wolf suggests that this may amount to a sense for girls and women not of power, but of both physical and mental vulnerability, as women's bodies are constantly "on display" for judgment and critique. The masculine body, by contrast, generally stays covered and protected, as Wolf notes. I am thus ambivalent, and concerned, about the cultural encouragement of girls and young women to display their selves and bodies via social media, and the way in which such encouragement reinforces cultural notions of the female body as "to be looked at" (Mulvey, 1975/1989, p. 19).

Girls and young women are expected to be "on display," not only to make their bodies visible, but also to speak, to be heard, to express their "inner" selves confidently, "authentically," and "transparently," and thus, to make themselves *known*. Anita Harris (2004, pp. 125–126) has documented the cultural push for girls and young women to display, confess, speak up, and generally participate in public discourse. Social media self-exposure and visibility sits within the broader culture of "confession and display" she outlines. As Harris suggests, projects of self-revelation and exposure are tied to self-actualization for girls and young women; and, as I argue in chapters 5 and 6, digital self-revelation is also tied to notions of moral, social, and material value. Young women are encouraged by parents, peers, marketers, politicians, health professionals, and educators to effectively make themselves available for scrutiny in all aspects of their lives, and new technologies aid them in doing so.

The promise that visibility leads to power, and wealth in particular, is one that is perpetuated by and in social media cultures, and has been true for a small minority of individuals already privileged in a variety of ways (Banet-Weiser, 2012; Marwick, 2013). But the kind of intense visibility and self-exposure encouraged of girls and young women is not only about self-actualization, power, and producing the self as valued and valuable. Rather, girls and young women make themselves open to public judgment, critique, and surveillance, while the cultural promises that circulate around their visibility may or may not cash out. As Sarah Banet-Weiser (2012, p. 70) explains, it is not that "online empowerment" through visibility is *always* a false hope or proposition, but that, rather, "online empowerment…is defined and circumscribed precisely by the architecture of the Internet, as well as by the cultural and political conditions that make the Internet seem an appropriate vehicle for gender empowerment." Specific kinds of empowerment may be realized by girls and young women online, she suggests, but are "realized within the context of a brand culture…where their performances of visibility and spectacular femininity are subject not only to the evaluative feedback of others but also to their own self-evaluation." While it has not been a focus of this book, it is also important to keep in mind that digital visibility and self-exposure does not only promise, and sometimes produce, power and value for girls and young women themselves, but is itself a product, and a vital source of profit for social media companies. As Mark Andrejevic reminds us:

> When we explore what people do on Facebook or MySpace and the forms of community such sites enable, we must also keep in mind what gets done with the products of this activity, who controls its use and re-use, who profits from its transformation into commercial commodities and marketing campaigns, as well as who is targeted by these campaigns and to what end. (Andrejevic, 2011, p. 97)

The central aim of *Postfeminist Digital Cultures* has been to unpack some of the deeper issues and social concerns that might underlie panicked debates about, and responses to girls' and young women's use of digital media. Part I of this book, in sum, illuminates how the panic around girls and sexualized media can serve to hide from view that girls' and young women's desire and sexual agency is still largely "missing" (Fine, 1988) as socially and culturally legitimate. These chapters on heterosexy SNS self-representations and sexting both point to the importance of keeping desire at the forefront of scholarship and of broader public debates and conversations about girls, sex, media, and digital self-representation. As adult stakeholders invested in the well-being of girls and young women, we need to make space for the possibility of *legitimate sexual attention-seeking*, and for experiences of sexual agency rather than only victimhood, in the way we discuss girls and young women's sexual media practices and representations and the way we address young people about sex and media. In Part II I have pointed to the cultural logics of value and worth that shape the way young women's digital self-representations are understood in the postfeminist context. These chapters point to ways in which the "authentic," transparent, self-actualized, independent, and highly confident female subject of postfeminism and girl power discourses places certain burdens and pressures on young women, both on those who are able to produce self-representations in line with these standards of confident self-exposure and those whose self-representations subvert, contradict, or fail against such standards.

Much scholarship has focused on the opportunities of social media participation and self-representation for girls and young women (Buckingham, 2008; Harris, 2008; McPherson, 2008; Bae and Ivashkevich, 2011; Keller, 2012, 2015; Brandes and Levin, 2013; Dean and Laidler, 2013; Tiidenberg, 2014). This book has located opportunities in the media practices discussed in each of the chapters too: for example in the expression of sexual desire and agency discussed in chapter 3; the *possibilities* for sexual attention seeking discussed in chapter 4, albeit not currently easy for young women to take up, but at least available for a future legitimation; the opportunities for self-making and performativity discussed in chapter 5, and the opportunities for feedback, support, and connection outside sanctioned sources of such discussed in chapter 6. Less scholarship has focused on the regulatory and disciplinary aspects of girls' and young women's social media practices and self-representations; that is, on "online spaces as postfeminist structures of surveillance" (Kanai, 2015a, see also, Ringrose, 2013; Banet-Weiser, 2011, 2012).

This has been a focus of my discussions throughout this book, and I suggest that structures of regulation and surveillance in networked publics, and the *costs* of visibility and self-exposure for girls and young women, as well as the material profit their visibility produces for others, should be central to future research agendas in this field.

* * *

Social media are transient and mutable, and MySpace is no longer the dominant SNS of choice. The other media practices and forms of self-representation discussed in this book will likely date quickly too. New social media are gaining popularity, particularly image blogs and photo-sharing sites such as Tumblr and Instagram (see Kanai, 2015b). These sites are often used more anonymously than SNSs such as MySpace and Facebook, where it is common for users to easily identify themselves and connect online with their offline network of peers, family, and friends. New ways of performing normative gender and sexuality and subverting it are no doubt emerging on such sites. But the social media practices and representations discussed in *Postfeminist Digital Cultures* have much to tell us that is vitally important about the kind of media conventions and discourses that constitute popular, valued femininity in the postfeminist cultural context, as well as the constitutive limits of postfeminist femininity, and the specific kind of visibility and self-exposure it requires. Girls' and young women's social media practices and representations have much to tell us about how they navigate complex and contradictory pressures to tell and show the self and body, and to be markedly visible and exposed in very specific and conditional ways. We have also seen how crisis is produced around girls whose digital self-representations are judged as having crossed the boundaries of girl power "can do" land. The media practices and representations I have explored in *Postfeminist Digital Cultures* are examples of the way girls and young women can, do, and are using media, popular culture, and digital networks and communities to get by, to survive, in what are difficult and complex cultural, social, economic, and political conditions. Albeit, they are doing so in ways that adults do not always approve of or understand. In supporting girls and young women as they negotiate and navigate these conditions, adults and stakeholders invested in their well-being need to be *slow and cautious* in judgment, as the meanings, values, and significance of new digital cultures and media practices emerge and are constituted.

Notes

1 Introduction

1. Hodkinson and Lincoln have described SNS profiles as akin to bedroom spaces for many youth, and Robards and Lincoln (2014) provide a critical evaluation of the SNS profile bedroom metaphor.
2. Panicked media coverage about the safety of girls' communicating online via SNSs has been mapped fruitfully by feminist scholars (see Shade, 2007; Cassel and Cramer, 2008; Cohen and Shade, 2008; Marwick, 2008; Thiel-Stern, 2009, 2014). For a mapping of media claims about narcissism and vanity see Tanner, Maher, and Fraser (2013). Recent panicked media coverage around "teen sexting" has generated its own small body of scholarly documentation and response (see Karaian, 2012; Hasinoff, 2013, 2015; Angelides, 2013; Simpson, 2013; Crofts, Lee, McGovern, and Milivojevic, 2015).
3. For an explanation of this case, see Heffernan and Zeller (2006) and Rushfield and Hoffman (2006).
4. See Bollmer (2012) for an insightful explanation and discussion of this case.

2 Postfeminism, Girls and Young Women, and Digital Media

1. A detailed survey of the literature and findings by feminist researchers on gender and sex-role stereotypes in representation is beyond my purposes here. Such has been fruitfully undertaken by Busby (1975), and more recently by scholars such as van Zoonen (1994), Gauntlett (2002), Gill (2007), and Thornham (2007).
2. Mulvey herself details some criticisms of her early essay on the male gaze, and addresses some of them in a later essay (see Mulvey, 1989).
3. Gill provides a useful discussion of some representational "sensibilities" she suggests are distinctive to "contemporary articulations of gender in the media." These sensibilities include:

   The notion that femininity is a bodily property; the shift from objectification to subjectification; the emphasis upon self-surveillance, monitoring and discipline; a focus upon individualism, choice and empowerment; the dominance of a makeover paradigm; the articulation or entanglement of feminist and anti-feminist ideas; a resurgence in ideas of natural sexual difference; a marked sexualization of culture; and an emphasis upon consumerism and the commodification of difference. (Gill, 2007, p. 255)

4. In brief, Zaslow describes neoliberalism as a political ideology and dominant discourse in late-modern societies that "places an emphasis on self-improvement, self-correction, and individual empowerment over social change or state support" (Zaslow, 2009, pp. 158–159). Discourses of "individualization" are discussed further in chapter 5. For further discussion of neoliberalism as related to gender, femininity, and the postfeminist social context, see Walkerdine, Lucey, and Melody (2001), Harris (2004), Gill and Scharff (2011), and Evans and Riley (2014).
5. see Hinton and Hjorth (2013) for further explanation of Web 2.0 technologies and the shift in internet use that is suggested by this term.
6. In suggesting that digital technologies are now more widely available and used around the world I do not mean to suggest that "digital divides" do not exist. Some scholars have suggested that the increased adoption of new technologies has served to further increase social inequality as those without access, motivation, and skills become further marginalized (see Norris, 2001; van Dijk, 2006; Murthy, 2008).

3 Heterosexy Images on Social Network Sites

1. The details of this study are discussed in chapter 1.
2. See Hearn (2008) for a detailed explanation of self-branding practices, and how these are central to subjectification processes in late-capitalism and neoliberalism.
3. See Van Doorn (2009) on the way such images and messages are exchanged among a group of Dutch youth, in what he suggests are potentially gender-queer or subversive media practices.
4. This is discussed further in chapter 1.
5. I refer to Sprinkle's work as both "porn" and "performance" as Sprinkle argues that she is engaged in both modes of performativity rather than suggesting that her work should be seen as strictly one or the other (Sprinkle, 1998).

4 Girls, Sexting, and Gender Politics

1. The details of this research, which I conducted in 2013 with Danielle Tyson, Mary Lou Rasmussen, and Adrian Farrugia, are discussed in chapter 1.

2. See Crofts and Lee (2013) and Hasinoff (2015), for a discussion of criminal cases and laws governing sexting.
3. See the Australian Cybersmart website for full details and a link to this film: http://www.cybersmart.gov.au/tagged.aspx

5 Postfeminist Self-Making: Textual Self-Representation and the Performance of "Authentic" Young Femininity on Social Network Sites

1. The details of this study are provided in chapter 1.
2. Beverley Skeggs (2004) has argued that class is lived at the intimate and everyday level on the basis of judgment. Class is experienced as a dialogic relationship, she suggests, between those who judge and those who are judged. Skegg's work gives us reason to consider the ways in which the "real- life" bodies of women who perform the kind of confident, autonomous, and "excessive" femininity discussed here are subject to judgment on the basis of strong existing axes of inequality, including class, background, race, and sexuality. This was beyond the scope of my study, however, as it dealt primiarly with representations rather than lived experiences and social identities.

6 Digital Girls in Crisis? Seeking Feedback and Representing Pain in Postfeminist Networked Publics

1. Their findings about Facebook and "emotional contragion" are highly questionable: see van Ryn and Fordyce, 2014.
2. see Quenqua (2014) for a recent explanation of the phenomenon.
3. Many thanks to Leo Keith for his help with this analysis. The videos we looked at for this analysis can be viewed at: https://www.youtube.com/watch?v=WoyZPn6hKY4&feature=youtu.be, https://www.youtube.com/watch?v=tLSFmYX45nc&feature=youtu.be, and https://www.youtube.com/watch?v=8xW_H4fow28&feature=youtu.be.
4. See Pavlidis and Fullagar (2014) for an account of similar processes of mediating pain in relation to roller derby.

Afterword Notes on Visibility and Self-Exposure

1. See https://www.youtube.com/user/thisgirlcanuk
2. See https://www.youtube.com/watch?v=aN7lt0CYwHg
3. Mulvey theorizes that cinematic narratives correspond primarily with one of two types of viewing pleasure or "scopophilia," structured around heterosexual male desire. These are *voyeuristic* scopophilia and *fetishistic* scopophilia. Voyeuristic scopophilia involves "investigating the woman, demystifying her mystery" (1975/1989, p. 21). Fetishistic scopophilia involves "build[ing] up the physical beauty of

the object, transforming it into something satisfying in itself," regardless of plot or story (p. 21). As such, a devaluation and humiliation of women or an overvaluation and idealization of the female body are two common ways the female body is constructed on screen.

4. These findings echo those of Ringrose and colleagues in the United Kingdom (Ringrose, 2010; Ringrose, Gill, Livingstone, and Harvey, 2012; Ringrose, Harvey, Gill, and Livingstone, 2013) on the contradictions and ambivalences around both SNS culture and sexting for girls.

Bibliography

Aapola, Sinnika, Marnina Gonick, and Anita Harris (2005). *Young Femininity: Girlhood, Power and Social Change*. Houndmills, Basingstoke, Hampshire; New York: Palgrave Macmillan.

Adler, Patricia and Peter Adler (2011). *The Tender Cut: Inside the Hidden World of Self-Injury*. New York: New York University Press.

Agustina, Jose, & Gomez-Duran, Esperanza. (2012). Sexting: Research Criteria of a Globalized Social Phenomenon. *Archives of Sexual Behavior*, 41, 1325–1328.

Ahmed, Sara (2004). *The Cultural Politics of Emotion*. New York: Routledge.

Akass, Kim and Janet McCabe (eds.) (2004). *Reading Sex and the City*. London, New York: I. B. Tauris.

Albury, Kath. (2015). Selfies, sexts, and sneaky hats: Young people's understandings of gendered practices of self-representation. *International Journal of Communication*, 9(2015), 1734–1745.

Albury, Kath and Kate Crawford (2012). Sexting, consent and young people's ethics: Beyond Megan's story. *Continuum: Journal of Media & Cultural Studies*, 3(26), 1–11.

Albury, Kath, Kate Crawford, Paul Byron, and Ben Mathews (2013). Young people and sexting in Australia: Ethics, representation and the law. ARC Centre for Creative Industries and Innovation/Journalism and Media Research Centre, University of New South Wales, Australia. Available at: http://jmrc.arts.unsw.edu.au/media/File/Young_People_And_Sexting_Final.pdf.

Albury, Kath, and Paul Byron. (2014). Queering sexting and sexualisation. *Media International Australia*, 153(Nov).

Alexa.com (2014). Actionable Analytics for the Web. Available at: http://www.alexa.com/.

Allen, Louisa (2013). Girls' portraits of desire: Picturing a missing discourse. *Gender and Education*, 25(3), 295–310. doi:10.1080/09540253.2012.752795.

American Psychological Association Task Force on the Sexualization of Girls (2007). *Report of the APA Task Force on the Sexualization of Girls*. Washington, DC: American Psychological Association. Available from: http://www.apa.org/pi/women/programs/girls/report-full.pdf.

American Psychological Association, Task Force on the Sexualization of Girls (2010). *Report of the APA Task Force on the Sexualization of Girls.* Washington, DC: American Psychological Association. Available from: http://www.apa.org/pi/women/programs/girls/report-full.pdf.

Andrejevic, Mark (2011). Social network exploitation. In Zizi Papacharissi (ed.), *A Networked Self: Identity, Community, and Culture on Social Network Sites.* New York: Routledge.

——— (2007). *iSpy: Surveillance and Power in the Interactive Era.* Kansas: University Press of Kansas.

——— (2004). *Reality TV: The Work of Being Watched.* Lanham: Rowman & Littlefield.

Ang, Ien (1985). *Watching Dallas: Soap Opera and the Melodramatic Imagination,* translated by D. Couling. London; New York: Routledge.

Angelides, Steven (2013). "Technology, hormones, and stupidity": The affective politics of teenage sexting. *Sexualities,* 16(5–6), 665–689. doi:10.1177/1363460713487289.

Arthurs, Jane (2004). *Television and Sexuality: Regulation and the Politics of Taste.* Maidenhead: Open University Press.

Attwood, Feona (2011). Through the looking glass? Sexual agency and subjectification online. In Christina Scharff and Rosalind Gill (eds.), *New Femininities: Postfeminism, Neoliberalism, and Subjectivity* (pp. 203–214). Houndmills: Palgrave Macmillan.

Attwood, Feona (ed.) (2009). *Mainstreaming Sex: The Sexualization of Western Culture.* London: I. B. Tauris.

Attwood, Feona (2006). Sexed up: Theorizing the sexualization of culture. *Sexualities,* 9(1), 77–94.

Australian Communications and Media Authority (ACMA) (2013). Communications report 2011–2012. Pyrmont, NSW: Australian Communications and Media Authority, Commonwealth of Australia. Available at: http://www.acma.gov.au/Home/theACMA/Library/researchacma.

Australian Parliament Senate Standing Committee on Environment, Communications and the Arts (2008). Sexualisation of children in the contemporary media. Canberra: Commonwealth of Australia. Available at: http://www.aph.gov.au/Parliamentary_Business/Committees/Senate/Environment_and_Communications/Completed_inquiries/2008–10/sexualisationofchildren/report/index.

Bae, Michelle and Olga Ivashkevich (2011). *Girls, Cultural Productions, and Resistance.* New York: Peter Lang.

Bail, Kathy (1996). *D.I.Y. Feminism.* St. Leonards, NSW: Allen & Unwin.

Bailey, Jane and Mouna Hanna (2011). The gendered dimensions of sexting: Assessing the applicability of Canada's child pornography provision. *Canadian Journal of Women & the Law,* 23(2), 405–441.

Bailey, Jane, Valerie Steeves, Jacqueline Burkell, and Priscilla Regan (2013). Negotiating with gender stereotypes on social networking sites: From bicycle face to Facebook. *Journal of Communication Inquiry,* 37(2): 91–112.

Bailey, Reg (2011). *Letting Children Be Children: The Report of an Independent Review of the Commercialisation and Sexualisation of Childhood*. London: British Home Office.

Baker, Darren and Sarah Fortune (2008). Understanding self-harm and suicide websites: A qualitative interview study of young adult website users. *Crisis*, 29(3), 118–122.

Baker, Joanne (2010). Claiming volition and evading victimhood: Post-feminist obligations for young women. *Feminism & Psychology*, 20(2), 186–204. doi:10.1177/0959353509359142.

Barker, Meg and Robbie Duschinsky (2012). Sexualisation's four faces: Sexualisation and gender stereotyping in the Bailey Review. *Gender and Education*, 24(3), 303–310. doi:10.1080/09540253.2012.660136.

Banet-Weiser, Sarah (2015). "Confidence you can carry!": Girls in crisis and the market for girls' empowerment organizations. *Continuum: Journal of Media and Cultural Studies*, 29(2), 182–193. doi: 10.1080/10304312.2015.1022938

——— (2014). Am I Pretty or Ugly? Girls and the market for self-esteem. *Girlhood Studies*, 7(1), 83–101.

——— (2012). *Authentic, TM: The Politics of Ambivalence in a Brand Culture*. New York: New York University Press.

——— (2011). Branding the post-feminist self: Girls' video production and YouTube. In Mary Celeste Kearney (ed.), *Mediated Girlhoods: New Explorations of Girls' Media Culture* (pp. 227–294). New York: Peter Lang.

Barad, Karen (2003). Posthumanist performativity: Toward an understanding of how matter comes to matter. *Signs: Journal of Women in Culture and Society*, 28(3), 801–831.

Bartky, Sandra Lee (1988). Foucault, femininity, and the modernization of patriarchal power. In Irene Diamond and Lee Quinby (eds.), *Feminism & Foucault: Reflections on Resistance* (pp. 61–86). Boston, MA: Northeastern University Press.

Baudrillard, Jean (1983). *Simulations*, translated by P. Foss, P. Patton, and P. Beitchman. New York: Semiotext(e).

Bauman, Zigmunt (1995). *Life in Fragments: Essays in Postmodern Morality*. Oxford; Cambridge, MA: Blackwell.

Bauman, Zigmunt (2001). *The Individualized Society*. Malden, MA: Polity Press.

Beck, Ulrich (1992). *Risk Society: Towards a New Modernity*, translated by M. Ritter. London: Sage.

Beer, David (2008). Social network(ing) sites. Revisiting the story so far: A response to danah boyd and Nicole Ellison. *Journal of Computer-Mediated Communication*, 13(2), 516–529.

Benjamin, Walter (1997). *One-way Street, and Other Writings*, translated by E. Jephcott and K. Shorter. London: Verso.

Berger, John (1972/2008). *Ways of seeing*. London: Penguin.

Berlant, Lauren (2008). *The Female Complaint*. Durham and London: Duke.

Best, Amy L. (2007). *Representing Youth: Methodological Issues in Critical Youth Studies*. New York: New York University Press.

Betterton, Rosemary (ed.) (1987). *Looking On: Images of Femininity in the Visual Arts and Media*. London; New York: Pandora.

Boero, Natalie and C. J. Pascoe (2012). Pro-anorexia communities and online interaction: Bringing the pro-ana body online. *Body & Society*, 18(2), 27–57. doi:10.1177/1357034x12440827.

Boler, Megan, Anne Harris, and Jenna Jacobson (forthcoming). Vlogging as self-curation: Mediating the male gaze on YouTube. *Feminist Media Studies*.

Bollmer, Grant (2012). Demanding connectivity: The performance of "true" identity and the politics of social media. *JOMEC Journal, Journalism, Media and Cultural Studies*, 1, 1–13.

Bond, Emma (2011). The mobile phone = bike shed? Children, sex and mobile phones. *New Media & Society*, 13(4), 587–604. doi:10.1177/1461444810377919.

Bordo, Susan (1997). The body and the reproduction of femininity. In Katie Conboy, Nadia Medina, and Sarah Stanbury (eds.), *Writing on the Body* (pp. 90–110). New York: Columbia University Press.

——— (1993). *Unbearable Weight: Feminism, Western Culture, and the Body*. Berkeley: University of California Press.

Bortree, Denise Sevick (2005). Presentation of self on the Web: An ethnographic study of teenage girls' weblogs. *Education, Communication & Information*, 5(1), 25–39.

boyd, danah (2014). *It's Complicated: The Social Lives of Networked Teens*. New Haven; London: Yale University Press.

——— (2008). Why youth (heart) social network sites: The role of networked publics in teenage social life. In D. Buckingham (ed.), *Youth, Identity, and Digital Media* (pp. 119–142). Cambridge, MA: MIT Press.

boyd, danah and Nicole Ellison (2007). Social network sites: Definition, history and scholarship. *Journal of Computer-Mediated Communication*, 13(1), 210–230.

boyd, danah, Alice Marwick, Parry Aftab, and Maeve Koeltl (2009). The conundrum of visibility. *Journal of Children and Media*, 3(4), 410–419.

boyd, danah, Jenny Ryan, and Alex Leavitt (2010). Pro-self-harm and the visibility of youth-generated problematic content. *I/S: A Journal of Law and Policy for the Information Society*, 7(1), 1–32.

Brandes, Sigal Barak and David Levin (2013). "Like My Status": Israeli teenage girls constructing their social connections on the Facebook social network. *Feminist Media Studies*, 1–16. doi:10.1080/14680777.2013.833533.

Brickman, Barbara Jane (2004). "Delicate" cutters: Gendered self-mutilation and attractive flesh in medical discourse. *Body & Society*, 10(4), 87–111.

Brown, Rebecca and Melissa Gregg (2012). The pedagogy of regret: Facebook, binge drinking and young women. *Continuum: Journal of Media & Cultural Studies*, 26(3), 357–369. doi:10.1080/10304312.2012.665834.

Brownmiller, Susan (1984). *Femininity*. New York: Linden Press/Simon & Schuster.

Brumberg, Joan J. (1997). *The Body Project: An Intimate History of American Girls*. New York: Random House.

Bruns, Axel (2008). The future is user-led: The path towards widespread produsage. *Fibreculture*, (11). Available at: http://journal.fibreculture.org/issue11/issue11_bruns.html.

Brunsdon, Charlotte (1993). Identity in feminist television criticism. *Media, Culture and Society*, 15(2), 309–320.

——— (2005). Feminism, postfeminism, Martha, Martha, and Nigella. *Cinema Journal*, 44(2), 110–116.

Buckingham, David (ed.) (2008). *Youth, Identity, and Digital Media*. Cambridge, MA: MIT Press.

Budgeon, Shelley (2001). Emergent feminist(?) identities: Young women and the practice of micropolitics. *European Journal of Women's Studies*, 8(1), 7–28.

Budgeon, Shelley and Dawn Currie (1995). From feminism to postfeminism: Women's liberation in fashion magazines. *Women's Studies International Forum*, 18(2), 173–186.

Bulbeck, Chila (2001). Articulating structure and agency: How women's studies students express their relationships with feminism. *Women's Studies International Forum*, 24(2), 141–156.

Busby, Linda (1975). Sex-role research on the mass media. *The Journal of Communication*, 25(4), 107–131.

Buszek, Maria Elena (2006). *Pin-up Grrrls: Feminism, Sexuality, Popular Culture*. Durham: Duke University Press.

Butcher, Helen, Ros Coward, Marcella Evaristi, Jenny Garber, Rachel Harrison, and Janice Winship (1974). *Images of Women in the Media*. Birmingham: Centre for Contemporary Cultural Studies, University of Birmingham.

Butler, Judith (2005). *Giving an Account of Oneself*. New York: Fordham University Press.

——— (1993). *Bodies That Matter: On the Discursive Limits of "Sex."* London: Routledge.

——— (1990). *Gender Trouble: Feminism and the Subversion of Identity*. New York: Routledge.

Callaghan, Dympna (1989). *Woman and Gender in Renaissance Tragedy: A Study of* King Lear, Othello, The Duchess of Malfi *and* The White Devil. New York; London: Harvester Wheatsheaf.

Calvert, Clay and Robert Richards (2009). When sex and cell phones collide: Inside the prosecution of a teen sexting case. *Hastings Communication and Entertainment Law Journal*, 32(1), 1–40.

Campbell, Scott and Yong Jin Park (2014). Predictors of mobile sexting among teens: Toward a new explanatory framework. *Mobile Media & Communication*, 2(1), 20–39. doi:10.1177/2050157913502645.

Carah, N. (2014). Curators of databases: Circulating images, managing attention and making value on social media. *Media International Australia, 150* (Feb), 137–142. Available at: http://www.uq.edu.au/mia/2014-issues#150

Case, Sue-Ellen (1988). *Feminism and Theatre*. New York: Routledge.

Cassel, Justine and Meg Cramer (2008). Moral panic and girls online. In Tara McPherson (ed.), *Digital Youth, Innovation, and the Unexpected* (pp. 53–75). Cambridge, MA: MIT Press.

Castells, Manuel (2012). *Networks of Outrage and Hope: Social Movements in the Internet Age*. Cambridge, UK: Polity Press.

Chesney-Lind, Meda and Katherine Irwin (2008). *Beyond Bad Girls: Gender, Violence and Hype*. New York: Routledge.

ChildLine UK, 2012. Online child safety: An overview from ChildLine 1st April 2011–31st March 2012. Unpublished report.

Cixous, Hélène (1980). The laugh of the Medusa. In Elaine Marks and Isabelle De Courtivron (eds.), *New French Feminisms: An Anthology* (pp. 245–264). Amherst: University of Massachusetts Press.

Cixous, Hélène and Catherine Clément (1996). *The Newly Born Woman*, translated by B. Wing. London: I. B. Tauris.

Clark, Lynn Schofield (2005). The constant contact generation: Exploring teen friendship networks online. In Sharon Mazzarella (ed.), *Girl Wide Web* (pp. 203–221). New York: Peter Lang.

Cohen, Nicole S. and Leslie Regan Shade (2008). Gendering Facebook: Privacy and commodification. *Feminist Media Studies*, 8(2), 210–214.

Cole, Ellen and Jessica Henderson Daniel (2005). *Featuring Females: Feminist Analyses of Media*. Washington, DC: American Psychological Association.

Cook, Daniel Thomas and Susan Kaiser (2004). Betwixt and be tween: Age ambiguity and the sexualization of the female consuming subject. *Journal of Consumer Culture*, 4(2), 203–227. doi:10.1177/1469540504043682.

Cook, Julia and Reza Hasmath (2014). The discursive construction and performance of gendered identity on social media. *Current Sociology*. doi:10.1177/0011392114550008.

Colebrook, Claire (2002). *Gilles Deleuze*. London; New York: Routledge.

Coleman, Rebecca (2009). *The Becoming of Bodies: Girls, Images, Experience*. Manchester: Manchester University Press.

Couldry, Nick (2012). *Media, Society, World: Social Theory and Digital Media Practice*. Cambridge, UK: Polity.

Cover, Rob (2012a). Performing and undoing identity online: Social networking, identity theories and the incompatibility of online profiles and friendship regimes. *Convergence: The International Journal of Research into New Media Technologies*, 18(2), 177–193. doi:10.1177/1354856511433684.

——— (2012b). *Queer Youth Suicide, Culture and Identity: Unliveable Lives?* London: Ashgate.

Cowie, Elizabeth (1997). *Representing the Woman: Cinema and Psychoanalysis*. Minneapolis: University of Minnesota Press.

Creed, Barbera (2003). *Media Matrix: Sexing the New Reality*. Crows Nest, NSW: Allen & Unwin.

Crofts, Thomas, Murray Lee, Alice McGovern, and Sanja Milivojevic (2015). *Sexting and Young People*. London: Palgrave Macmillan.

Crofts, Thomas and Murray Lee (2013). "Sexting," children and child pornography. *Sydney Law Review*, 35(1), 85–106.

Currie, Dawn, Deirdre M. Kelly, and Shauna Pomerantz (2009). *"Girl Power": Girls Reinventing Girlhood*. New York: Peter Lang.

Daugherty, Anne Millard (2001). Just a girl: Buffy as icon. In Roz Kaveney (ed.), *Reading the Vampire Slayer: The Unofficial Critical Companion to* Buffy *and* Angel (pp. 148–165). London: Tauris Parke.

Day, Katy (2010). Pro-anorexia and "binge-drinking": Conformity to damaging ideals or "new," resistant femininities? *Feminism & Psychology*, 20(2), 242–248.

Day, Katy, Brendan Gough, and Majella McFadden (2004). "Warning! Alcohol can seriously damage your feminine health": A discourse analysis of recent British newspaper coverage of women and drinking. *Feminist Media Studies*, 4(2), 165–183.

Day, Katy and Tammy Keys (2008). Starving in cyberspace: A discourse analysis of pro-eating disorder websites. *Journal of Gender Studies*, 17(1), 1–15.

Dean, Marissa and Karen Laidler (2013). A new girl in town: Exploring girlhood identities through Facebook. *First Monday*, 18(2–4). Available at: http://firstmonday.org/ojs/index.php/fm/article/view/4230.

de Beauvoir, Simone (1949/1972). *The Second Sex*, translated by H. M. Parshley. Harmondsworth: Penguin.

de Lauretis, Teresa (1984). *Alice Doesn't: Feminism, Semiotics, Cinema*. Bloomington: Indiana University Press.

——— (1989). *Technologies of Gender: Essays on Theory, Film, and Fiction*. Basingstoke: Macmillan.

Dennis, Kelly (2009). *Art/Porn: A History of Seeing and Touching*. New York: Bloomsbury.

Diamond, Elin (1997). *Unmaking Mimesis: Essays on Feminism and Theater*. London; New York: Routledge.

Dobson, Amy Shields (2015). Girls' "pain memes" on YouTube: The production of pain and femininity in a digital network. In Sarah Baker, Brady Robards, and Bob Buttigieg, (eds.), *Youth Cultures and Subcultures: Australian Perspectives* (pp. 173–182). Farnham: Ashgate.

——— (2014a). Laddishness online: The possible significations and significance of "performative shamelessness" for young women in the post-feminist context. *Cultural Studies*, 28(1), 142–164. doi:10.1080/09502386.2013.778893.

——— (2014b). Performative shamelessness on young women's social network sites: Shielding the self and resisting gender melancholia. *Feminism & Psychology*, 24(1): 97–114.

——— (2014c). "Sexy" And "Laddish" Girls: Unpacking complicity between two cultural imag(inations)es of young femininity. *Feminist Media Studies*, 14(2): 253–269. doi: 10.1080/14680777.2012.713866.

——— (2011). The representation of female friendships on young women's MySpace profiles: The all-female world and the feminine "other." In Elza Dunkels, Gun-Marie Franberg, and Camilla Hallgren (eds.), *Youth Culture and Net Culture: Online Social Practices* (pp. 126–152). Hershey, PA: IGI Global.

——— (2008). Femininities as commodities: Cam girl culture. In Anita Harris (ed.), *Next Wave Cultures: Feminism, Subcultures, Activism* (pp. 123–148). New York: Routledge.

Dobson, Amy Shields, and Jessica Ringrose (2015). *Sext Education: Pedagogies of sex, gender and shame in the schoolyards of Tagged and Exposed*. Sex Education. Available at: http://www.tandfonline.com/doi/full/10.1080/14681811.2015.1050486#abstract.

Dolan, Jill (1991). *The Feminist Spectator as Critic*. Ann Arbor: University of Michigan Press.

Douglas, Susan (2010). *The Rise of Enlightened Sexism: The Seductive Message that Feminism's Work is Done*. New York: Henry Holt.

Driscoll, Catherine (2008). Girls today: Girls, girl culture and girl studies. *Girlhood Studies*, 1, 13–32.

——— (2002). *Girls: Feminine Adolescence in Popular Culture and Cultural Theory*. New York: Columbia University Press.

Driscoll, Catherine and Melissa Gregg (2011). Convergence culture and the legacy of feminist cultural studies. *Cultural Studies*, 25(4–5), 566–584.

Driver, Susan (2007). *Queer Girls and Popular Culture: Reading, Resisting and Creating Media*. New York: Peter Lang.

Drotner, Kirsten (2001). *Media for the Future: Children, Youth and the New Media Landscape*. Copenhagen: Høst & Søn.

Drouin, Michelle, Kimberly Vogel, Alisen Surbey, and Julie Stills (2013). Let's talk about sexting, baby: Computer-mediated sexual behaviors among young adults. *Computers in Human Behavior, 29*(5), A25–A30.

Duggan, Maeve (2014). Online harassment. Washington, DC: Pew Internet. Available at: http://www.pewinternet.org/2014/10/22/online-harassment/.

——— (2013). Photo and video sharing grow online. Washington, DC: Pew Internet. Available at: http://www.pewinternet.org/2013/10/28/photo-and-video-sharing-grow-online/.

Duggan, Maeve and Aaron Smith (2013). Social media update. Washington, DC: Pew Internet. Available at: http://www.pewinternet.org/2013/12/30/social-media-update-2013/.

Duguay, S. (2014). "He has a way gayer Facebook than I do": Investigating sexual identity disclosure and context collapse on a social networking site. *New Media & Society*. doi: 10.1177/1461444814549930.

Duits, Linda and Pauline van Romondt Vis (2009). Girls make sense: Girls, celebrities and identities. *European Journal of Cultural Studies*, 12(1), 41–58.

Duits, Linda and Liesbet van Zoonen (2011). Coming to terms with sexualization. *European Journal of Cultural Studies,* 14(5), 491–506. doi:10.1177/1367549411412201.

——— (2007). Who's afraid of female agency? A rejoinder to Gill. *European Journal of Women's Studies,* 14(2), 161–170.

——— (2006). Headscarves and porno-chic: Disciplining girls' bodies in the European multicultural society. *European Journal of Women's Studies,* 13(2), 103–117.

Durham, M. Gigi (2009). *The Lolita Effect: The Media Sexualization of Young Girls and What We Can Do About It.* New York: The Overlook Press.

Dvorak, John C. (2013). Last word. *PC Magazine*, December 2013.

Dyer, Richard. (1997). *White.* London; New York: Routledge.

Edwards, Lynne (2005). Victims, villains, and vixens: Teen girls and Internet crime. In Sharon Mazzarella (ed.), *Girl Wide Web: Girls, the Internet, and the Negotiation of Identity* (pp. 13–30). New York: Peter Lang.

Edgar, Patricia and Hilary McPhee (1974). *Media She.* Melbourne: Heinemann.

Egan, R. Danielle (2013). *Becoming Sexual: A Critical Appraisal of the Sexualisation of Girls.* Cambridge, UK: Polity Press.

Egan, R. Danielle and Gail Hawkes (2012). Sexuality, youth and the perils of endangered innocence: How history can help us get past the panic. *Gender and Education*, 24(3), 269–284. doi:10.1080/09540253.2012.666232.

——— (2009). The problem with protection: Or, why we need to move towards recognition and the sexual agency of children. *Continuum: Journal of Media & Cultural Studies*, 23(3), 389–400.

——— (2008a). Endangered girls and incendiary objects: Deconstructing the discourse of corporate paedophilia. *Sexuality and Culture,* 12(4), 291–312.

——— (2008b). Girls, sexuality and the strange carnalities of advertisements. *Australian Feminist Studies*, 23(57), 307–322.

Elliott, Anthony (2001). *Concepts of the Self.* Cambridge, UK: Polity Press.

Elliott, Anthony and Charles Lemert (2006). *The New Individualism: The Emotional Costs of Globalisation.* London; New York: Routledge.

Elm, M. Sveningsson (2009). Teenagers get undressed on the Internet: Young people's exposure of bodies in a Swedish Internet community. *Nordicom Review* 30(2): 87–103.

Esch, Kevin and Vicki Mayer (2007). How unprofessional: The profitable partnership of amateur porn and celebrity culture. In Susanna Paasonen, Kaarina Nikunen, and Laura Saarenmaa (eds.), *Pornification: Sex and Sexuality in Media Culture* (pp. 99–111). Oxford; New York: Berg.

Evans, Adrienne and Sarah Riley (2014). *Technologies of Sexiness: Sex, Identity, and Consumer Culture.* New York: Oxford University Press.

Evans, Adrienne, Sarah Riley, and Avi Shankar (2010). Technologies of sexiness: Theorizing women's engagement in the sexualization of culture. *Feminism & Psychology,* 20(1), 114–131. doi:10.1177/0959353509351854.

Fairbain, J. (2015). Rape threats and revenge porn. In J. Bailey and V. Steeves (eds.), eGrils, eCitizens (pp. 229–252). Ottawa: University of Ottawa Press.

Faludi, Susan (1992). *Backlash: The Undeclared War Against Women*. London: Chatto & Windus.

Ferreday, Debra (2003). Unspeakable bodies: Erasure, embodiment and the pro-ana community. *International Journal of Cultural Studies*, 6(3), 277–295. doi:10.1177/13678779030063003.

Ferris, Lesley (1990). *Acting Women: Images of Women in Theatre*. Basingstoke: Macmillan.

Fine, Michelle (1988). Sexuality, schooling, and adolescent females: The missing discourse of desire. *Harvard Educational Review*, 58(1), 29–54.

Foucault, Michel (1984). *The History of Sexuality: An Introduction*. London: Penguin.

——— (1991). The body of the condemned. In Paul Rabinow (ed.), *The Foucault Reader* (pp. 170–178). London: Penguin.

Fraser, Nancy (1992). Rethinking the public sphere: A contribution to the critique of actually existing democracy. In Craig Calhoun (ed.), *Habermas and the Public Sphere*. Boston: Massachusetts Institute of Technology.

Fraser, Suzanne (2003). *Cosmetic Surgery, Gender and Culture*. New York: Palgrave Macmillan.

Fredrickson, Barbara and Tomi-Ann Roberts (1997). Objectification theory. *Psychology of Women Quarterly*, 21(2), 173–206. doi:10.1111/j.1471-6402.1997.tb00108.x.

Fritzsche, Bettina (2004). Spicy strategies: Pop feminist and other empowerments in girl culture. In Anita Harris (ed.), *All About the Girl: Culture, Power, and Identity* (pp. 155–162). New York: Routledge.

Fuchs, Elinor (1989). Staging the obscene body. *The Drama Review*, 33(1), 33–58.

Fullagar, Simone and Jessica Francombe-Webb (2015). This Girl Can campaign is all about sex, not sport. *The Conversation*, January 15. Available at: http://theconversation.com/this-girl-can-campaign-is-all-about-sex-not-sport-36236.

Funnell, Nina (September 10, 2011). There's no shame in teenage sextual relations. *The Sydney Morning Herald*. Retrieved November 18, 2011 from: http://www.smh.com.au/opinion/society-and-culture/theres-no-shame-in-teenage-sextual-relations-20110909-1k1nb.html.

Gabriel, Fleur (2014). Sexting, selfies and self-harm: Young people, social media and the performance of self-development. *Media International Australia*, 151, 104–112.

García-Gómez, Antonio (2011). Regulating girlhood: Evaluative language, discourses of gender socialization and relational aggression. *European Journal of Women's Studies* 18(3): 243–264.

Gauntlett, David (2002). *Media, Gender, and Identity: An Introduction*. London; New York: Routledge.

Gerbaudo, Paolo (2012). *Tweets and the Streets: Social Media and Contemporary Activism*. London: Pluto Press.

Gibson, Pamela Church (2004). *More Dirty Looks: Gender, Pornography and Power* (2nd ed.). London: British Film Institute.

Giddens, Anthony (1991). *Modernity and Self-identity: Self and Society in the Late Modern Age*. Stanford, CA: Stanford University Press.

Gilbert, Jen (2015). *Sexuality in Schools: The Limits of Education*. Minneapolis: University of Minnesota Press.

Gill, Rosalind (2011). Sexism reloaded, or, it's time to get angry again! *Feminist Media Studies*, 11(1), 61–71. doi:10.1080/14680777.2011.537029.

——— (2008). Empowerment/sexism: Figuring female sexual agency in contemporary advertising. *Feminism & Psychology*, 18(1), 35–60. doi:10.1177/0959353507084950.

——— (2009). Beyond the "sexualization of culture" thesis: An intersectional analysis of "Sixpacks," "Midriffs" and "Hot Lesbians" in advertising. *Sexualities*, 12(2), 137–160.

——— (2007). *Gender and the Media*. Cambridge; Malden: Polity Press.

——— (2003). From sexual objectification to sexual subjectification: The resexualisation of women's bodies in the media. *Feminist Media Studies*, 3(1), 100–106.

Gill, Rosalind and Jane Arthurs (2006). Editors' introduction: new femininities? *Feminist Media Studies*, 6(4), 443–451.

Gill, Rosalind and Christina Scharff (eds.) (2011). *New Femininities: Postfeminism, Neoliberalism, and Subjectivity*. Houndmills, Basingstoke, Hampshire; New York: Palgrave Macmillan.

Gilligan, Carol (1982). *In a Different Voice: Psychological Theory and Women's Development*. Cambridge, MA: Harvard University Press.

Goffman, Erving (1969). *The Presentation of Self in Everyday Life*. London: Allen Lane.

——— (1979). *Gender Advertisements*. New York: Harper & Row.

Goldman, Robert (1992). *Reading Ads Socially*. London; New York: Routledge.

Gonick, Marnina, Emma Renold, Jessica Ringrose, and Lisa Weems (2009). Rethinking agency and resistance: What comes after girl power? *Girlhood Studies* 2(2), 1–9.

Gordon-Messer, Deborah, Jose Arturo Bauermeister, Alison Grodzinski, and Marc Zimmerman (2013). Sexting among young adults. *Journal of Adolescent Health*, 52(3), 301–306.

Green, Leila, Danielle Brady, Kjartan Ólafsson, John Hartley, and Catherine Lumby (2011). Risks and safety for Australian children on the internet CS vol 4, no 1: AU Kids Online (vol. 4). Brisbane: ARC Centre for Creative Industries and Innovation, Queensland University of Technology.

Greer, Germaine (1970). *The Female Eunuch*. London: MacGibbon & Kee.

Gregg, Melissa (2011). *Work's Intimacy*. Cambridge, MA: Polity.

Grisso, Ashley D. and David Weiss (2005). What are gURLS talking about? Adolescent girls' construction of sexual identity on gURL.com. In Sharon Mazzarella (ed.), *Girl Wide Web: Girls, the Internet, and the Negotiation of Identity* (pp. 31–49). New York: Peter Lang.

Grodin, Debra and Thomas R. Lindlof (eds.) (1996). *Constructing the Self in a Mediated World*. Thousand Oaks, CA: Sage.

Hains, Rebecca (2012). *Growing Up With Girl Power: Girlhood on Screen and in Everyday Life*. New York: Peter Lang.

Hakim, Catherine (2011). *Honey Money: The Power of Erotic Capital*. London: Allen Lane.

Halberstam, Judith (1998). *Female Masculinity*. Durham, NC: Duke University Press.

Hall, P. Cougar, Joshua West, and Emily McIntyre (2012). Female self-sexualization in MySpace.com personal profile photographs. *Sexuality & Culture* 16(1), 1–16.

Hasinoff, Amy Adele (2015). *Sexting Panic: Rethinking Criminalization, Privacy, and Consent*. Champaign: University of Illinois Press

——— (2014). Blaming sexualization for sexting. *Girlhood Studies, 7*(1), 102–120.

——— (2013). Sexting as media production: Rethinking social media and sexuality. *New Media & Society,* 15(4), 449–465. doi:10.1177/1461444812459171.

Haraway, Donna (1991/2000). A manifesto for cyborgs. In David Bell and Barbara M. Kennedy (eds.), *The Cybercultures Reader* (pp. 291–324). Abingdon, Oxon: Routledge.

Harris, Anita (2008). Young women, late modern politics, and the participatory possibilities of online cultures. *Journal of Youth Studies,* 11(5), 481–495.

——— (2005). Discourses of desire as governmentality: Young women, sexuality and the significance of safe spaces. *Feminism & Psychology* 15(1): 39–43.

——— (2004). *Future Girl: Young Women in the Twenty-First Century*. New York: Routledge.

Harris, Anita and Dobson, Amy Shields (2015). Theorizing agency in post-girlpower times. *Continuum,* 29(2), 145–156. doi: 10.1080/10304312.2015.1022955.

Harris, Andrew, Judith Davidson, Elizabeth Letourneau, Karl Paternite, and Karin Tusinski Miofsky (2013). *Building a Prevention Framework to Address Teen "Sexting" Behaviors*. Boston, MA: NCJRS. Available at: https://www.ncjrs.gov/pdffiles1/ojjdp/grants/244001.pdf.

Hartley, John, Jean Burgess and Axel Bruns, Axel (2013). *A Companion to New Media Dynamics*. Malden, MA: Wiley-Blackwell.

Hatton, Erin and Mary Trautner (2011). Equal opportunity objectification? The sexualization of men and women on the cover of *Rolling Stone*. *Sexuality & Culture,* 15(3), 256–278. doi:10.1007/s12119-011-9093-2.

Hearn, A. (2008). "Meat, Mask, Burden": Probing the contours of the branded "self." *Journal of Consumer Culture, 8*(2), 197–217. doi: 10.1177/1469540508090086.

Heffernan, Virginia and Tom Zeller (September 12, 2006). "Lonely Girl" (and friends) just wanted movie deal, *New York Times*. Retrieved 15/10/09 from http://www.nytimes.com/2006/09/12/technology/12cnd-lonely.html?_r=1&hp&ex=1158120000&en=a56f0e777a707f56&ei=5094&partner=homepage.

Henderson, Lisa (2008). Slow love. *The Communication Review*, 11(3), 219–224.

Hermes, Joke (1995). *Reading Women's Magazines: An Analysis of Everyday Media Use*. Cambridge, UK: Polity Press.

Hess, Thomas and Elizabeth Baker (eds.) (1973). *Art and Sexual Politics: Women's liberation, Women Artists, and Art History*. New York: Collier Books.

Hess, Thomas and Nochlin, Linda (eds.) (1973). *Woman as Sex Object: Studies in Erotic Art, 1730–1970*. London: Allen Lane.

Hine, Christine (2000). *Virtual Ethnography*. London: Sage.

Hinton, Sam and Larissa Hjorth (2013). *Understanding Social Media*. London: Sage.

Hochschild, Arlie (1979). Emotion work, feeling rules, and social structure. *American Journal of Sociology* 85(3), 551–575.

Hodkinson, Paul (2007). Interactive online journals and individualization. *New Media and Society*, 9(4), 625–650.

Hodkinson, Paul and Sian Lincoln (2008). Online journals as virtual bedrooms? Young people, identity and personal space. *Young: Nordic Journal of Youth Research*, 16(1), 27–46.

Hollows, Joanne (2000). *Feminism, Femininity, and Popular Culture*. Manchester: Manchester University Press.

Hollway, Wendy (1984). Gender Difference and the Production of Subjectivity. In J. Henriques, W. Hollway, C. Urwin, C. Venn, and V. Walkerdine (eds.), *Changing the Subject: Psychology, Social Regulation and Subjectivity* (pp. 227–263). London: Routledge.

Hopkins, Susan (2002). *Girl Heroes: The New Force in Popular Culture*. Annandale, NSW: Pluto Press.

Horst, Heather and Daniel Miller (2012). *Digital Anthropology*. London: Berg.

Horvath, M., L. Alys, K. Massey, A. Pina, M. Scally, and J. Adler (2013). *"Basically...porn is everywhere": A Rapid Evidence Assessment on the Effect That Access and Exposure to Pornography Has on Children and Young People*. London: Middlesex University.

Howe, Neil and William Strauss (2000). *Millennials Rising: The Next Great Generation*. New York: Vintage Books.

Hunsinger, Jeremy and Theresa M. Senft (2013). *The Social Media Handbook*. New York: Routledge.

Illouz, Eva (2008). *Saving the Modern Soul: Therapy, Emotions, and the Culture of Self-Help*. Los Angeles: University of California Press.

——— (2007). *Cold Intimacies: The Making of Emotional Capitalism*. Oxford: Polity.

Inness, Sherrie (1999). *Tough Girls: Women Warriors and Wonder Women in Popular Culture*. Philadelphia: University of Pennsylvania Press.

——— (ed.) (2004). *Action Chicks: New Images of Tough Women in Popular Culture*. New York: Palgrave Macmillan.

Italie, Leanne (2012). YouTube phenomenon has girls asking: Am I pretty? *Yahoo News*, March 3. New York. Available at: http://news.yahoo.com/youtube-phenomenon-girls-asking-am-pretty-164721902.html.

Ito, Mizuko, Heather Horst, Matteo Bittanti, danah boyd, Becky Herr-Stephenson, Patricia Lange, et al. (2008). Living and learning with new media: Summary of findings from the Digital Youth Project. Chicago: The MacArthur Foundation. Available at: http://digitalyouth.ischool.berkeley.edu/report.

Jackson, Carolyn (2006). "Wild" girls? An exploration of "ladette" cultures in secondary schools. *Gender and Education*, 18(4), 339–360.

Jackson, Carolyn and Penny Tinkler (2007). "Ladettes" and "Modern Girls": "Troublesome" young femininities. *The Sociological Review*, 55(2), 251–272.

Jackson, Sue (2006). "Street Girl." "New" sexual subjectivity in a NZ soap drama? *Feminist Media Studies*, 6(4), 469–486.

Jackson, Sue and Sarah Goddard (2015). "I'd say 14 is too young": Pre-teen girls negotiations of "sexualized" media. *Continuum: Journal of Media and Cultural Studies*, 29.

Jackson, Sue, Tiina Vares, and Rosalind Gill (2013). "The whole playboy mansion image": Girls' fashioning and fashioned selves within a post-feminist culture. *Feminism & Psychology*, 23(2), 143–162. doi:10.1177/0959353511433790.

Jane, E. A. (2012). "Your a Ugly, Whorish, Slut." *Feminist Media Studies, 14*(4), 531–546. doi: 10.1080/14680777.2012.741073.

Janus, Noreen (1977). Research on sex-roles in the mass media: Toward a critical approach. *Insurgent Sociologist*, 7(3), 19–31.

Jeffreys, Sheila (2005). *Beauty and Misogyny: Harmful Cultural Practices in the West*. East Sussex; New York: Routledge.

Jenkins, Henry (2006). *Convergence Culture: Where Old and New Media Collide*. New York; London: New York University Press.

Jhally, Sut (2006). *The Spectacle of Accumulation: Essays in Culture, Media, and Politics*. New York: Peter Lang.

Johansson, Anna (2014). Hybrid embodiment: Doing respectable bodies on YouTube. In Simon Lindgren (ed.), *Hybrid media culture: Sensing place in a world of flows*. London: Routledge.

Joint Select Committee on Cyber-Safety (2011). *High-Wire Act: Cyber-Safety and the Young*. Canberra: Commonwealth of Australia. Available at: http://www.aph.gov.au/parliamentary_business/committees/house_of_representatives_committees?url=jscc/report.htm.

Jowett, Lorna (2005). *Sex and the Slayer: A Gender Studies Primer for the Buffy Fan*. Middletown, CT: Wesleyan University Press.

Kanai, Akane (2015a). Thinking beyond the Internet as a tool: Girls' online spaces as postfeminist structures of surveillance. In Jane Bailey and

Valerie Steeves (eds.), *eGirls, eCitizens* (pp 83–108). Ottawa: University of Ottawa Press.

——— (2015b). WhatShouldWeCallMe? Self-Branding, Individuality and Belonging in Youthful Femininities on Tumblr. *M/C Journal*, 18(1).

Kaplan, E. Ann (1983). *Women and Film: Both Sides of the Camera*. New York: Methuen.

Karaian, Lara (2014). Policing "sexting": Responsibilization, respectability and sexual subjectivity in child protection/crime prevention responses to teenagers' digital sexual expression. *Theoretical Criminology*, 18(3), 228–299. doi:10.1177/1362480613504331.

——— (2012). Lolita speaks: "Sexting," teenage girls and the law. *Crime, Media, Culture*, 8(1), 57–73. doi:10.1177/1741659011429868.

Kearney, Mary Celeste (ed.) (2011). *Mediated Girlhoods: New Explorations of Girls' Media Culture*. New York: Peter Lang.

——— (2006). *Girls Make Media*. New York: Routledge.

Kehily, Mary Jane (2012). Contextualising the sexualisation of girls debate: Innocence, experience and young female sexuality. *Gender and Education*, 24(3), 255–268.

Kelly, Deidre, Shauna Pomerantz, and Dawn Currie (2006). "No boundaries?" Girls' interactive, online learning about femininities. *Youth and Society*, 38(1), 3–28.

Keller, Jessalyn (2015). Girl power's last chance? Tavi Gevinson, feminism, and girls' media culture. *Continuum: Journal of Media and Cultural Studies*, 29 (2), 274–285. doi: 10.1080/10304312.2015.1022947

——— (2012). Virtual feminisms: Girls' blogging communities, feminist activism, and participatory politics. *Information, Communication & Society* 15(3): 429–447.

Kenway, Jane and Sue Willis (1990). *Hearts and Minds: Self-esteem and the Schooling of Girls*. London; New York: Falmer Press.

Köhl, Margarita Marie and Gerit Götzenbrucker (2014). Networked technologies as emotional resources? Exploring emerging emotional cultures on social network sites such as Facebook and Hi5: A trans-cultural study. *Media, Culture & Society*, 36(4), 508–525. doi:10.1177/0163443714523813.

Koffman, Ofra (2013). *Children Having Children? Morality, Psychology and the Emergence of the Teenage Pregnancy Problem*. Manchester: Manchester University Press.

Koffman, Ofra, Rosalind Gill, and Shani Orgad (2015). Girl power and "selfie humanitarianism." *Continuum: Journal of Media and Cultural Studies*, 29(2), 157–168. doi: 10.1080/10304312.2015.1022948.

Kramer, Adam, Jamie Guillory, and Jeffrey Hancock (2014). Experimental evidence of massive-scale emotional contagion through social networks. *Proceedings of the National Academy of Sciences*, 111(24), 8788–8790. doi:10.1073/pnas.1320040111.

Kruger, Barbara (artist) (1981). *Untitled (Your gaze hits the side of my face)* [Photography]. New York: Mary Boone Gallery.

Kustow, Lis (1972). Television and women. In Michelene Wandor (ed.), *The Body Politic: Writings from the Women's Liberation Movement in Britain, 1969–1972* (pp. 60–71). London: Stage 1.

Lamb, Sharon, Kelly Graling, and Emily Wheeler (2013). "Pole-arized" discourse: An analysis of responses to Miley Cyrus's Teen Choice Awards pole dance. *Feminism & Psychology*, 23, 163–183.

Lamb, Sharon and Zoë Peterson (2012). Adolescent girls' sexual empowerment: Two feminists explore the concept. *Sex Roles*, 66(11), 703–712. doi:10.1007/s11199-011-9995-3.

Lange, Patricia (2007). Publicly private and privately public: Social networking on YouTube. *Journal of Computer-Mediated Communication*, 13(1), 361–380.

Law Reform Committee (2013). *Report of the Law Reform Committee for the Inquiry into Sexting*. Victoria: Parliament of Victoria. Available at: http://www.parliament.vic.gov.au/lawreform/article/944.

Leage, Rodda and Ivana Chalmers (2010). Degrees of caution: Arab girls unveil on Facebook. In Sharon Mazzarella (ed.), *Girls Wide Web 2.0: Revisitng Girls, the Internet, and the Negotiation of Identity* (pp. 27–44). New York: Peter Lang.

Lenhart, Amanda, Kristen Purcell, Aaron Smith, and Kathryn Zickhuyr (2010). Social media and mobile internet use among teens and young adults. Washington, DC: Pew Internet. Available at: http://www.pewinternet.org/2010/02/03/social-media-and-young-adults/.

Lenhart, Amanda (2009). Teens and sexting: How and why minor teens are sending sexually suggestive nude or nearly nude images via text messaging. Washington, DC: Pew Internet. Available at: http://www.pewinternet.org/2009/12/15/teens-and-sexting/.

——— (2009). Adults and social network websites. Washington, DC: Pew Internet. Available at: http://www.pewinternet.org/Reports/2009/Adults-and-Social-Network-Websites.aspx.

Lenhart, Amanda and Mary Madden (2007). Social networking websites and teens: An overview. Washington, DC: Pew Internet. Available at: http://www.pewinternet.org/Reports/2007/Social-Networking-Websites-and-Teens.aspx.

Lenhart, Amanda, Mary Madden, Aaron Smith, and Alexandra Macgill (2007). *Teens and Social Media*: Washington, DC: Pew Internet. Available at: http://www.pewinternet.org/Reports/2007/Teens-and-Social-Media.aspx.

Levy, Ariel (2005). *Female Chauvinist Pigs: Women and the Rise of Raunch Culture*. Melbourne: Schwartz Publishing.

Lewis, Stephen, Nancy Heath, Michelle Sornberger, and Alexis Arbuthnott (2012). Helpful or harmful? An examination of viewers' responses to nonsuicidal self-injury videos on YouTube. *Journal of Adolescent Health*, 51(4), 380–385.

Liu, Hugo (2007). Social network profiles as "taste performances." *Journal of Computer-Mediated Communication*, 13(1), 252–275.

Livingstone, Sonia (2008). Taking risky opportunities in youthful content creation: Teenagers' use of social networking sites for intimacy, privacy and self-expression. *New Media and Society,* 10(3), 393–411.

Livingstone, Sonia, Leslie Haddon, Anke Görzig, and Kjartan Ólafsson (2011). Risks and safety on the internet: The perspective of European children: Full findings and policy implications from the EU Kids Online survey of 9–16 year olds and their parents in 25 countries. London: London School of Economics.

Lumby, Catherine (1997). *Bad Girls: The Media, Sex and Feminism in the 90s.* St. Leonards, NSW: Allen & Unwin.

Lumby, Catharine and Kath Albury (2010). Too much too young? The sexualisation of children debate in Australia. *Media International Australia* 135, 141–152.

Lumby, Catharine and Nina Funnell (2011). Between heat and light: The opportunity in moral panics. *Crime, Media, Culture,* 7(3), 277–291.

Lundby, Knut (ed.) (2008). *Digital Storytelling, Mediatized Stories: Self-representations in New Media.* New York: Peter Lang.

Madden, Mary (2013). Older adults and Internet use: (Some of) what we know. Washington, DC: Pew Internet. Available at: http://www.pewinternet.org/2013/10/21/older-adults-and-internet-use-some-of-what-we-know/.

Maguire, Emily (2008). *Princesses & Pornstars: Sex, Power, Identity.* Melbourne: Text Publishing Company.

Maldonado, Elisha (2013). "Am I ugly?" YouTube trend is disturbing. *New York Post,* October 27. Available at: http://nypost.com/2013/10/27/girls-shouldnt-be-obsessed-with-physical-beauty/.

Mann, Sally (artist). (1989). *Candy Cigarette* [photography]. Chicago: Museum of Contemporary Photography.

Marwick, Alice (2013). *Status Update: Celebrity, Publicity, and Branding in the Age of Social Media.* New Haven, CT: Yale University Press.

——— (2012). The Public Domain: Surveillance in Everyday Life. *Surveillance Studies,* 9(4).

——— (2008) To catch a predator? The MySpace moral panic. *First Monday* 13(6). Available at: http://firstmonday.org/article/view/2152/1966.

May, Roxanne (2013a). Cybersexual Violence Series Part 1: Amanda Todd and Why We Need to Quit Calling it (Cyber)bullying. Available at: https://jhruoftmag.wordpress.com/2013/03/01/cybersexual-violence-series-part-1-amanda-todd-and-why-we-need-to-quit-calling-it-cyberbullying/.

——— (2013b). Cybersexual Violence Series Part 3: "Respect Yourself." Available at: http://jhruoftmag.wordpress.com/2013/03/12/cybersexual-violence-series-part-3-respect-yourself/.

Mazzarella, Sharon (2010). *Girl Wide Web 2.0: Revisiting Girls, the Internet, and the Negotiation of Identity.* New York: Peter Lang.

McClelland, Sara and Michelle Fine (2008). Rescuing a theory of adolescent sexual excess: Young women and wanting. In Anita Harris (ed.), *Next*

Wave Cultures: Feminism, Subcultures, Activism (pp. 83–102). New York: Routledge.

McNair, Brian (2002). *Striptease Culture: Sex, Media and the Democratization of Desire*. London; New York: Routledge.

McPherson, Tara (ed.) (2008). *Digital Youth, Innovation, and the Unexpected*. Cambridge, MA: MIT Press.

McRobbie, Angela (2009). *The Aftermath of Feminism: Gender, Culture and Social Change*. Los Angeles; London: Sage.

——— (2008). Young women and consumer culture. *Cultural Studies*, 22(5), 531–550.

——— (2007). Top Girls? Young women and the post-feminist sexual contract. *Cultural Studies*, 21(4–5), 718–737.

——— (2004). Notes on postfeminism and popular culture: Bridget Jones and the new gender regime. In Anita Harris (ed.), *All About the Girl: Culture, Power, and Identity* (pp. 3–14). New York: Routledge.

Megarry, Jessica (2014). Online incivility or sexual harassment? Conceptualising women's experiences in the digital age. *Women's Studies International Forum*, 47, Part A, 46–55. doi:http://dx.doi.org/10.1016/j.wsif.2014.07.012.

Miller, Daniel and Jolynna Sinanan (2014). *Webcam*. Cambridge, UK: Polity.

Mitchell, Anne, Patrick Kent, Wendy Heywood, Pamela Blackman, and Marion Pitts (2014). *National Survey of Australian Secondary Students and Sexual Heath 2013*. La Trobe University Melbourne: Australian Research Centre in Sex, Health and Society.

Mitchell, Kimberly, David Finkelhor, Lisa Jones, and Janis Wolak (2012). Prevalence and characteristics of youth sexting: A national study. *Pediatrics*, 129(1), 13–20. doi:10.1542/peds.2011-1730.

Molyneaux, Heather, Susan O'Donnell, Kerri Gibson, and Janice Singer (2008). Exploring the gender divide on YouTube: An analysis of the creation and reception of vlogs. *American Journal of Communication*, 10(2), 1–14.

Moreno, Megan, Libby Brockman, Judith Wasserheit, and Dimitri Christakis (2012). A pilot evaluation of older adolescents' sexual reference displays on Facebook. *Journal of Sex Research*, 49(3), 390–399. doi:10.1080/00224499.2011.642903.

Moreno, Megan, Malcom Parks, Frederick Zimmerman, Tara Brito, and Dimitri Christakis (2009). Display of health risk behaviors on MySpace by adolescents: Prevalence and associations. *Archives of Pediatrics and Adolescent Medicine*, 163(1), 27–34.

Moreno, Megan, Michael Swanson, Heather Royer, and Linda Roberts (2011). Sexpectations: Male college students' views about displayed sexual references on females' social networking web sites. *Journal of Pediatric and Adolescent Gynecology*, 24(2), 85–89.

Mulvey, Laura (1975/1989). Visual pleasure and narrative cinema. In L. Mulvey (ed.), *Visual and Other Pleasures* (pp. 14–26). Houndmills, Basingstoke: Palgrave.

——— (1989). Afterthoughts on "Visual Pleasure and Narrative Cinema" inspired by King Vidor's *Duel in the Sun* (1946). In Laura Mulvey (ed.), *Visual and Other Pleasures* (pp. 29–38). Houndmills, Basingstoke: Palgrave.

Murray, Craig and Jezz Fox (2006). Do Internet self-harm discussion groups alleviate or exacerbate self-harming behaviour? *Australian e-Journal for the Advancement of Mental Health,* 5(3), 1–9.

Murthy, Dhiraj (2008). Digital ethnography: An examination of the use of new technologies for social research. *Sociology,* 42(5), 837–855.

Negra, Diane (2009). *What a Girl Wants? Fantasizing the Reclamation of Self in Postfeminism.* New York: Routledge.

Nelson, Olympia (2013). Dark undercurrents of teenage girls' selfies: Pouty self portraits have turned boy-girl relations into a cut-throat sexual rat race. *The Sydney Morning Herald,* July 11. Available at: http://www.smh.com.au/comment/dark-undercurrents-of-teenage-girls-selfies-20130710-2pqbl.html.

Nochlin, Linda (1971/1989). Why have there been no great women artists? In Linda Nochlin (ed.), *Women, Art, and Power and Other Essays* (pp. 145–178). London: Thames and Hudson.

——— (1973). Eroticism and female imagery in nineteenth-century art. In Thomas Hess and Linda Nochlin (eds.), *Woman as Sex Object: Studies in Erotic Art, 1730–1970* (pp. 8–15). London: Allen-Lane.

Norris, Pipa (2001). *Digital Divide: Civic Engagement, Information Poverty, and the Internet Worldwide.* Cambridge: Cambridge University Press.

North, Louise (2009). *The Gendered Newsroom: How Journalists Experience the Changing World of Media.* New York: Hampton Press.

Nurka, Camille (2014). Public Bodies. *Feminist Media Studies,* 14(3), 485–499.

Oppliger, Patrice (2008). *Girls Gone Skank: The Sexualization of Girls in American Culture.* Jefferson, NC: McFarland.

Orenstein, Peggy (1994). *Schoolgirls: Young Women, Self-esteem, and the Confidence Gap.* New York: Doubleday.

Orlowski, Andrew (2003, 23/04/08). Most bloggers "are teenage girls"—survey. *The Register* Retrieved 04/12/06, from http://www.theregister.co.uk/2003/05/30/most_bloggers_are_teenage_girls/.

Owen, Susan, Sarah Stein, and Leah Vande Berg (2007). *Bad Girls: Cultural Politics and Media Representations of Transgressive Women.* New York: Peter Lang.

Paasonen, Susanna, Kaarina Nikunen, and Laura Saarenmaa (eds.) (2007). *Pornification: Sex and Sexuality in Media Culture.* Oxford; New York: Berg.

Papacharissi, Zizi (ed.) (2011). *A Networked Self: Identity, Community and Culture on Social Network Sites.* New York: Routledge.

Papadopoulos, Linda (2010). *Sexualisation of Young People Review.* London: Home Office. Available at: http://webarchive.nationalarchives.gov.uk/20100418065544/homeoffice.gov.uk/about-us/news/sexualisation-young-people.html.

Patraka, Vivian (1992). Binary terror and feminist performance: Reading both ways. *Discourse*, 14(2), 163–185.

Paul, Pamela (2005). *Pornified: How the Culture of Pornography is Changing Our Lives, Our Relationships, and Our Families*. New York: Times.

Pavlidis, Adele and Simone Fullagar (2014). The pain and pleasure of roller derby: Thinking through affect and subjectification. *International Journal of Cultural Studies*, 1–17. doi: 10.1177/1367877913519309.

Piepmeier, Alison (2009). *Girl Zines: Making Media, Doing Feminism*. New York: New York University Press.

Phelan, Phelan (1993). *Unmarked: The Politics of Performance*. London; New York: Routledge.

Phippen, Andy (2009). *Sharing Personal Images and Videos among Young People*. Exeter: South West Grid for Learning.

Pipher, Mary (1994). *Reviving Ophelia: Saving the Selves of Adolescent Girls*. New York: Putnam.

Pitcher, Karen (2006). The staging of agency in *Girls Gone Wild*. *Critical Studies in Media Communication*, 23(3), 200–218.

Playdon, Zoe-Jane (2001). "What you are, what's to come": Feminism, citizenship and the divine. In Roz Kaveney (ed.), *Reading the Vampire Slayer: The Unofficial Critical Companion to* Buffy *and* Angel (pp. 120–147). London: Tauris Parke.

Pollock, Griselda.(1987). What's wrong with images of women? In Rosemary Betterton (ed.), *Looking On: Images of Femininity in the Visual Arts and Media* (pp. 40–49). London; New York: Pandora.

——— (1988). *Vision and Difference: Femininity, Feminism, and Histories of Art*. London; New York: Routledge.

Powell, A. (2015). Young Women, Activism, and the "Politics of (Sexual) Choice": Are Australian Youth Cultures Post-Feminist? In Sarah Baker, Brady Robards and Bob Buttigieg (eds.), *Youth Cultures and Subcultures: Australian Perspectives* (pp. 215–226). Farnham: Ashgate.

Powell, Anastasia (2010). Configuring consent: Emerging technologies, unauthorised sexual images and sexual assault. *Australian & New Zealand Journal of Criminology*, 43(1), 76–90.

Powell, Anastasia and Nicola Henry (2014). Blurred lines? Responding to "sexting" and gender-based violence among young people. *Children Australia*, 39(2), 119–124.

Pozner, Jennifer (2010). *Reality Bites Back: The Troubling Truth About Guilty Pleasure TV*. Berkeley, CA: Seal Press.

Projansky, Sarah (2014). *Spectacular Girls: Media Fascination and Celebrity Culture*. New York; London: New York University Press.

Quenqua, Douglas (2014). Tell Me What You See, Even if It Hurts Me "Am I Pretty?" Videos Posed to the Internet, Raise Questions. *The New York Times*, Fashion and Style, August 1. Available at: http://www.nytimes.com/2014/08/03/fashion/am-i-pretty-videos-posed-to-the-internet-raise-questions.html?_r=0.

Radway, Janice (1984). *Reading the Romance: Women, Patriarchy, and Popular Literature*. Chapel Hill: University of North Carolina Press.

Railton, Diane and Paul Watson (2007). Sexed authorship and pornographic address in music videos. In Susanna Paasonen, Kaarina Nikunen, and Laura Saarenmaa (eds.), *Pornification: Sex and Sexuality in Media Culture* (pp. 115–126). Oxford; New York: Berg.

——— (2005). Naughty girls and red blooded women: Representations of female heterosexuality in music video. *Feminist Media Studies*, 5(1), 51–63.

Rasmussen, Mary Lou (2006). *Becoming Subjects: Sexualities and Secondary Schooling*. New York: Routledge.

Reid-Walsh, Jacqueline and Claudia Mitchell (2004). Girls' web sites: A virtual "room of one's own?" In Anita Harris (ed.), *All About the Girl: Culture, Power, and Identity* (pp. 173–182). New York: Routledge.

Renold, Emma and Jessica Ringrose (2011). Schizoid subjectivities? Re-theorizing teen girls' sexual cultures in an era of "sexualization." *Journal of Sociology*, 47(4), 389–409. doi:10.1177/1440783311420792.

Rich, Emma (2005). Young women, feminist identities and neo-liberalism. *Women's Studies International Forum*, 28(6), 495–508.

Ringrose, Jessica (2013). *Postfeminist Education? Girls and the Sexual Politics of Schooling*. New York: Routledge.

——— (2010). Sluts, whores, fat slags and playboy bunnies: Teen girls' negotiations of "sexy" on social networking sites and at school. In Carolyn Jackson, Carrie Paechter, and Emma Renold (eds.), *Girls and Education* (pp. 170–182). Maidenhead, Berkshire: Open University Press.

——— (2008). "Every time she bends over she pulls up her thong": Teen girls negotiating discourses of competitive, heterosexualized aggression. *Girlhood Studies*, 1, 33–59.

Ringrose, Jessica and Katarina Eriksson Barajas (2011). Gendered risks and opportunities? Exploring teen girls' digitized sexual identities in postfeminist media contexts. *International Journal of Media & Cultural Politics*, 7(2), 121–138.

Ringrose, Jessica, Rosalind Gill, Sonia Livingstone, and Laura Harvey (2012). A Qualitative study of children, young people "sexting": A report prepared for the NSPCC. London: National Society for the Prevention of Cruelty to Children. Available at: http://eprints.lse.ac.uk/44216/.

Ringrose, Jessica and Laura Harvey (2015). Boobs, back-off, and small bits: Mediated body parts, sexual reward and gendered shame in teens' networked images. *Continuum: Journal of Media and Cultural Studies*, 29(2), 205–217. doi: 10.1080/10304312.2015.1022952.

Ringrose, Jessica, Laura Harvey, Rosalind Gill, and Sonia Livingstone (2013). Teen girls, sexual double standards and "sexting": Gendered value in digital image exchange. *Feminist Theory*, 14(3), 305–323. doi:10.1177/1464700113499853.

Ringrose, Jessica and Valerie Walkerdine (2008). Regulating the abject: The TV make-over as site of neo-liberal reinvention toward bourgeois femininity. *Feminist Media Studies*, 8(3), 227–246.

Robards, Brady (2014). Digital traces of the persona through ten years of Facebook. *M/C Journal*, 17(3).

——— (2010). Randoms in my bedroom: Unsolicited contact on social network sites. *Prism*, 7(3).

Robards, Brady and Siân Lincoln (2014). Being strategic and taking control: Bedrooms, social network sites and the narratives of growing up. *New Media & Society* (online ahead of print, October 8) doi:10.1177/1461444814554065.

Robards, Brady and Andy Bennet (2014). *Mediated Youth Cultures: The Internet, Belonging, and New Cultural Configurations*. New York: Palgrave Macmillan

Rodham, K., J. Gavin, S. P. Lewis, J. M. St. Denis, and P. Bandalli (2013). An investigation of the motivations driving the online representation of self-injury: A thematic analysis. *Archives of Suicide Research*, 17(2), 173–183.

Rodley, Chris (2014). Facebook's real name policy won't stop queers getting bullied. In *The Conversation*, September 26. Available at: http://theconversation.com/facebooks-real-name-policy-wont-stop-queers-getting-bullied-32205.

Rose, Nicholas (1996). *Inventing Our Selves: Psychology, Power, and Personhood*. Cambridge: Cambridge University Press.

Ross, Karen (2010). *Gendered Media: Women, Men, and Identity Politics*. Lanham, MD: Rowman & Littlefield.

Ross, Sharon (2004). "Tough enough": Female friendship and heroism in Xena and Buffy. In Sherrie Inness (ed.), *Action Chicks: New Images of Tough Women in Popular Culture* (pp. 231–256). New York: Palgrave Macmillan.

Rossie, Amanda (2015). Moving beyond "Am I pretty or ugly?": Disciplining girls through YouTube feedback. *Continuum: Journal of Media and Cultural Studies*, 29. (2), 230–240. doi: 10.1080/10304312.2015.1022953.

Rottenberg, Catherine (2014). The rise of neoliberal feminism. *Cultural Studies*, 28(3), 1–20. doi:10.1080/09502386.2013.857361.

Rubin, Jennifer, and McClelland (2015). "Even though it's a small checkbox, it's a big deal": Stresses and strains of managing sexual identity(s) on Facebook. *Culture, Health & Sexuality*, 17(4), 512–526. doi: 10.1080/13691058.2014.994229.

Rush, Emma and Andrea La Nauze (2006). Corporate paedophilia: Sexualisation of children in Australia. Canberra: The Australia Institute. Available at: https://www.tai.org.au/?q=node/9&pubid=969.

Rushfield, Richard and Clarie Hoffman (September 8, 2006). Mystery fuels huge popularity of Web's Lonelygirl15, *Los Angeles Times*. Retrieved 09/12/07. Available at: http://articles.latimes.com/2006/sep/08/entertainment/et-lonelygirl8.

Sandberg, Sheryl (2013). *Lean In: Women, Work, and the Will to Lead.* New York: Alfred A. Knopf.

Salter, Michael (forthcoming). Privates in the online public: Sex(ting) and reputation on social media, *New Media and Society.*

——— (2013). Justice and revenge in online counter-publics: Emerging responses to sexual violence in the age of social media. *Crime Media Culture,* 9(3), 225–242.

Salter, Michael and Thomas Crofts (2015). Responding to revenge porn: Challenging online legal impunity. In L. Comella and S. Tarrant (eds.) *New Views on Pornography: Sexuality, Politics and the Law.* Praeger Publisher: Westport.

Salter, Michael, Thomas Crofts, and Murray Lee (2013). Beyond criminalisation and responsibilisation: Sexting, gender and young people. *Current Issues in Criminal Justice,* 24(3), 301–316.

Sarkeesian, Anita [writer/producer] (2013). *Damsel in Distress: Part 1—Tropes vs Women in Video Games* [video presentation]. Available at: https://www.youtube.com/watch?v=X6p5AZp7r_Q&list=PLn4ob_5_ttEaA_vc8F3fjzE62esf9yP61&index=1.

Scarry, Elaine (1985). *The Body in Pain.* New York: Oxford University Press

Scharff, Christina (2012). *Repudiating Feminism: Young Women in a Neoliberal World.* Farnham: Ashgate.

Schneider, Rebecca (1997). *The Explicit Body in Performance.* New York: Routledge.

Senft, Theresa M. (2008). *Camgirls: Celebrity & Community in the Age of Social Networks.* New York: Peter Lang.

Senft, Theresa M. and Nancy K. Baym, Nancy (2015). What Does the Selfie Say? Investigating a Global Phenomenon. *International Journal of Communication,* 9, 1588–1606

Shade, Leslie Regan (2007). Contested spaces: Protecting or inhibiting girls online? In Sandra Weber and Shanly Dixon (eds.), *Growing Up Online: Young People and Digital Technologies* (pp. 229–248). New York: Palgrave Macmillan.

Sherman, Yael (2004). Tracing the carnival spirit in Buffy the Vampire Slayer: Feminist reworkings of the grotesque. *Thirdspace: A Journal of Feminist Theory and Culture,* 3(2).

Simpson, Brian (2013). Challenging childhood, challenging children: Children's rights and sexting. *Sexualities,* 16(5–6), 690–709. doi:10.1177/1363460713487467.

Skeggs, Beverley (2014). Values beyond value? Is anything beyond the logic of capital? *The British Journal of Sociology,* 65(1), 1–20. doi:10.1111/1468–4446.12072.

——— (2005). The making of class and gender through visualizing moral subject formation. *Sociology,* 39(5), 965–982. doi:10.1177/0038038505058381 2005.

——— (2004). *Class, Self, Culture.* London: Routledge.

Skeggs, Beverley and Helen Wood (2012). *Reacting to Reality Television: Performance, Audience and Value*. Oxon: Routledge.

Spelman, Elizabeth (1997). *Fruits of Sorrow: Framing Our Attention to Suffering*. Boston, MA: Beacon Press.

Sprinkle, Annie (1998). *Post-porn Modernist: My 25 Years as a Multi-media Whore*. San Francisco: Cleis Press.

Stern, Susannah (2008). Producing sites, exploring identities: Youth online authorship. In David Buckingham (ed.), *Youth, Identity, and Digital Media* (pp. 95–117). Cambridge, MA: MIT Press.

——— (2002). Virtually speaking: Girls' self-disclosure on the WWW. *Women's Studies in Communication* 25(2), 223–253.

——— (1999). Adolescent girls' expression on web home pages: Spirited, sombre and self-conscious sites. *Convergence: The Journal of Research into New Media Technologies*, 5(4), 22–41.

Stokes, Carla (2010). "Get on my level": How Black American adolescent girls construct identity and negotiate sexuality on the Internet. In Sharon Mazzarella (ed.), *Girls Wide Web 2.0: Revisitng Girls, the Internet, and the Negotiation of Identity* (pp. 45–67). New York: Peter Lang.

Stokes, Katrina (May 7, 2012). Raunchy pop stars a bad influence on kids. *The Advertiser*. Available at: http://www.adelaidenow.com.au/raunchy-popstars-a-bad-influence-on-kids/story-e6frea6u-1226349286325.

Strassberg, Donald, Ryan McKinnon, Michael Sustaíta, and Jordan Rullo (2013). Sexting by high school students: An exploratory and descriptive study. *Archives of Sexual Behavior*, 42(1), 15–21. doi:10.1007/s10508-012-9969-8.

Szostak, Natasha (2013). Girls on YouTube: Gender politics and the potential for a public sphere. *The McMaster Journal of Communication*, 8, 46–58. Available at: http://digitalcommons.mcmaster.ca/mjc/vol10/iss1/4/.

Subrahmanyam, Kaveri, Stephanie Reich, Natalia Waechter, and Guadalupe Espinoza (2008). Online and offline social networks: Use of social networking sites by emerging adults. *Journal of Applied Developmental Psychology*, 29(6), 420–433.

Subrahmanyam, Kaveri and Patricia Greenfield (2008). Online communication and adolescent relationships. *The Future of Children*, 18(1), 119–146.

Subrahmanyam, Kaveri, David Smahel, and Patricia Greenfield (2006). Connecting developmental constructions to the Internet: Identity presentation and sexual exploration in online teen chat rooms. *Developmental Psychology*, 42(3), 395–406.

Sunrise [television program] (2014). Teen girls asking "Am I pretty?" *Sunrise Extra*, Wednesday August 6, episode 938. Available at: https://au.tv.yahoo.com/sunrise/.

Takayoshi, Pamela, Emily Huot, and Megan Huot (1999). No boys allowed: The World Wide Web as a clubhouse for girls. *Computers and Consumption*, 16, 89–106.

Tallon, Kelly, Ahram Choi, Matthew Keely, Julianne Elliott, and Debra Maher (2012). New Voices New Laws: School-age young people in New South Wales speak out about the criminal laws that apply to their online behaviour. NSW: National Children's and Youth Law Centre.

Tanner, Claire, JaneMaree Maher, and Suzanne Fraser (2013). *Vanity: 21st Century Selves*. New York: Palgrave Macmillan.

Tasker, Yvonne and Diane Negra (2007). *Interrogating Postfeminism: Gender and the Politics of Popular Culture*. Durham, NC: Duke University Press.

Taylor, Anthea (2012). *Single Women in Popular Culture: The Limits of Postfeminism*. Basingstoke: Palgrave Macmillan.

——— (2003). What's new about "the new femininity?" Feminism, femininity and the discourses of the new. *Hecate: An Interdisciplinary Journal of Women's Liberation*, 29(2), 182–198.

Taylor, Charles (1989). *Sources of the Self: The Making of Modern Identity*. Cambridge, MA: Havard University Press.

Temple, Jeff, Jonathon Paul, Patricia van den Berg, Vi Donna Le, Amy McElhany, and Brian Temple (2012). Teen sexting and its association with sexual behaviors. *Archives of Pediatric and Adolescent Medicine*, 166(9), 828–833.

Thelwall, Mike (2008a). Social networks, gender, and friending: An analysis of MySpace member profiles. *Journal of the American Society for Information Science and Technology*, 59(8), 1321–1330.

——— (2008b). Fk yea I swear: Cursing and gender in MySpace. *Corpora*, 3(1), 83–107.

Thiel-Stern, Shayla (2014). *From the Dance Hall to Facebook: Teen Girls, Mass Media, and Moral Panic in the United States*, 1905–2010. Amherst; Boston: University of Massachusetts Press.

——— (2009). Femininity out of control on the Internet: A critical analysis of media representations of gender, youth, and MySpace.com in international news discourses. *Girlhood Studies*, 2, 20–39.

Thiel, Shayla (2005). "IM me": Identity construction and gender negotiation in the world of adolescent girls and instant messaging. In Sharon Mazzarella (ed.), *Girls Wide Web* (pp. 179–201). New York: Peter Lang.

Thomas, Marc, Hannah Waldram, and Ed Walker (2014). *Connected: The Power of Modern Community*. London, UK: Guardian Shorts.

Thomson, Rachel, Mary Jane Kehily, Lucy Hadfield, and Sue Sharpe (2011). *Making Modern Mothers*. Bristol, UK: Policy.

Thornham, Sue (2007). *Women, Feminism and Media*. Edinburgh, UK: Edinburgh University Press.

Thumin, Nancy (2012). *Self-Representation and Digital Culture*. Basingstoke: Palgrave Macmillan.

Tiidenberg, Katrin (2014). Bringing sexy back: Reclaiming the body aesthetic via self-shooting. *CyberPsychology*, 8(1). doi:10.5817/CP2014-1-3.

Tincknell, Estella, Deborah Chambers, Joost Van Loon, and Nichola Hudson (2003). Begging for it: "New femininities," social agency, and moral discourse in contemporary teenage and men's magazines. *Feminist Media Studies,* 3(1), 47–63.

Tolman, Deborah (2002). *Dilemmas of Desire: Teenage Girls Talk About Sexuality.* Cambridge, MA: Harvard University Press.

Tsolidis, Georgina (1986). *Educating Voula: Prepared by Georgina Tsolidis for Ministerial Advisory Committee on Multicultural and Migrant Education.* Melbourne: Ministry of Education, Victoria.

Tsoulis-Reay, Alexa (2009). OMG I'M ONLINE...AGAIN! MySpace, MSN and the everyday mediation of girls. *Screen Education,* 53, 48–55.

Tuchman, Gaye (1979). Women's depiction by the mass media. *Signs,* 4(3), 528–542.

Tufekci, Zeynep and Kasey Spence (May 24–28, 2007). *Emerging Gendered Behavior on Social Network Sites: Negotiating between the Pull of the Social and the Fear of the Stalker.* Paper presented at the International Communication Association 2007 Annual Meeting, San Francisco, CA.

Tufte, Birgitte (2003). Girls in the new media landscape. *Nordicom Review,* 24(1), 71–78.

Turkle, Sherry (1995). *Life on the Screen: Identity in the Age of the Internet.* New York: Simon & Schuster.

——— (1996). Parallel lives: working on identity in virtual space. In Debra Grodin and Thomas R. Lindlof (eds.), *Constructing the Self in a Mediated World* (pp. 156–175). Thousand Oaks, CA: Sage.

Turner, Graeme (2010) *Ordinary People and the Media: The Demotic Turn.* London: Sage.

Twenge, Jean (2006). *Generation Me: Why Today's Young Americans Are More Confident, Assertive, Entitled—And More Miserable than Ever Before.* New York: Free Press.

Valenti, Jessica (2011). *The Purity Myth: How America's Obsession with Virginity Is Hurting Young Women.* Berkeley, CA: Seal Press.

van Dijck, Jose (2013a). "You have one identity": Performing the self on Facebook and LinkedIn. *Media, Culture & Society,* 35(2): 199–215.

——— (2013b). *The Culture of Connectivity: A Critical History of Social Media.* Oxford: Oxford University Press.

van Dijk, Jan. (2006). Digital divide research, achievements and shortcomings. *Poetics,* 34(4–5), 221–235.

Van Doorn, Niels (2009). The ties that bind: The networked performance of gender, sexuality and friendship on MySpace. *New Media and Society,* 11(8), 1–22. doi:10.1177/1461444809342766.

van Ryn, Luke and Robbie Fordyce (2014). Facebook emotions can be "viral" but aren't very contagious. *The Conversation,* June 3. Available at: http://theconversation.com/facebook-emotions-can-be-viral-but-arent-very-contagious-27437.

van Zoonen, Liesbet (2013). From identity to identification: Fixating the fragmented self. *Media, Culture & Society,* 35(1), 44–51.

——— (1994). *Feminist Media Studies.* London: Sage.

Walker, Shelley, Lena Sanci, and Meredith Temple-Smith (2013). Sexting: Young women's and men's views on its nature and origins. *Journal of Adolescent Health,* 52(6), 697–701. doi:http://dx.doi.org/10.1016/j.jadohealth.2013.01.026.

Walker, Shelley, Lena Sanci, and Meredith Temple-Smith (2011). Sexting and young people: Experts' views. *Youth Studies Australia,* 30(4), 8–16.

Walkerdine, Valerie, Helen Lucey, and June Melody (2001). *Growing Up Girl: Psychosocial Explorations of Gender and Class.* New York: New York University Press.

Walter, Natasha (2010). *Living Dolls: The Return of Sexism.* London: Virago.

Warner, Michael (2002). *Publics and Counterpublics.* New York: Zone Books.

Weber, Sandra and Shanly Dixon (eds.) (2007). *Growing Up Online.* New York: Palgrave Macmillon.

Wehlage, Gary (1989). *Reducing the Risk: School Communities as Communities of Support.* Philadelphia: The Falmer Press, Taylor and Francis.

Westlake, E. J. (2008). Friend me if you Facebook: Generation Y and performative surveillance. *The Drama Review,* 52(4), 21–40.

Whelehan, Imelda (2000). *Overloaded: Popular Culture and the Future of Feminism.* London: Women's Press.

Whitehead, Kally and Tim Kurz (2009). "Empowerment" and the pole: A discursive investigation of the reinvention of pole dancing as a recreational activity. *Feminism & Psychology,* 19(2), 224–244. doi:10.1177/0959353509102218.

Williams, Linda (1993). A provoking agent: The pornography and performance art of Annie Sprinkle. In P. C. Gibson and R. Gibson (eds.), *Dirty Looks: Women, Pornography, Power* (pp. 176–191). London: British Film Institute.

Williamson, Judith (1978). *Decoding Advertisements: Ideology and Meaning in Advertising.* London: Boyars.

Williamson, Milly (2005). *The Lure of the Vampire: Gender, Fiction and Fandom from Bram Stoker to Buffy.* London; New York: Wallflower.

Willson, Jacki (2008). *The Happy Stripper: Pleasures and Politics of the New Burlesque.* London; New York: I. B. Tauris.

Winch, A. (2013). *Girlfriends and Postfeminist Sisterhood.* New York: Palgrave Macmillan.

Winship, Janice (2000). Women outdoors: Advertising, controversy and disputing feminism in the 1990s. *International Journal of Cultural Studies,* 3(1), 27–55.

Wiseman, Rosalind (2002). *Queen Bees & Wannabes: Helping your Daughter Survive Cliques, Gossip, Boyfriends, and Other Realities of Adolescence.* New York: Three Rivers Press.

Wolf, Naomi (1991). *The Beauty Myth: How Images of Beauty Are Used against Women.* London: Vintage.

Woodiwiss, Jo (2014). Beyond a single story: The importance of separating "harm" from "wrongfulness" and "sexual innocence" from "childhood" in contemporary narratives of childhood sexual abuse. *Sexualities*, 17(1–2), 139–158. doi:10.1177/1363460713511104.

Young, E. Alex (2014). Is it time to quit Facebook? *Aljazeera America*, August 27. Available at: http://america.aljazeera.com/opinions/2014/8/facebook-unpaid-labordataadvertising.html.

Zaslow, Emilie (2009). *Feminism, Inc.: Coming of Age in Girl Power Media Culture*. New York: Palgrave Macmillan.

Index

CPSIA information can be obtained
at www.ICGtesting.com
Printed in the USA
LVHW081156110819
627229LV00011B/422/P

9 781137 408396